the
BIG BOOK
of backyard
projects

the
BIG BOOK
of
backyard
projects

WALLS
FENCES
PATHS
PATIOS
BENCHES
CHAIRS
& MORE

paige gilchrist

LARK
BOOKS

A Division of
Sterling Publishing Co., Inc.
New York

Library of Congress Cataloging-in-Publication Data

The big book of backyard projects : walls, fences, paths, patios,
benches, chairs & more / editor, Paige Gilchrist.
    p. cm.
  Includes index.
  ISBN 1-57990-681-8 (pbk.)
  1. Garden structures. I. Gilchrist, Paige.
TH4961.B54 2005
690'.89—dc22

                                  2004025712

10 9 8 7 6 5 4 3 2 1

Published by Lark Books, A Division of
Sterling Publishing Co., Inc.
387 Park Avenue South, New York, N.Y. 10016

This book is composed of the following titles, published by Lark Books,
a division of Sterling Publishing Co., Inc.:
Making Paths & Walkways © 1999, Lark Books
Making Garden Floors © 2001, Lark Books
Garden Walls, Fences, and Hedges © 2001, Lark Books
The Complete Book of Garden Seating © 2001, Lark Books

© 2005, Lark Books

Distributed in Canada by Sterling Publishing, c/o Canadian Manda Group,
165 Dufferin Street, Toronto, Ontario, Canada M6K 3H6

Distributed in the U.K. by Guild of Master Craftsman Publications Ltd.,
Castle Place, 166 High Street, Lewes, East Sussex, England BN7 1XU
Tel: (+ 44) 1273 477374, Fax: (+ 44) 1273 478606, "email": pubs@thegmcgroup.com,
Web: www.gmcpublications.com

Distributed in Australia by Capricorn Link (Australia) Pty Ltd.,
P.O. Box 704, Windsor, NSW 2756 Australia

If you have questions or comments about this book, please contact:
Lark Books, 67 Broadway, Asheville, NC 28801. Tel: (828) 253-0467

Manufactured in China

All rights reserved

ISBN 13: 978-1-57990-681-8
ISBN 10: 1-57990-681-8

For information about custom editions, special sales, premium and corporate purchases, please
contact Sterling Special Sales Department at 800-805-5489 or specialsales@sterlingpub.com.

cover photographers
clockwise from top left:

CHARLES MANN
garden design by Keeyla Meadows

RICHARD HASSELBERG

EVAN BRACKEN

RICHARD BABB

CHARLES MANN
garden design by Nan Raymond

editors:
PAIGE GILCHRIST
JANICE EATON KILBY
KATHY SHELDON

art directors:
CHRIS BRYANT
THOM GAINES

principal photographers:
RICHARD BABB
EVAN BRACKEN
RICHARD HASSELBERG

cover designer:
BARBARA ZARETSKY

illustrators:
ORRIN LUNDGREN
DON OSBY
OLIVIER ROLLIN

assistant editor:
NATHALIE MORNU

associate art director:
SHANNON YOKELEY

editorial assistance:
DELORES GOSNELL

editorial interns:
KELLY J. JOHNSON
JANNA NORTON
MATTHEW M. PADEN

contents

introduction

Okay, first of all, calm down. Just because you have a very fat book in your hands that contains the words *big* and *projects* in the title, does not mean you need to overdo it. The title also includes the word *back-yard*, and backyards are all about relaxing. So grab a glass of something cool to drink, find a shady spot to sit, and peruse these pages awhile. What's that? You don't have a comfortable place to sit outside? Then you really do need this book!

But before you lift that first hammer or raise your shovel, remember: turning your yard into the sanctuary of your dreams can and should be fun. Think back to when you were young and your job was to go outside and play. Try to capture a bit of that spirit as you pick and choose among the dozens of projects presented here. To help, we've divided the book into four sections: garden floors, paths and walkways, walls and fences, and garden seating.

Like their indoor counterparts, garden floors can define—or redefine—the entire character of a yard, whether you want to add elegance, incorporate whimsy, update a look that's outmoded, or visually link scattered landscaping elements. Floors can take the form of everything from traditional brick terraces and rustic stone patios to intimate seating areas paved with decorative pebbles. But they all have the potential to perform their practical functions and, at the same time, set the tone for your outdoor design.

Addressing those twin concerns of practicality and style, we start with a thorough overview of all the technical information you need to plan and lay an outdoor floor. How-to photographs, color illustrations, and step-by-step instructions take you

GARDEN FLOORS

from putting your first stake in the ground to building a solid foundation and settling your pavers firmly in place. Supporting chapters help you compare and contrast paving options and take you on a visual tour of the accessible list of tools you'll need for the job. In the detailed chapters that follow, we show you how to apply that technical information to create floors that not only function, but do so with flair—and in every form imaginable. We give you detailed specifics for installing basic floors of brick, tile, ornamental gravel and pebbles, various types of stone, concrete pavers, poured concrete, and recycled and nontraditional materials. But the basics are only the beginning. Each chapter also features scores of full-color photographs that illustrate how the material and techniques have been adapted in a wide range of settings to create floors of all sizes, shapes, and styles.

The timeless pleasure of paths is that, while making your outdoor space more useful and accessible, they also make it more beautiful. In addition to providing a dry place to step while picking vegetables or a more convenient route for rolling a wheelbarrow, a path or walkway can add interest, movement, color, texture, and—most notably—individual character to your plot of land, whether you have a tiny side yard or acres in the country.

PATHS AND WALKWAYS

At the beginning of this section of the book, we guide you through the steps of getting started; help you make choices about layout, materials, and design; and walk you through the tools and techniques you need for building a standard path base.

Then, we take you down many walkways: humble tracks of pine needles that wind through garden gates, classic brick walks leading to patios and porches, stepping stones that make their way through shady patches of moss—even clever concrete walks colored in every shade of the rainbow. Detailed sections cover the procedures for making paths of materials ranging from grass and cut stone to decorative pebbles and flagstone paving.

The words *garden* and *yard* both trace their ancestry to a word meaning enclosure. The word *paradise* comes from the Persian word for a walled garden. Today, a wall or fence can still enclose and, at the same time, transform the look of your yard or garden.

In the wall and fence section of the book we first look at all the functions these borders can perform—some that may already be on your wish list and some that you'll want to add. We then give you all the information you'll need to evaluate your specific site and look at other considerations (including legal ones) to help you avoid making costly mistakes when enclosing your yard.

The individual chapters on walls and fences examine each category of border in depth and offer criteria for choosing a wall or fence that will most meet your needs. Would a board or a lattice fence work best for you? Are you attracted to the crisp symmetry of a brick wall or the more natural curves of a stone wall? You'll find dozens of gorgeous photos of different types of borders to inspire you and help you narrow your search. If you choose a border that calls for the skills and equipment of a professional, the information here will insure that you get the most for your money. In addition, detailed instructions and illustrations are provided for making several borders, ranging from somewhat challenging (a picket fence or low brick wall) to downright simple (a stick fence).

WALLS AND FENCES

Many people design and plant wonderful gardens but think it's much too hard or complicated to make their own outdoor seating. Wrong! You can make seating that's perfect for your own yard and have fun doing it! There are some classic seating designs that work so well they'll be used and loved forever, and they're in this book. Who doesn't love roomy Adirondack chairs with armrests that are actually designed to hold arms (and a drink, and a book) comfortably? How many of us still cherish warm childhood memories of the fan-backed metal lawn chairs and squeaky gliders that resided in our grandmothers' gardens? Many a weary gardener has turned over a milk crate or tipped a wheelbarrow upright to make an instant seat from which to contemplate the day's work. Simple ideas are frequently the best, and easy is good.

GARDEN SEATING

The garden seating section of the book contains projects for readers at all skill levels. You'll learn how to create seating classics that last, including comfortable chairs, benches, loveseats, lounges, swings, and tree surrounds. The how-to projects feature a wide range of materials, handsome and witty designs, and surface treatments ranging from the traditional to the unexpected. In addition, we'll give you useful suggestions about how to choose seating that works for you, how to decide where to put it, and how to build and plant easy structures to give your seating areas shade and privacy.

Finished with that cool drink? Then turn the page and get started transforming your backyard.

GARDEN FLOORS

the big book of backyard projects

planning your
design

IF only there were an easy-to-follow formula for planning your garden floor's design. Maybe a nice, foolproof computer program that would allow you to key in a set of variables, hit "enter," and receive a perfectly tailored plan, complete with recommendations for your floor's location, shape, size, and paving material.

Then again, one of the main reasons we're lured away from the computer screen and all our other planning gadgets and out into the garden is that we like the more natural flow we find there. Rules are never quite as rigid as they seem inside. And that, oddly, makes everything a bit more clear. Once we've wandered around out there for awhile, it begins to dawn on us that we're not simply bringing together the right combination of pavers and mortar and decorative edging. We're creating a place where we'll drink lemonade with friends or serve birthday cake to five-year-olds or sit and quietly watch our garden grow-a place that will likely be central to our living and our lives.

This going outside, in other words, and the subsequent wandering is essential to planning the design of your garden floor. It will, of course, lead to some actual pencil-to-paper plotting and figuring (we'll get to that at the end of this section). But for now, get out, walk around, and simply ponder three basic questions:

■ **How do you plan to use your garden floor?**

■ **What is your personal style?**

■ **What are the characteristics of your site?**

Following are some suggestions for exploring each question as you stroll.

your floor's use

▪ What is the main purpose of your garden floor? If it's to serve as a base for a piece of garden sculpture, for example, your floor will likely be relatively small. If it's to provide a place for pool parties, on the other hand, you're embarking on a larger job.

▪ Do you plan to use your floor frequently or only on special occasions? Your answer may influence the paving material you choose and what sort of foundation you create.

▪ Do you plan to use your floor as an eating and entertaining area? If so, you may want it near the door that leads inside and toward the kitchen. You might also want to consider incorporating utilities such as electricity and running water as well as space for a grill into your plan.

L E F T: **Consider other features you want to incorporate into your design when you plan your floor.**

▦ Do you want your floor to form the foundation for a quiet and meditative space? In this case, you may want it farther from the house.

▦ Will you place furniture on the floor? Think about what kind and how much; both will affect the size of your floor. Also, consider whether you want to incorporate seating into your design through seat walls or other structures.

▦ What time of day do you think you'll most often be using the floor? Pay attention to sun patterns and wind activity during that time of day; they may affect where you place your floor. If you'll be using your floor frequently in the evenings, you may want to incorporate lighting into your plan (which could involve installing wiring before you actually lay your floor).

▦ Are there other features you want to incorporate into your floor design, such as a hot tub or a fishpond?

your style

▦ What sort of look do you want in general? Classic and elegant? Contemporary? Charmingly lived-in? Consider the style of existing landscaping elements and of the architecture of your house as you answer these questions. Each paving material lends itself to a certain style. You'll also find that small details, such as growing moss in the joints between your pavers instead of mortaring them, can help set a specific tone.

On a more subtle level, what's the atmosphere you want to create? Shady and intimate (maybe even half hidden)? Sunny and open? One that beckons to early morning coffee drinkers? One that's hospitable to flocks of young swimmers and all of their pool paraphernalia?

Will you often entertain people wearing evening dress or parents pushing strollers? If so, you'll want to keep in mind that gravel and pebbles are hard on high heels and wheels. Pavers with unmortared joints can pose problems, too. A smooth surface will probably best suit your style.

How much interest do you have in caring for your floor? Would you prefer a floor that requires minimal maintenance (maybe sweeping off once a season), or is puttering (perhaps replenishing sand in the joints between bricks or raking gravel) a welcome bit of backyard therapy for you?

How much money do you want to spend on your floor, and do you want to do all of the work yourself?

LEFT AND ABOVE: **The same material, used differently in different settings, can look casually rustic or formal and polished.**

your site

◗ Study the structural elements on your site. In addition to your house, is there a deck, shed, wall, fence, or other structure your floor will share space with? Take into consideration their materials, sizes, colors, and textures, and think about how you want your floor to blend or contrast with these other elements.

◗ Study your site's natural and living features, from gardens and flowerbeds to trees and hedges. How do you want your floor to relate to them? Could it wrap around a favorite tree or connect to the path that winds through the rose garden? Is there a special view you'd like to be able to see from the patio?

◗ Walk your site after a good rain to see how well your soil drains. Check for especially soggy (poorly draining) areas, and notice your site's natural water runoff patterns. There's a lot you can do to improve drainage (see page 39), but you'll have the best success if you're working with rather than against your site's natural tendencies.

◗ Walk some more (you can do this when your site is dry), and get to know the topography of your site. Does it slope quite a bit? You might consider terraced floors with connecting steps. Is it completely flat? If so, you'll want to build in some slope to both aid drainage and add visual interest.

Do all of this walking at various times of day to get a sense of sun patterns, wind patterns, even noise patterns. What you find out may prompt you to consider incorporating screens, hedges, trellises, arbors, or even fences into your overall design. While you're at it, take a mental trip through the seasons that affect your site. Will there be times when your floor is subjected to heavy rains or lots of snow and ice-or will the sun beat down on it most of the year?

As you'll see in the next chapter, some paving materials are better suited to harsh weather conditions; others drain better in wet climates.

Notice the circulation patterns throughout your site. Where do people naturally sit, stand, gather, and travel back and forth? They'll offer some of the most helpful clues of all about where to locate your floor and how to provide access to it.

The paving material you use—and how you use it— may depend on the atmosphere you want to create. The photos (ON THE FACING PAGE AND ABOVE) **show how decorative gravel alone can create a range of different moods.**

developing the plan

If your left brain is now demanding that you put something down on paper, you can go back inside, jot down what you observed, and prepare to make a scaled drawing.

Making a Scaled Drawing

A scaled drawing is simply a bird's-eye view of your site, on which a unit of measurement is equal to a longer dimension on the actual site. For example, one common formula is to let ⅛ inch on your plan represent 1 foot on the ground. If you have a survey of your house site, use it as your scaled drawing (increasing its size on a photocopy machine, if necessary). If not, create one for your site (or for only the portion where you think your floor will go, if you already have a clear idea).

1 Measure all existing structures and features (such as drives, walks, utilities, planting beds, and trees).

2 Use a pencil, ruler, and drafting triangle to transfer scaled versions of the structures and features to a piece of plain paper. (If your drawing is too big for a regular piece of paper, you can buy large vellum sheets for drawings of this sort at graphic supply stores. You can also use graph paper, which makes scaled drawings easy; let each square represent an actual dimension on the ground.)

ABOVE: **Think about blending your garden floor with your site's natural and other landscaping elements.**

Adding Your Floor to the Drawing

A scaled base map allows you to play with options on paper, adjusting your floor's shape and size and moving it around (which is a whole lot easier than moving actual dirt and pavers).

1 Make several photocopies of your base map, or tape tracing paper over your master copy.

2 Armed with the information you gathered during all that time outside, begin sketching design ideas. Start with rough concepts, and refine them as you go-maybe a round patio becomes an oval, or a seating area moves from

one spot to a better one under a tree. Don't worry about the exact shape and size of your floor at this point.

3 Back outside! Take your plans out and evaluate them. Drag a chair with you, sit on the spot you've picked for your floor, and notice how it feels. Lay out a hose or stick survey flags in the ground to roughly mark the perimeter of the floor and see how it looks, both while you're standing in the space and when you view it from other points.

4 Once you're satisfied with your concept, pull out a clean copy of your base map (or tape a new sheet of tracing paper on top of your master), and draw your planned floor to scale in its exact position. Your final scaled drawing will help you calculate the amount of foundation and paving materials you need, and it will guide you as you lay your floor.

At this point, of course, your plan still has some blanks you need to fill in. The paving material you choose, the technique you use to lay it, and whether you add decorative touches such as edging or plants in the gaps between pavers will all affect your floor's design. The chapters that follow give you the details you need on materials and techniques. And the thinking you did earlier in this chapter provides a basis for sifting through those details, making decisions, and coming up with a complete plan for your project. But when you're outside once again, your shovel finally in hand and a pile of paving materials nearby, don't be sur-

prised to find yourself making minor adjustments and shifting your thinking now and then. Even the best drawn plans often become a little better once you're out there digging in the dirt. It's all part of that natural flow.

BELOW: Let the topography of your site help guide your choices about material (poured concrete does well on this sloping terrain) and influence whether you incorporate terraced levels or other features into your design.

paving
materials

Nothing affects the character of your garden floor as much as the material you pave it with. Each choice creates a distinct look, from the old-world charm of recycled bricks and cobbles to the contemporary appeal of concrete. In addition, each material has its own pros and cons as far as ease of installation, cost, durability, and climate considerations. This chapter gives you an overview of the qualities of common paving materials, making it easy to compare, contrast, and determine which one is best for your project.

brick

The Look

With its plentiful range of colors and textures and diverse array of laying patterns, brick is one of the most versatile materials you can choose. Whether you want picturesque (maybe reclaimed brick from a former city street with plants creeping out of the joints), formal (try crisp new brick in a precise, traditional pattern), or something in between, chances are you can find a brick to achieve the effect.

Pros

Because of its standard size, brick is easier than randomly shaped stone to both quantify and lay. As a paving material, it provides a nice complement to brick houses and other structures, and it's often right at home in historic neighborhoods. Plus, it's easy to clean, and those with a rough texture create a surface with good traction. Brick also mixes well with other materials, from concrete to stone, and makes especially effective and attractive edging. Finally, if laid on a flexible foundation, a brick floor is relatively easy to remove if you find you must improve drainage or repair utilities beneath it.

Cons

Brick can be difficult to match if you want your new patio or terrace to blend perfectly with your home's exterior or an existing path or wall. Brick is also susceptible to efflorescence (white streaks), and light colors of brick can stain easily because they're less dense and more absorbent. Frost heaves and growing tree roots can cause brick floors to buckle, and brick can crack under extreme weight.

Climate Considerations

Brick tends to grow mossy and slick in rainy climates, old bricks may crack or crumble in winter climates, and brick floors make for an especially hot surface for barefooted travelers in sunny climates.

Durability

If the quality of your brick is good, its durability will be good, too. Unfortunately, sometimes older brick with more character doesn't weather well. Bricks designed specifically for paving are the best choice. Paving bricks are pressed densely into molds by machine and baked longer than building bricks, making them less absor-bent and, as a result, better for outdoor flooring.

Ease of Installation

To ensure a smooth brick surface, you need to invest the time in laying a firm foundation. And if you're laying your floor on a flexible (as opposed to a concrete) foundation, you can't do without edging, so you need to plan for that, too. Finally, laying brick requires careful attention to detail, especially if you're laying intricate patterns.

Calculating Quantity

Though they come in various sizes and thicknesses, brick pavers are typically ⅝ to 2¼ inches thick, 3⅝ inches wide, and 7⅝ inches long. Using that standard size (and allowing for joints between the bricks), it takes approximately five bricks to pave a square foot (this allows you a few extra for breakage or for replacing bricks in the future). Multiply the length of your floor by the width to determine total square feet (and remember that brick laid on edge, which creates a more unusual-looking surface, will cover less area).

Purchasing

You can get brick through brick suppliers, tile companies, and home-and-building supply centers. If you have a brick home or other brick you want to match, it's a good idea to take one brick home for comparison before you have an entire load delivered. Be sure you purchase paving bricks rather than facing bricks, which are intended for walls, and if you live in an area where temperatures dip below freezing, purchase SW (severe weather) bricks. With a full-sized pickup truck that's got good suspension, you can typically haul about 1000 pounds or more of brick. Most suppliers also deliver for a fee, and many rent load-and-go vehicles that you can drive back to your site and unload.

Pricing

Because bricks are sold individually, the cost will depend on how many you need and what style you choose. The three most common colors-red, tan, and gray-sell for the same price, but the price of other styles and colors of brick will vary.

tile

The Look

Paving tiles range from natural, unglazed terra-cotta squares to less traditional shapes featuring brightly colored glazes and intricate patterns, all available in a multitude of sizes. Depending on the type you choose, you can use tiles to add regional flavor, ethnic flair, or whimsy, color, and fun to your garden setting.

Pros

Tiles made for exterior use, especially those that are unglazed, are very dense and highly resistant to scratching and marring. If you want to make glazed tiles less slippery, you can add an abrasive coat-

ing. All except the lightest tiles resist dirt and staining. Best of all, tiles offer vivid colors and customized designs you can't find in other paving materials.

Cons

Because they're thin, tiles can't withstand much load, and without a well-prepared concrete foundation set with expansion joints (see page 51), they're susceptible to cracking. Tiles are also labor intensive to lay (you've got to grout between every joint), and custom-designed tiles, especially, can be expensive.

Climate Considerations

If your floor will have to withstand freezing and thawing, be sure you use tiles designed specifically for outdoor use. Also, the air and surface temperatures should be between 60 and 90 °F (16 and 32 °C) when you're installing tiles.

Durability

Without the most stable of foundations, tile is prone to cracking.

Ease of Installation

Creating a tile floor is more time-consuming than working with many paving materials. If you want your floor to last, you don't have the option of dry laying tile on a flexible foundation. You've got to first construct a concrete foundation, then mortar the tiles in place.

Calculating Quantity

Multiply the length of your floor by the width to determine the amount of tile you need in square feet.

Purchasing

You'll find the best selection at centers that specialize in tile distribution. Some brick suppliers also sell tile. Again, be sure to specify vitreous or impervious tile for exterior use when you place your order. And choose tiles that have a non-skid surface.

Pricing

Tile is sold by the square foot, with price depending on the material and design you choose. Clay tile such as terra-cotta, for example, is less expensive than quarried tile.

ornamental gravel and pebbles

The Look

This most eclectic category of paving material includes smooth water-washed pebbles dredged from riverbeds, bright white angular chippings from larger rocks, and much in between. You can find gravel or pebbles to blend—or contrast—with virtually any surrounding plants and land-scaping elements. And any type you go with will create a garden floor with much more sense of movement than you get with a fixed paving material.

Pros

In addition to its versatility (at home every-where from crisp, formal gardens to medita-tive rock gardens), loose rock is one of the least expensive materials you can choose. It also drains well, conforms easily to curving layouts and gentle slopes, holds its shape if the ground underneath it heaves, and acts as a mulch for surrounding plants.

Cons

If your stone is larger than ¾ inch, it'll be difficult to walk on. In general, a floor of loose rock isn't the best choice for an area where you expect heavy traffic from strollers, wheelbarrows, or people sporting high-heeled shoes. Loose rock also tends to travel outside its borders, meaning periodic raking back in may be necessary-and edg-ing is pretty much a must. If your garden floor is near the door and lots of tracking back and forth is common, it can even tend to migrate inside the house. Weeds can also pop up in a loose-rock floor, and pure white rocks can discolor over time.

Climate Considerations

Use the information beginning on page 39 to solve any drainage problems ahead of time if you're laying a loose-rock floor in a wet climate.

Durability

You'll need to replenish your rock occa-sionally and rake spillage back in place, but outside of this easy maintenance, loose-rock floors feature good durability.

Ease of Installation

Moderately easy-and much quicker than mortaring pavers in place. However, you should allow time, energy, and a budget for the step of installing edging around any gravel floor (it helps keep the rock from straying).

Calculating Quantity

Many types of loose rock are sold in bags by the cubic foot. You can also purchase bulk amounts in cubic yards or tons. To figure the amount of rock you need in cubic feet, multiply the width and length of your floor layout by how deep you want your rock, keeping all measurements in feet. Divide cubic feet by 27 to convert to cubic yards.

Purchasing

Sand and gravel yards and quarries sell a variety of loose rock in bulk; you can cart it home in a truck or have it delivered for a fee. You can also often find smaller amounts of loose rock (usually sold by the bag) at nurseries and home-and-garden centers.

Pricing

You'll get the best prices by buying in bulk—typically by the ton (2000 pounds). Special, decorative stone will cost you more than standard gravel.

stone

Natural stone pavers come in three major categories: fieldstone, flagstone, and cut stone. Fieldstone is just what the name suggests—rough, irregular, uncut stone collected from fields, streambeds, or old stone walls. For paving projects, you want smooth, flat fieldstones. Flagstone is quarried stone that is flat, thin, and cut or broken into irregular shapes, typically with jagged, angular edges. Cut stone (also called ashlar), is cut into uniform shapes, usually squares or rectangles ranging in size from about 1 square foot to 4 square feet.

There are four main types of stone; availability of each type varies by region.

SEDIMENTARY STONES, such as sandstone, limestone, and bluestone, are somewhat soft and easy to cut. They can feature intricate patterns and a textured surface that's non-slippery. However, they are subject to staining and weathering because they are so porous.

SLATE is a hard and durable stone, ranging in color from blue to gray to black. It's thinly cut, so it's best laid only on a concrete foundation.

GRANITE is very hard and durable. Colors range from white to pink to dark gray. It's an expensive material, but useful for edging and surfacing.

MARBLE is an expensive stone with stunning colors and patterns. It's easy to cut, but can make for a slippery paved surface.

The Look

Fieldstone is the material to use if you're after a rustic, heavily textured floor that looks as if it was lifted from the yard of a quaint country cottage and placed among the flowers in your garden. Flagstone, with its random shapes and aged surfaces, creates a similar effect, but gives you a more even surface. Both lend themselves to imaginative patterns, with lots of irregular gaps in between the stones—perfect for plantings if you're laying your floor on a flexible (rather than concrete) foundation. Cut stone, on the other hand, with its uniform shape and size, will typically create a more elegant and formal-looking floor. In all cases, if you use a type of stone found in your area, your floor will more naturally blend with its surroundings.

Pros

You can use fieldstone and flagstone on both level and gently sloping surfaces. Flagstone is easy to cut and shape as you piece together the puzzle of your floor (see page 93). Cut stone creates a very smooth surface (ideal if your floor will be home to lots of outdoor furniture). And if it's mortared in place, it becomes a nearly permanent surface. Choosing any of these stone types gives you an opportunity to build your floor with locally available material and to blend your floor with other stone elements in your landscape.

Cons

Stones (particularly fieldstones) that have irregular surfaces will collect puddles when it rains, and they can be difficult to walk on if they're extremely bumpy. Very smooth pavers, on the other hand, such as slate and marble, become slick when they're wet. Cut stone can also be expensive. Oh, and stone is typically heavy.

Climate Considerations

In winter climates, the puddles that collect on the surfaces of uneven stones will form pools of ice, creating walking hazards; small, dry-laid stones will be subject to frost heaves; and cut stone can crack.

Durability

Good to excellent, though some types of stone (limestone, for example) will wear down under years of weathering and use.

Ease of Installation

Laying fieldstone or flagstone is a bit like putting together a very large—and very heavy—jigsaw puzzle. Because each piece is different, you may find yourself spending a lot of time cutting and shaping your stones so they fit the way you want them to. Cut stone will be slightly easier to dry lay, but mortaring it in place is a labor-intensive (and again, heavy) undertaking.

Calculating Quantity

Multiply the length of your floor by its width to determine the amount of stone you need in square feet. Fieldstone and flagstone are usually sold by the ton, but your figure in square feet will give your supplier enough information to roughly calculate the amount you need.

Purchasing

If you're lucky enough to have a stone-studded field, you can collect fieldstones yourself (though it could be a time-consuming job, depending on the size of your floor). Stone yards are also a good source for all types of paving stone, and some tile companies sell cut stone, as well. Suppliers will typically load your truck or car with small amounts of stone. Many also offer delivery for a fee.

Pricing

If the stone you're buying is sold by the ton, size and thickness of the stone will affect the price. Some colors and types are also more expensive than others, with rare colors of cut stone being the most expensive of all. Also, you'll pay a premium if you want to hand-pick your stones at a stone yard.

concrete pavers

The Look

Concrete pavers have become wildly popular because they lend themselves to nearly any look. Some are excellent imitations of natural stone, with the real thing's range of colors and textures. Others come in artificial shapes, from circles to hexagons, or feature faux stamped finishes that mimic materials such as brick or wood. You can also find concrete pavers in block form resembling brick or granite. Finally, specially designed interlocking concrete pavers have an artificial but neat (and exceptionally sturdy) design.

Pros

Lay your pavers properly on a well-prepared foundation, and your floor can last for decades with very little maintenance. Concrete pavers can withstand severe weather and heavy loads without losing their color or structural integrity. What's more, they're about half the cost of stone pavers. They're also easier to cut than brick if you need to shape them to fit your floor space, and they lend themselves to intricate and interesting laying patterns. If you're laying your pavers on a flexible foundation, it will be relatively easy to remove a section temporarily, if necessary, to improve drainage or reach any utility lines running below the floor.

Cons

Poor-quality pavers trying to imitate brick or some other material can create an unnatural look, and wide expanses of interlocking concrete pavers may have a monotonous effect. Also, with pavers you should plan for the extra step of installing edging to help hold them in place.

Climate Considerations

Prepare your foundation properly, and concrete pavers will work well in any climate.

Durability

Excellent.

Ease of Installation

Because of their uniform size and shape, concrete pavers are somewhat easier to lay than fieldstone or flagstone, but mortaring them in place, if you choose to do so, is still a labor-intensive undertaking. Laying non-interlocking concrete blocks is quite similar to the detailed work of laying brick; interlocking concrete pavers are much easier to lay. And again, investing the time and work preparing a good foundation to start with is key.

Calculating Quantity

Pavers are sold by the square foot. Multiply the length of your floor by its width to determine the amount you need. Paving blocks are slightly smaller than standard-size bricks, but you can still calculate quantity the same way you would for brick, figuring on approximately five blocks to pave a square foot.

Purchasing

Concrete material suppliers are your best bet for purchasing pavers. Pavers are also often sold at home-and-building supply centers. Some distribution centers have demonstration areas, where laid sections of pavers make it easy to evaluate different colors and styles.

Pricing

You'll spend about the same amount on concrete pavers as you would on brick, and considerably less than you would on stone.

poured concrete

The Look

Sometimes referred to as "liquid stone," the cement-and-water mixture that hardens into concrete can be poured into any form imaginable. It can also be colored, texturized with everything from floats and brooms to imprints of leaves, stamped with patterns, and embedded with materials from random shells to elaborate tile mosaics. Though it lends itself easily to urban and contemporary settings, it can be adapted to many others.

Pros

In addition to being one of the most cost-effective paving materials, concrete makes for a highly durable and long-lasting garden

floor that requires very little maintenance. Its design versatility is a big plus; it also combines well with other materials to create interesting patterns and unique finishes.

Cons

It's true. Concrete can look sterile if it's used unimaginatively in large, sweeping sections. It's also a more complicated paving material to work with than others; beginners may want some help (a well-prepared foundation is crucial). And, once concrete is in, it's in. If you change your mind about what you've done, you'll need to break up your floor and start over.

Climate Considerations

Cracking concrete can be a problem in harsh winter climates (or on sites with growing tree roots). Concrete can also ice over in the winter. You may want to watch the weather as you plan for pouring your floor, as well. Extremes of heat and cold can cause damage during the concrete's "curing."

Durability

Excellent.

Ease of Installation

Concrete floors are more time-consuming to create than any other. They also require more careful planning and more equipment.

Calculating Quantity

You can use either premixed cement, which comes in bags (you simply add water), or bulk materials (Portland cement, sand, and aggregate) that you mix yourself in a rented mixer (or a wheelbarrow for small amounts). A bag of premix will typically tell you how much coverage it provides. If you're buying in bulk, your supplier can help you figure out how much you need, which may vary, depending on what region you live in. Start with the standard formula: multiply the length by the width and depth of your floor and foundation area to determine the cubic feet you need to cover (dividing by 27 if you want to convert cubic feet to cubic yards). With cement, add 10 percent to your total for spillage or waste.

Purchasing

Home-and-building supply centers sell bagged cement. If you're buying bulk materials and mixing them yourself, you can get the cement from a building supply store or a concrete materials supplier, and the sand and aggregate from a sand-and-gravel yard, all sold in cubic yards or by the ton. For larger jobs, it may be worthwhile to have a concrete supplier mix and deliver your cement.

Pricing

Overall, concrete is one of the least expensive paving materials. Use pre-mixed bags only for small jobs (they're too pricey for big ones). For other jobs, it may be a bit more expensive but worth the time savings to have a supplier deliver ready-mix cement. The cost will depend on your location, ease of access to your site, and the size of your order.

paving
tools

IF a quick word-association exercise has you linking the *floor* in garden floors with words such as *house* or *building* and then, worriedly, *construction site*, *work crews*, and *large, expensive equipment*, this is the chapter to read to set your mind at ease.

The list of tools you need to lay a basic garden floor is surprisingly short—not to mention familiar. If you've already tackled a do-it-yourself project involving measuring and marking and some digging and moving of dirt, chances are you've got most of what you need. None of the tools required is specialized or hard to find. In fact, most are so common you could buy those you don't already have at bargain prices at a good flea market—or borrow them from a friendly neighbor.

Following is an overview of all you'll need for each of the major stages of building a floor. In addition, when we get to the details about specific kinds of floors (starting on page 56), we let you know about additional tools you might need for that type of project. Some of those are one-time-use pieces of equipment (such as brick saws or power compactors) that you won't want to buy; you can easily rent those items at a local equipment rental service.

marking tools

PIN FLAGS (also called survey flags) or **STAKES AND STRING**. Use these markers to outline the perimeter of your planned floor. Simply stick the flags in the ground at regular intervals, or pound in wooden stakes or lengths of rebar at the corners and run a taut string from marker to marker. For a floor with a rounded or curving shape, you may want to use a rope or a garden hose as the marker, instead.

LEFT TO RIGHT: **Marking paint, level, line levels, tape measure, carpenter's square, smaller level, pin flags, rebar and string**

TAPE MEASURE. To know exactly where to plant your flags or stakes (and for numerous other measuring jobs throughout the floor-building process), you'll need a good, sturdy measuring tool. A standard-model tape measure with a 25-foot retractable steel tape is ideal.

CARPENTER'S SQUARE or **FRAMING SQUARE**. These tools, which feature right angles, will help you quickly test the squareness of any corners in your floor's layout.

MARKING PAINT. Once you've marked the perimeter of your floor with flags, stakes, or a hose, you'll want to spray the lines on the ground, so you've got a guide when you start digging. (You could also snap a chalk line if you're marking a straight line between two points.)

FOUR-FOOT LEVEL. You'll use this must-have tool to check the slope of your floor at every stage of the process, beginning with the grading of the site you're marking. If you already own a slightly smaller or larger level, what you have should work fine.

LINE LEVEL (also called a string level). This small, lightweight device that clips onto a taut string does the same job as a 4-foot level, but it's handier for leveling longer stretches of your floor.

LEFT TO RIGHT: **Square-bladed shovel, hand tamper, mattock, round-nose shovel**

excavating tools

ROUND-NOSE SHOVEL. For good, old-fashioned digging, you can't beat this all-purpose tool. You'll also reach for it when you're spreading foundation materials into the excavated area later.

SQUARE-BLADED SHOVEL. This shovel is good for cutting out the edges of your floor and leveling rough spots-and later for scooping crushed rock to fill your foundation.

MATTOCK. A broad, slightly curved digging blade at one end and a small chopping blade or pick at the other make a mattock the perfect tool for loosening packed earth and embedded rocks and cutting out roots.

HAND TAMPER. You'll need to compact your floor's foundation to start with, then tamp down each layer of the foundation materials as you add them to create a firm base for your paving material. Hand tampers feature metal plates that are typically 8 or 10 inches square. For an especially large site, you may want to rent a power compactor.

WHEELBARROW. You'll need a wheelbarrow for hauling out dirt at this stage and for hauling in materials to fill the foundation at the next one. If you'll be mixing concrete, get a heavy-duty wheelbarrow.

Other optional excavating tools include **LOPPING SHEARS** or a **PRUNING SAW**, which are helpful in cutting back small roots, and a **FOOT ADZE HOE**, useful for skimming the sod off the surface of your site and for breaking up clay.

foundation material and paving tools

METAL RAKE. We're not talking about a leaf rake here; you need one you can put some force behind. As you begin dumping in loads of crushed rock and later sand to fill the floor's foundation, you'll use the teeth of this versatile tool to spread the material into place and the other side to smooth and level it.

SCREED. Forget the fancy name. A screed is simply a scrap piece of 2 x 4 you'll drag across your foundation's sand setting bed or across just-poured concrete to level the surface. When you're leveling a setting bed, you'll want to cut notches out of each end of your screed, so it fits over your floor's edging (or temporary supports such as metal pipes) and levels the sand to the appropriate height.

RUBBER MALLET. After laying your pavers, this is just the hand tool you need to tap them and settle them in.

MASON'S CHISEL. When working with some pavers, especially flagstone, you can use a mason's chisel to carefully chip them here and there (or score them and make clean cuts), helping them to better fit in place.

LEFT TO RIGHT: **Metal rake, mason's chisel, rubber mallet**

ABOVE: **Screed**

finishing tools

STIFF-BRISTLED BROOM. A broom is indispensable for sweeping sand into your floor's joints (a small stiff-bristled brush can help in tight areas, too)—and for cleaning the surface of your floor when you're finished.

TROWELS. With their variety of shapes and sizes, trowels come in handy for everything from spreading out mortar beds for laying paving materials to neatly filling the joints in between them.

HOSE. A fine spray of water will help settle floors of pavers laid with sand or dry mortar in the joints.

CLOCKWISE FROM LEFT: **Stiff-bristled broom, brush, trowels**

ABOVE: **Ear, eye, and knee protection**

safety tools

EYE PROTECTION is important if you're chipping bricks or cutting stones. Add **EAR PROTECTION** if you're using power equipment for either job or if you're operating a power compactor.

KNEEPADS make kneeling in sand for hours as you carefully position pavers a much more comfortable undertaking. And sturdy **WORK GLOVES** make everything from carrying rocks to swinging a mattock happier tasks.

floor
basics

J ust like the ones that keep us upright and comfortable inside, outdoor floors, whatever the type, need to be level and dry. That means well before you begin busying yourself with paving materials, you've got to devote some attention to slope, drainage, and preparing a proper foundation.

slope

Too Much

Every garden floor needs to slope somewhat (we'll get to that in a minute). But slope is also one of those good things you *can* have too much of.

If the patch of ground where you want to put your patio slants just slightly more than is comfortable for walking, standing, or sitting, you can smooth the grade fairly simply. Use a mattock to loosen the earth, a square-bladed shovel to skim soil from high spots, and a wheelbarrow to carry it to places you need to build up to make the site more level.

If, on the other hand, the place you've picked for your patio features a steep, downhill drop, an uphill climb, or lots of undulating contours, you may want to either rent a small, front-end-loading garden tractor to even it out or hire a professional grader. (These are also options if your site is just plain too big to tackle with a shovel.) When faced with a whole lot more slope than you want, however, remember that working with what you've got (rather than fighting it) will produce the least expensive and most natural-looking results. Instead of using heavy machinery to completely rearrange the grade on a large chunk of your yard, for example, you might want to consider putting in terraced garden floors linked by steps. The box on page 38 tells you how to build some simple steps to connect one floor to another along a steeply sloped area. If your job is a more complicated one, you'll probably want input and perhaps hands-on help from a landscape architect or a contractor.

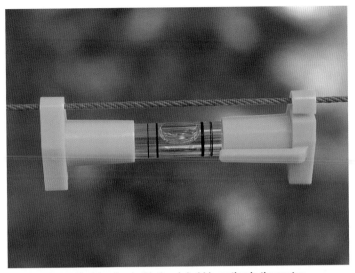

PHOTO 1. **A string level with the air bubble resting in the center (indicating a level line)**

Just Enough

Though you do need to even out steep slopes when you're laying a garden floor, a *completely* flat piece of ground is not what you're after. A gently sloping site is critical for directing water off the surface of your floor (and away from a nearby house or building foundation). A standard two-percent slope is nearly imperceptible to the eye (not to mention the feet), but it's just enough to direct water flow. To achieve it, grade your site, adding soil or skimming it away as necessary, so it falls about ¼ inch per foot of horizontal distance.

To establish a two-percent slope for your site, use a string level with double lines attached to the middle of a taut string tied to two stakes, one at what should be the high end of your floor site (near your house foundation, for example), the other at the low end:

▣ First, level the line, so the air bubble in the level rests in the center of the vial (photo 1).

▣ Next, adjust the line (see figure 1) so the bubble in the vial rests against the outer line on the level's vial, reflecting a two-percent slope (or a ¼-inch drop per horizontal foot). If, for example, you're planning a patio that will be 12 feet wide, the top edge of the site needs to be 3 inches higher than the bottom edge.

FIGURE 1. **Adjusting a string level to establish a two-percent slope**

adding simple steps

Often, rises and dips in a garden landscape add visual interest you want to preserve. Rather than flattening your space into a featureless slab, you can level areas where you want to put paving, then connect them to others with informal steps cut into natural slopes. Spaced-landing timber steps are some of the simplest.

1 Clear the step area of plants, leaves, and topsoil.

2 Measure the distance in height between the spots where you want the top and bottom steps.

3 Divide the measurement by the step height (the width of your timbers) to get the number of steps you need.

4 Install the timbers, spacing them evenly and working from the bottom of the slope to the top, compacting the soil behind each timber as you go.

5 Before anchoring the timbers, walk the steps to make sure the layout is comfortable. Once you're satisfied, drill two $5/8$-inch holes through the center of each timber about 6 inches in from each end. Drive 24-inch pieces of #5 rebar down through the holes into the ground below until they're flush with the top of the timber.

Flat pieces of fieldstone installed by excavating spots for them to fit into the slope also make stable and especially natural-looking steps.

When you excavate your site to lay your floor's foundation, use the sloped string as a guide (measuring from the string down to the base of the foundation), to make sure the foundation floor is sloping appropriately.

You can also use a 4-foot-long level with double lines on the vial to monitor the slope of the foundation as you excavate and, later, to monitor the slope of your paving material as you lay it:

Place the level so that one end sits at the high end of your site.

When the ground is sloping two percent, the level's air bubble will rest against the outer line on the level's vial (see figure 2). As you grade (working your way down the site's slope), periodically rest the level on the ground and adjust the soil, as necessary, to achieve your two-percent slope.

FIGURE 2. **Using a level to check slope**

drainage

In addition to sloping your site so that rainwater will flow gently off your future floor's surface, you'll also want to check for any serious drainage problems, and, if necessary, improve your site's drainage before you lay your floor. If your site is plagued by large amounts of storm water runoff or subsurface water, you probably have one or more telltale signs, such as muddy areas, persistent puddles, particularly lush growth, or wet basement walls.

You can also conduct this simple test to determine how well your site's soil drains.

1 Dig a hole roughly 4 inches in diameter by 12 inches deep, and fill it with water.

2 Let the water drain, then fill the hole with water again.

3 After 12 hours, check the hole. If all the water is gone, the soil is porous or sandy and drains well. If there is still standing water after 24 hours, the soil is too dense or full of clay; you'll want to improve its drainage before laying your floor. If the water in the hole gradually rises instead of falls, the site's water table is very high, making it a less than ideal spot for laying a floor directly in the ground; a floor constructed on a raised wooden platform might be a good alternative.

Improving drainage is always a site-specific job, but in general, identifying the nature of your drainage problem will help you determine the best way to correct it. Here are some basic solutions to common drainage problems.

Splash Blocks and Downspout Extensions

Make sure your roof downspouts are effectively directing water away from your house and not dumping it into the soil right at the foundation. If they're not directing water away, you can often correct the problem by placing purchased concrete splash blocks or several large stones at the places where the spouts release water; the splash blocks or stones will help dissipate the water. On a properly sloped site, you may also be able to solve the problem by simply adding a 2 to 4-foot downspout extension.

Drainpipes

You can lay a flexible, non-perforated, PVC drainpipe underground to solve a surface-water problem that doesn't respond to splash blocks or downspout extensions. Dig a 12-inch-deep trench

FIGURE 3. **You can lay a drainpipe to solve a surface-water problem.**

running from the source of the problem to an appropriate place for runoff water to drain. (You can use a special adaptor to connect the drainpipe to a downspout outlet, if necessary.) Storm sewers, community gutters, and the dry wells and catch basins described later in this section are good spots for directing the water. Sanitary sewers aren't, and directing runoff water onto a neighbor's property is not only impolite, but in many areas it's illegal. Make the trench 4 inches wider than the drainpipe, and slope it a minimum of ⅛ inch per horizontal foot. Lay 2 inches of gravel in the trench, install the pipe, cover it with more gravel, then add grass or plantings on top.

You can also use drainpipes to redirect subsurface water. Prepare a trench like the one described above, but lay a perforated PVC drainpipe, with the holes in the pipe facing down, so water will rise into the pipe and the holes won't become clogged with silt and debris.

Swales

Digging a shallow trench known as a swale is a good way to slow or redirect runoff water that courses down a hillside. Pitch it in the direction you want the water to go, mound and compact the soil on the downhill side, then re-lay your sod or plant over the trench with ground cover. To control erosion in a particularly steep swale, line it with landscape cloth that's specifically designed for erosion control and/or with rock (4- to 8-inch river rock or fieldstone works well).

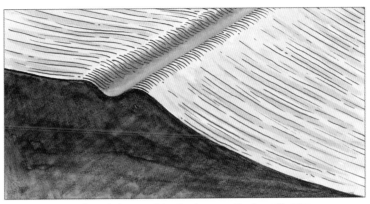

FIGURE 4. **A swale is a good way to slow or redirect runoff water.**

Catch Basins

To improve the drainage of a low spot where constant puddling is a problem, a catch basin is your best bet. Catch basins are typically about 1 or 2 feet square and 2 to 6 feet deep. You can either pour your own concrete basin or purchase a plastic one. Install a sloping drainpipe to carry water from the catch basin to a drainage spot and put a grate on top, so you can clean silt and debris out of the basin periodically.

FIGURE 5. **Catch basins improve drainage of low spots.**

Dry Wells

If you don't have a good location for emptying water you've diverted with a drain or a swale, you can dig a dry well. It's a gravel-filled hole approximately 3 feet deep and 2 to 4 feet wide that is covered with landscape fabric, then topped with a layer of gravel or topsoil and sod. (See figure 6.)

FIGURE 6. **Dig a dry well for emptying diverted water.**

marking the design

Once you've assessed your site's slope and solved any drainage problems, you're ready to mark out your floor. If leveling your site requires some major grading, you may want to smooth and clear the ground and even out the slope of the overall area before this step. If not, you can mark your site first, then simply slope the floor's foundation as you excavate it.

For informal shapes featuring curves, use rope or a garden hose to mark your floor's outline. If your floor features straight edges, use a tape measure to plot its exact position, then mark the perimeter with stakes and string or with pin flags (also called survey flags). (Be sure to mark the perimeter several inches outside your planned floor if you're pouring a concrete floor, which requires that you put form boards around the edges.)

To square up the corners, apply a bit of basic geometry known as the triangle method: measure 3 feet along one leg of the triangle formed by the corner and mark that point; measure 4 feet along the other leg of the triangle and mark that

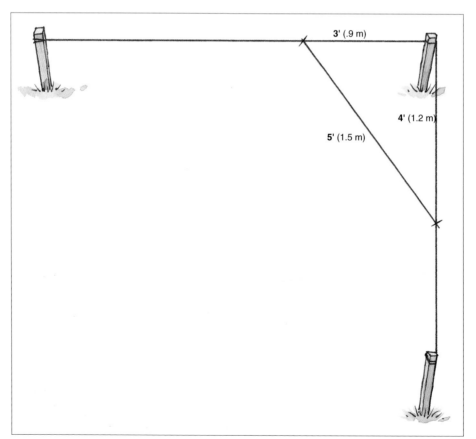

3' (.9 m)

4' (1.2 m)

5' (1.5 m)

FIGURE 7. **Using the triangle method to square corners**

PHOTO 2. **Marking the floor outline with paint**

point; the diagonal between the two points will measure 5 feet if the corner is square (see figure 7). If you need to mark a precise, circular shape, use a stake and string as a compass, and place stakes at 1-foot intervals along the resulting arc.

After outlining your floor, use the rope, hose, or string lines as guides and mark the ground with powdered chalk, lime, sand, or marking paint. The marked lines will be easy to follow as you begin to dig out your floor's foundation (photo 2).

preparing the foundation

A strong, well-constructed foundation helps keep your garden floor stable and firm, it minimizes cracking and settling of your paving material, and it aids the area in draining properly. In short, you can't do without it. Whether you're creating a flagstone patio, a brick pad to put your picnic table on, or any other type of floor, you'll start the same way: by excavating your marked-out area and then adding materials to prepare one of three foundation options.

making a move

As you clear, smooth, and grade the site that will become your garden floor, chances are, you'll come up against existing plants and perhaps even a tree or two. It's best for them, easiest for you, and often much more interesting in terms of overall design if you simply leave them where they are and incorporate them into your plan. Wrap a patio around a towering oak, for example, and your new floor has good shade and an instant focal point. Try not to cut or fill more than a couple of inches or centimeters around the base of the tree, since most of the roots grow just under the surface. (The roots generally extend to the drip line of the tree, which is the area beneath the entire canopy.)

When you do have to move a plant or a tree to make room for your floor, prepare a spot for replanting it ahead of time, or ready a temporary place, then replant it permanently later. Spring and fall are the best times of year for relocating trees and shrubs; cloudy days and late afternoons or evenings offer the most ideal conditions. To remove a plant, shrub, or small tree, use a sharp spade to cut a circle around the roots, then shape the roots and their surrounding soil into a ball by undercutting the lower roots. Pick up the tree or shrub by the base of the root ball, not by the trunk; the weight of the soil can damage the roots. Put the transplant into the hole you prepared in its new location, and water it well. If you've got a large tree to relocate, enlist the help of a professional.

excavating
the foundation

If you've ever moved soil with a shovel, you've got all the specialized training you need to take on this step. The goal is to hollow out a base that is deep enough to hold your foundation materials and your paving material. The depth will vary from floor to floor, depending on the type and amount of foundation materials you're using (standard "recipes" follow), the thickness of your paving material, and the amount you want your floor surface to rise above the surrounding grade (½ to 1 inch is standard; however, if you're laying a floor that abuts the door to a house, you want the floor's surface to be 1 inch below the door sill). For a typical project, you'll excavate a foundation 6 to 10 inches deep.

You can start with a sod cutter to remove the top layer of your ground's organic matter if you have a lawn, or you can simply make vertical cuts with a square-bladed shovel. Once you're down to packed earth, try a mattock or foot adze hoe to loosen the soil, remove rocks embedded in the ground, and cut out small roots (photos 3 and 4). Toss what you excavate into a wheelbarrow as you go, and move it to a nearby storage spot. It'll come in handy later for backfilling your floor's edging and for adjusting the slope of the foundation floor, if necessary. At this stage, you should also excavate a trench around the perimeter of your floor for

PHOTO 3. **Making vertical cuts with a square-bladed shovel**

PHOTO 4. **Loosening the soil with a mattock**

PHOTO 5. **Excavating a trench around the foundation for edging**

PHOTO 6. **Checking the slope of the foundation**

PHOTO 7. **Tamping the soil**

setting edging, if you plan to use it (photo 5) (see Adding Edging, page 50). Measure the depth of your edging material, then subtract the amount you want it to sit above the ground surface to determine how deep to dig the edging trench.

Once you reach the point of smoothing out and leveling your foundation floor, be sure to use a level to check its slope (photo 6), and adjust it as necessary to achieve the standard two-percent fall described on page 37. Finish by tamping and firming the soil well (photo 7). A poorly compacted foundation can cause settling and unevenness in a floor's surface. For a large area, you may want to rent a power compactor, but for most home projects, a hand tamper works fine. You can also do a lot of good tamping with nothing more than a couple of feet. (It's best if you wear work boots rather than tennis shoes for the job.)

PHOTO 8. **Adding the foundation's first layer: crushed rock**

adding foundation materials

Option 1: Flexible Foundation of Rock and Sand

A flexible foundation of rock and sand is the most common type used for home yard and garden projects. It's durable, yet flexible enough to withstand most frost heaves, and it provides a stable underpinning for either dry laying or mortaring in place any paving material.

■ Begin with a layer of crushed rock or gravel. Use an even mix of washed rock pieces ranging from a maximum of ¾ inch to fine particles. In most cases, a 2- to 4-inch layer of crushed rock is sufficient. If your soil drains poorly, make the crushed-rock layer of the foundation about 2 inches deeper, and if you're laying a drive or some other surface that will need to accommodate vehicles, make this bottom layer of rock 6 to 10 inches deep. For an extra-strong foundation, instead of crushed rock you can substitute the same material your local grading contractors use for road bases, called road bond or ABC (aggregate base course). Be sure to specify that you want the road base mix used in the top rather than the bottom of the road base. And use this mixture only if you have well-draining soil; because it compacts so

PHOTO 9. **Spreading and leveling the crushed rock**

PHOTO 10. **Checking the depth of the foundation's first layer**

densely, it doesn't provide much percolation. Spread and level this first layer of base material with a shovel and rake, checking to make sure you're maintaining a two-percent slope (photos 8 through 10).

If you're especially concerned about weed growth, spread non-woven landscape fabric over the layer of crushed stone and into your edging trenches. The fabric will also help keep the sand, added next, from settling into the stone layer. Overlap sheets of the landscape fabric, as necessary, and cut 1-inch holes in it every 12 inches, so the foundation will drain well.

Set your edging material in place (photo 11). (See Adding Edging, page 50.)

PHOTO 11. **Setting edging and checking to make sure it's level**

---

calculating quantity for foundation material

You can buy the crushed rock and sand you need to build your floor foundation at a sand and gravel yard. Suppliers typically sell by the cubic yard, cubic foot, or the ton, and they'll be glad to help you calculate the amount you need. If you want to come up with an estimate yourself, here's the formula to follow.

1 Multiply the length of your floor by its width to determine your floor's surface area. (If your floor is circular, multiply its radius squared by 3.14 to determine the area.)

2 Multiply the surface area of your floor by the depth of crushed rock or sand you need, converting the depth from inches or centimeters to feet or meters before multiplying. The result is the amount of material you need in cubic feet. For example, say you have a patio that is 12 feet by 12 feet in surface area and you want to add 3 inches of crushed rock. You would multiply 12 by 12 by .25 to come up with 36 cubic feet. (You divide the depth in inches by 12 to convert it to feet before multiplying.

3 If you'd like to convert the results of step 2 to cubic yards, simply divide the number of cubic feet by 27. (For example, 36 divided by 27 is 1.33 cubic yards.)

Once you've got your figure, increase it. You should always order approximately 10 percent more loose base material than the compacted volume you want to end up with, to allow for the compaction and any settling.

PHOTO 12. **Adding the sand setting bed on top of the crushed rock**

PHOTO 13. **Smoothing and leveling the sand setting bed with a rake**

PHOTO 14. **Checking the setting bed's level**

Spread on 1 inch of clean, washed, coarse concrete sand. This final layer is the setting bed for your paving material. If you have a source of river sand, it will also work well for this layer, but don't use fine mason's sand or the silica sand sold by the bag at home improvement stores. Save finer sand for filling the joints between your paving material later. Rock dust, also known as granite fines and available from quarries in certain regions, makes a good setting bed, as well. Don't rely on this final layer as a leveling layer; rather, make sure your foundation is level and properly sloped before adding the sand (photo 12).

Smooth the sand setting bed with a rake. You can also spray it with water to gently compact it. Then level it (photos 13 and 14). If you're planning to lay thick, heavy paving stone, you can level the sand by simply dragging the flat end of your rake over the surface. If, instead, you're preparing the bed for brick, tile, or another surface material that requires a more precise and uniform level, drag a screed across the surface (see figure 8). For areas that are too large to rest the notched ends of the screed on the edging material as you move it across the sand, set up temporary boards or even long, thin, metal pipes, and move them as you screed the entire surface.

Figure 9 shows a side view of a flexible foundation of rock and sand.

Option 2: Flexible Foundation of Sand Only

For smaller jobs on sites that feature good drainage and a solid subgrade, you can adapt the full flexible foundation recipe above, and lay a foundation of sand only (eliminating the crushed rock). This scaled-down version is easier and less expensive to lay, but it's also less stable. It's best for areas that won't be getting a lot of pedestrian traffic-maybe a small floor where you'll stand a birdbath, for example. Don't ever lay a sand-only foundation for a floor that will have to accommodate vehicle traffic.

▪ If you choose to use it, spread the non-woven landscape fabric directly on the foundation soil.

▪ Spread on 2 inches of sand or rock dust.

▪ Set your edging material in place, if you're using edging.

FIGURE 8. **Using a screed to achieve a precise level on the setting**

▪ Smooth the sand setting bed with a rake, spray it with water to gently compact it, then level it by dragging a rake back or a screed across the surface, as described in Option 1.

Figure 10 shows a side view of flexible foundation of sand only.

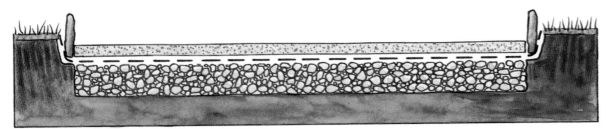

FIGURE 9. **Side view of a flexible foundation of rock and sand**

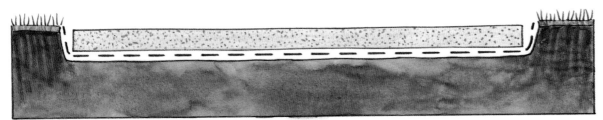

FIGURE 10. **Side view of a flexible foundation of sand only**

trench around your foundation, so the top of your edging material will be flush with any lawn area (so mowing is easy) or just above the surrounding ground. Add a 1-inch sand setting bed and (before laying your paving material), set your edging and level it (adjusting the setting bed as necessary). Use a rubber mallet to tap the edging pieces firmly into place, and backfill around them until they're stable. For extra-strong edging, you can substitute 3 to 4 inches of wet concrete for the sand setting bed.

■ Modern reproductions of traditional Victorian molded clay edging units will give your floor a more ornamental edge. Install them the same way you would brick edging.

■ Pressure-treated timber edging contrasts nicely with most paving materials. One option is to lay 2 x 4s on edge in trenches deep enough that the top of the wood will be flush with the paved floor (you don't need a sand setting bed; you can lay the 2 x 4s directly on the trench's soil). Make sure the trenches are also wide enough to accommodate 2 x 2 stakes on the outside of the edging to hold it in place. Set the stakes about every 4 feet, with their tops below the surface, then backfill to cover them up. Another option is to set 4 x 4 timbers in edging trenches, drill $5/8$-inch holes in the timbers about every 4 feet, and drive 2-foot lengths of #5 rebar through each hole and into the foundation to hold them in place (making sure the tops of the rebar lengths are flush with the timber). Heavy, unsawn logs make appealingly rustic edging, especially for floors of gravel and rock. They're also weighty enough that you can simply lay them on well-compacted ground.

adding edging

In some cases, you've got to add edging to hold your floor together physically (to contain the pebbles, for example, or to keep the bricks you set on sand from shifting out of place). In others, the main job of edging is to pull everything together visually (often giving a floor a more finished and unified look).

Either way, you've got lots of choices.

■ Many paving materials, including bricks, tiles, stones, and small concrete pavers, make equally effective edging. They also offer the most versatile design options; most can be set on edge, side-by-side, or on end at a diagonal, and smaller pavers work well on curved edges. Excavate the edging

Finally, if you need the stability of edging but don't like the idea of visible trim, preformed metal and plastic edging will do the job while remaining hidden underground. These are the only types of edging you install after your floor is in place. For details, see page 113.

PHOTO 15. **Dry laying pavers, adjusting the sand setting bed underneath, as necessary**

Option 3: Concrete Foundation

If you want a very long-lasting and absolutely level floor, you can't beat a concrete foundation. It won't settle or shift, and it provides an even, finished surface for dry laying or mortaring in place your paving material. It's also quite a bit more labor intensive. The process is the same as pouring a concrete floor, except that you don't have to go to the trouble of finishing the surface, since you'll cover it with sand or mortar and your paving material. Turn to page 122 for step-by-step instructions.

laying your paving material

You've got three basic options for putting in your paving material, as well. Whichever you choose, you'll need to adapt the technique somewhat, depending on the material you're working with. We've outlined each approach here, then provided detailed instructions for laying each type of paving material in the chapters that follow.

Option 1: Dry Laying

With this simplest of paving options, you place your pavers directly on the foundation's sand setting bed, sweep additional sand into the joints between the pavers, and (despite the technique's name), lightly spray your new floor with water to compact the added sand and flush away any excess. You may need to repeat the process a couple of times, until the sand is well packed and the pavers are firmly set (photos 15 through 18).

PHOTO 16. **Checking the slope of the pavers**

PHOTO 17. **Sweeping sand into the joints**

PHOTO 18. **Spraying the floor to compact the setting bed**

You can dry lay on either a flexible foundation or on a concrete foundation to which you've added an inch or so of sand. And dry laying is the method to use if you want to plant in the joints between your pavers; just sweep in topsoil rather than sand.

Option 2: Mortaring on a Flexible Foundation

Mortaring your floor on a flexible foundation gives it a more finished appearance and some added stability. (Be sure to use the foundation option that includes crushed rock—at least 4 inches of it—it will help prevent the mortar from cracking.) The technique is essentially the same as dry laying, but the finishing ingredient is different. Rather than sweeping sand into the joints between your pavers, you sweep in dry mortar mix. Once the mortar is evenly distributed, spray the floor with water to soak the mix, wait approximately 15 minutes, then spray it again. After the floor is dry and the mortar has hardened, you may need to repeat the process to firmly set all of your pavers.

(A note of caution: though this method is much easier than installing a concrete foundation and laying pavers in mortar on top of it, it's also not as durable, and your mortar may eventually crack.)

To create a standard mortar mix, combine one part Portland cement with three parts dry, fine sand.

FIGURE 11. **Coating a concrete slab with outdoor epoxy**

Option 3: Mortaring on a Concrete Foundation

Whether you've poured a concrete foundation for an extra-sturdy floor or you've got a plain concrete patio slab you want to dress up, here's how to mortar your pavers on top of it.

1   If you're working with an existing slab, clean it first with a commercial cleaner or a mix of one part trisodium phosphate (TSP) to five parts water. Scrub the slab with a heavy brush or broom, rinse it, and let it dry.

2   If you're laying thin pavers, such as tile, use a trowel to coat a section of the concrete surface with a thin layer of outdoor epoxy (figure 11). Work on only one manageable section at a time. (A 10-foot-square section is about right.) If

tip

When you're laying pavers, don't kneel on the ones you've just set to work on the next row; you'll risk upsetting the level surface you worked to establish. Instead, use a scrap of wood on the foundation's sand as a kneeling board. Place it just behind the row you're laying, and work from there.

FIGURE 12. **Spreading mortar on a concrete slab**

you're using heavier pavers, use a mason's trowel to spread a ½- to ¾-inch layer of mortar on the concrete, again working on only one manageable section (figure 12). You can use ready-mix mortar (which comes dry by the bag with instructions for adding water). Or, you can mix your own, using a hoe to stir together one part Portland cement and three parts fine sand. Use a sturdy wheelbarrow as your mixing container, and add water (about 2 to 2½ gallons per bag of cement) until your mix has the consistency of soft mud. It helps to add half of the sand first, then the cement, and then the rest of the sand before adding the water. Use a screed to level the mortar.

3 Lay your pavers on either the epoxy or the mortar, tap each one with a mallet to level it, then let the area rest overnight (figure 13). If you're laying out a precise pattern of brick, tile, or cut stone, you may want to use spacers between each paver to ensure that your spacing is uniform. You can cut your own plywood spacers to place between bricks, then remove them before you grout the joints. For tile or cut stone, you may want to purchase plastic spacers that fit in the corners of each joint. In most cases, you can mortar the joints (step 4) right over the plastic spacers.

FIGURE 13. **Laying pavers on epoxy or mortar**

keeping it straight

If you want your pavers to form a precise pattern, you need a guide that keeps you from laying crooked rows. Stretch a straight and level line of string across the edge of where you're working, and use it to keep everything in line.

FIGURE 14. **Filling joints with mortar**

4 For mortaring the joints, again you can purchase commercial mortar or mix your own, using a recipe of one part Portland cement and three parts mortar sand. You can also add tinting agents (available in powder form at home-and-building supply stores) to color your mortar so it better matches or accents your pavers. Add water until the mixture is spreadable. Use a trowel (a small pointed trowel works well) or a grout bag to fill the floor's joints with mortar (figure 14). As you work, use a damp sponge to immediately clean any misplaced mortar from the surfaces of your pavers. Once the mortar begins to set (you can tell because it will hold the impression of your finger), finish it off by pulling a jointing tool across it to compact and shape it (figure 15). A thin copper tube makes an excellent jointing tool.

FIGURE 15. **Compacting and shaping the joints to finish them**

planting in the gaps

Plants in the pockets, crevices, and joints of your garden floor are a delightful way to blur lines, making your floor less of a separate landscape element and more an extension of the garden itself.

Planting Steps

◾ Fill gaps where you want to add plants with a mixture of equal parts sand and topsoil (plus some compost for added nutrients).

◾ Transplant seedlings or sow seeds into the mixture.

◾ Water the seeds or transplanted seed-lings well and shade transplants for a few days.

◾ Mulch the young plants with pine needles or shredded hardwood mulch for several weeks until they're established.

Design Tips

◾ If your paved area is spacious and in danger of appearing featureless, open up holes in the paving (by removing pavers or breaking up sections of paving), fill the holes with a soil-and-sand mixture, and set in plants or sow seeds.

◾ Use strategically placed plants to help soften the appearance of a floor that looks more formal than you'd like or to add a wonderful contrast of color and texture.

◾ Tight positioning helps plants in gaps fill in more quickly, and it gives weeds less of a chance to get established.

Planting in the Gaps boxes throughout the book offer suggestions on plants that do well in various garden floor settings.

brick
floors

Brick is one of the most evocative materials you can use to pave your garden floor. Whether the warm, sun-baked surfaces of these familiar clay pavers bring to mind Italian piazzas, college quads, or a favorite grandparent's backyard, for most of us, brick represents something pleasing and enduring. Happily, these adaptable paving modules come in such a broad range of color, texture, and finish that you can use them to bring to life nearly any image they conjure up.

special tools and supplies

You may need to trim your brick pavers to help them conform to the edges of your floor, especially if the edges curve or if you're laying your bricks in a pattern that runs diagonally. You can either hire a masonry professional to help, or use the following tools to make the cuts yourself.

■ Pencil or chalk for marking cuts

■ Power masonry saw or brick cutter (if you've got lots of cuts to make) or a brick sett (a wide-bladed chisel) and a hammer (if you need to trim only a few pavers)

■ Eye and ear protection (for using power equipment)

In addition, if you're installing a flexible base with crushed rock, you may want to rent a power compactor, which will help you create a firmer base.

design options

PREVIOUS PAGE:
Brick doesn't have to be laid in a tidy pattern—or any pattern at all. In this quaint garden-pond surround, whole and broken pavers mix randomly with fieldstones. And forget tight mortaring; grass fills the joints in between.

ABOVE: An alternating circular pattern of brick blends with the curved elements in this garden's landscape.

FACING PAGE:
Here, formal planting beds were incorporated into the paving design, making garden and floor one and the same.

Traditional patterns used for laying brick are known as bonds. A few of the best loved and most widely used are shown in figure 1. Some bonds create a sense of movement. Others have a much more fixed and formal feel. And fortunately, none come with rules that say you can't mix, match, adapt, or change your paving pattern mid-floor. Combining more than one brick color or incorporating other paving materials can help you emphasize aspects of your paving pattern or add original accents to your overall design.

In addition to the paving pattern you choose, how closely you lay the bricks together and what you use to fill the joints in between will affect your floor's character. Crisp, new bricks laid with tight joints-or mortared with a stark, contrasting color-might make a very formal front drive, for example. Weathered pavers laid with wide gaps filled with topsoil and herbs, on the other hand, could be perfect for a seating area

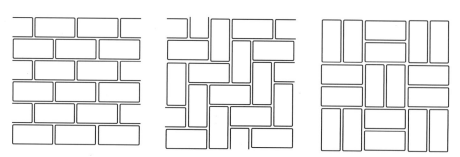

FIGURE 1. **Common brick laying patterns include, left to right, running bond, herringbone, and basket weave.**

purchasing tips

■ Purchase bricks that are low in soluble salts, and they'll be less susceptible to efflorescence, a whitish surface stain caused by salts leaching from the brick or surrounding areas.

■ Specify that you want paving bricks, which are designed to withstand winter freezing and thawing.

■ For bricks that resist chipping and help direct water flow into the floor's foundation, specify chamfered bricks, which are beveled on each edge.

near the potting shed. When you're choosing the brick itself, you'll also want to consider how well the color and style will blend with brick on surrounding structures.

Finally, your edging choice will figure into your design, too. If you're dry laying your brick on a flexible base, you'll want an edge to help stabilize your floor. Edging isn't as critical if you're mortaring on a concrete base, but you can still add it as a decorative feature. If you're laying your brick beside asphalt (a driveway, for example), an edge in between will be critical. Asphalt tends to settle more than brick. Without a band of edging in between, that settling will create a messy and hazardous ridge.

installation:
flexible foundation

Foundation

Clear and grade your site, mark your floor layout, and prepare one of the two flexible foundation options described on page 46. As you calculate the depth of your foundation, plan for your brick surface to end up about ½ to 1 inch above the surrounding grade; the elevation will help with the floor's drainage. If you're laying a very informal and small floor, you can get by with the simpler, sand-only foundation (Option 2). For most brick floors, however, you'll want the sturdier foundation of rock and sand (Option 1). Increase the layer of crushed rock in the foundation to 6 to 8 inches if your floor is part of an entryway drive or some other area that will need to bear the load of vehicles as well as foot traffic.

Setting Bed

The top layer of leveled sand in the foundation serves as your setting bed.

Laying the Brick

Begin by stretching level string lines across your floor area to use as guides for keeping your pattern lines straight and your surface level (see page 54). Then, start at one of your floor's outer edges, and lay a small section of brick

LEFT: **Brick in a traditional herringbone pattern**

RIGHT: **This floor-within-a-floor look is actually a clever expansion of an existing brick patio.**

(about 4 to 5 feet), following your pattern. The size of the joints between the bricks can vary according to your design, but for a traditional-looking floor, you'll want a gap of about ⅟₁₆ to ⅛ inch. Adjust the sand setting bed underneath, as necessary, to make sure the tops of the bricks are up against the string level. After laying each row, lay a short length of 2 x 4 across the bricks, and tap it to level them. Use a rubber mallet to level individual bricks, if necessary.

Continue laying the rest of your floor the same way. Always kneel in the sand behind where you're working, so you won't dislodge the bricks you've just set in place. And check your work occasionally with a level to make sure you're maintaining the slope you established when you graded your site.

Joints

After laying all the bricks, sprinkle clean, fine, dry sand across the surface of your floor, sweep it into the joints with a stiff push broom, and use a hose to sprinkle the floor lightly with water to settle the sand. Repeat the sweeping-and-watering process until the sand is well packed, the joints are full, and the bricks don't wobble.

Variation

If you've laid your floor on a sturdy foundation of at least 4 inches of crushed rock, rather than sweeping sand into the joints between your bricks, you can sweep in dry mortar mix. Once the mor-

ABOVE: **A simple, circular brick floor helps set off a focal point and connect this garden's paths.**

tar is evenly distributed, spray the floor lightly with water to soak the mix, wait approximately 15 minutes, then spray it again. After the floor is dry and the mortar has hardened, you may need to repeat the process to firmly set all of your bricks. (A note of caution: though this method is much easier than installing a concrete foundation and laying bricks in mortar on top of it, it's also not as durable, and your mortar may eventually crack.)

installation:
concrete foundation

It involves more work and more expense, but for a crisper look and unquestioning stability, you can lay your brick floor on a concrete foundation.

Foundation

Clear and grade your site, mark your floor layout, and prepare the concrete foundation (Option 3) described on page 51. Make sure you have installed the expansion joints properly, or you'll get cracking later. Finish the foundation with a rough texture, using a screed or a float, and let it cure for at least seven days before adding the brick.

Setting Bed

You can add ½ to 1 inch of sand on top of the concrete foundation, screed it to level it, then dry lay your bricks in the sand, as described above. Or, for ultimate stability, you can lay your bricks in a bed

B E L O W : **Salvaged bricks mortared tightly together in a basket-weave pattern create the floor for this outdoor retreat.**

cutting brick

Cutting large quantities of brick (for a herringbone pattern, for example) is a job best tackled with a power masonry saw or brick cutter and the assistance of someone with experience using the equipment. But if you want to cut a few bricks yourself, you can do it with a brick sett (a wide-bladed chisel) and a hammer. Wearing eye protection, mark the cut line on your paver, place the chisel on the mark, tap the chisel with the hammer to score the line, then strike the chisel with more force to make the final cut. You can finish by using the chisel to lightly smooth any rough edges along the cut. It's a good idea not to cut a brick you're using for paving into pieces less than one-third the brick's original size. Tinier pieces will too easily dislodge from their paved position.

of mortar. For the mortar setting bed, use a mason's trowel to spread a ½ to ¾ inch layer of mortar over one workable section of the foundation at a time (about 5 square feet). Mortar sets quickly, so you don't want to apply it to the entire foundation at once. Screed the mortar to level it. If your brick pavers are especially thin, apply an epoxy coat to the concrete prior to spreading on the mortar, then add only ½ inch of mortar.

BELOW: **Brick works especially well with other paving materials. Here, it's combined with stones embedded in concrete.**

RIGHT: **This tiny tree surround is made of handmade Sussex brick laid in a bed of crushed flint, in which pockets were opened up and planted with thyme.**

Laying the Brick

Press the bricks into the mortar according to your design, placing spacers between each to keep the spacing even (typically about ⅜ inch). You can either place the bricks onto the mortar and add more mortar between the joints later after they've set, or you can "butter" one end and one side of each brick with mortar before laying it. As you set each one, lightly tap it with a mallet to settle it. After laying each row, lay a short length of 2 x 4 across the bricks, and tap it to level them. It's a good idea to keep a bucket of water and a piece of burlap nearby. Dampened burlap is a good tool for rubbing off any mortar that makes its way to the surface of a brick. Continue laying the rest of your bricks, then let the floor rest overnight.

Joints

Use a small pointed trowel or a grout bag to fill the joints between the bricks with mortar. If you used the "buttering" method for laying your bricks, you'll simply be filling in any spots that aren't completely full. (This is another good time to keep a piece of burlap and water handy, to immediately clean any misplaced mortar from the surfaces of your bricks.) Once the mortar begins to set (you can tell because it will hold the impression of your fin-

ger), finish it off by pulling a jointing tool across it to compact and shape it.

Let your newly mortared floor settle for a day before walking on it. A week later, brush the surface with a stiff brush to clean up stray mortar drips and dust.

Maintenance

If you dry lay your brick on sand, individual pavers will dislodge or settle in too deeply now and then. Use a flat-headed screwdriver to remove problem pavers, adjust (and in many cases add to) the sand underneath, then position the brick back in place. Occasionally, you'll also need to replace washed-out sand in the joints between bricks and do a bit of weeding.

Efflorescence, the whitish mineral that leaches out of brick, creating stains or streaks, won't compromise the strength of your floor, but it can be unattractive. If it doesn't disappear with normal weathering, choose a warm, dry day to wash it off with water and a rag, or brush it away with a stiff, dry brush. In the winter, choose a rubber-tipped shovel for removing snow from your brick floor; metal shovels will chip the brick, and de-icing chemicals and rock salt will discolor it.

tile
floors

IF your garden environment is in need of a tad more flair, tile paving could give it just the lift you're looking for. Colorful glazed tiles invoke images of outdoor floors surrounding ancient Persian pools. Configure the tiles into a mosaic pattern, and your new patio will look as if it was plucked from a traditional Moroccan garden. Or, choose rough, sun-drenched terracotta tile, and you can create a terrace with the stark beauty of a desert setting. Whether you want warmth, color, regional flavor, or humor and whimsy, incorporating this adaptable paving material is one of the most effective ways to add character to your garden setting.

special tools and supplies

▪ Tile cutter and/or a wet saw (You may need to trim your tiles to help them conform to your laying pattern or to the edges of your floor. A tile cutter is good for straight cuts. Rent a wet saw for making curved or angled cuts.)

▪ Notched trowel (This tool with a flat bottom and a toothed comb on the sides is perfect for preparing a mortar setting bed for tile.)

▪ Rubber-faced grout float (for spreading grout into your floor's joints)

▪ Power compactor (If you're installing a flexible base with crushed rock, you may want to rent a power compactor, which will help you create a firmer base.)

design options

You can achieve a whole lot of effect with tile-without a lot of tile. Sure, you can pave an entire patio with 12-inch squares of earth-toned terra cotta and end up with a handsomely textured floor. But you can also scatter inserts of randomly sized patterned tiles among sandstone pavers, embed cut pieces of glazed tile into a poured concrete slab, or create a small tiled focal point within a floor paved with another material. Because tile pavers come in a range of sizes and they're fairly easy to reshape by cutting, they lend themselves to more intricate laying patterns than most other materials. (Flipping through books that feature photos of centuries-old tile floors in warm, sunny climates around the world can be a wonderful source of inspiration.) One especially interesting pattern, traditionally laid with slate, is to surround flat tiles by tiles set on edge (see figure 1).

The type of tile you choose will also affect the tone of your design. Machine-shaped tiles, with their crisp, uniform edges, will have a more contemporary look, while hand-molded tiles, which will vary slightly from paver to paver, tend to have a more rustic appearance.

ABOVE: **Bluestone pavers edged with unglazed tile joints and glazed tile inserts**

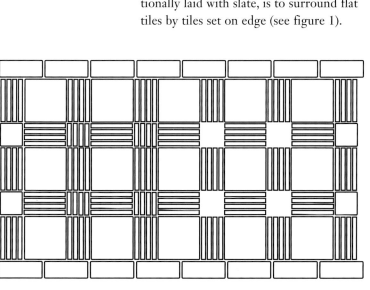

FIGURE 1. **Flat tiles surrounded by tiles laid on edge. For added effect, you can inset smaller flat tiles at the corner joints.**

installation

Foundation

Clear and grade your site, mark your floor
layout, and prepare the concrete foundation (Option 3) described on page 51.
(Tiles are too thin to lay on a flexible
foundation; they need firmer support to
prevent them from cracking under the
pressure of feet and furniture.) Make sure
you incorporate expansion joints into the
concrete foundation (again, to prevent
future cracking). Finish the foundation
with a rough texture, using a screed or a
float, and let it cure for at least seven days
before adding the tile.

LEFT: **The various understated shades of glazed quarry tile in this terrace do a nice job of matching the nearby brick without upstaging all the surrounding blooms.**

Setting Bed

Again, a sand setting bed won't provide enough stability for tile; you should lay your tile pavers on a bed of latex-Portland cement mortar. Dampen the concrete foundation, then use the flat side of a notched trowel to spread a ¼- to ⅜-inch-thick layer of the mortar over one workable section of the foundation at a time (about 5 square feet). (Mortar sets quickly, so you don't want to apply it to the entire foundation at once.) With the notched side of the trowel, comb the mortar, holding the trowel at a 45° angle to the foundation.

Laying the Tile

Press the tiles into place on the combed mortar. Use tile spacers (available from most masonry suppliers) in the joints if you want uniform spaces between each paver. When you set the tiles, do so gently. You don't want the mortar filling more than one-third of the depth of the joints.

If your tiles have textured backs, you may want to coat their backs with grout before laying them. The grout coating will ensure full mortar coverage, with no voids to collect water that can freeze and cause your tiles to crack.

After laying each row, lay a short length of 2 x 4 across the tiles, and tap each lightly with a mallet to settle and level it. It's a good idea to keep a bucket of water and a sponge nearby, so you can quickly sponge off any mortar that makes its way to the surface of a tile. Continue laying the rest of your tiles, then let the floor rest overnight.

cutting tile

Rent a tile cutter from a masonry supplier, and making simple, straight cuts will be a snap. First, you position the tile in the cutter's metal frame and draw its carbide-tipped blade or wheel across the tile to score it. Then, you simply press down on the cutter's handle until the tile breaks cleanly along the score line. For more intricate cuts, either hire a masonry professional to help, or, if you have some experience using the equipment, rent a wet saw.

Joints

The following day, remove all your tile spacers (or leave them in and grout over them). Dampen the tiles, and spread a commercial tile grout mix over the surface, preparing and applying the mix according to the manufacturer's instructions. Push the grout into the joints with a rubber-faced grout float, let it set for the manufacturer's recommended amount of time (typically about 15 minutes), then wipe the tile faces clean with a damp sponge. Let the grout dry for

BELOW: **In this radiant setting, unglazed tile blends beautifully with poured concrete, concrete blocks, flagstones, and bright decorative tile.**

LEFT: **Terra-cotta tiles were cut in squares and filler strips to surround this curved planter.**

the second recommended amount of time (about 40 minutes), wipe off the tiles with a soft, dry cloth, then cover the floor with plastic and let it damp cure for three to seven days.

Maintenance

Tiles mortared on a concrete foundation will be pretty firmly set and won't require much maintenance, though individual tiles may crack and need to be replaced.

planting in the gaps: *moss*

If your floor is in a shady spot, moss can be an especially picturesque plant for carpeting the gaps between the pavers.

Growing moss yourself is a bit of a challenge, but you can transplant sections from construction sites, drainage ditches, or anyplace where high-acid soil has been compacted and neglected. (Collect moss that is already wet—after a good rain is the best time.) Prepare the gaps where you want the moss to go by pulling up all existing growth and watering until the soil is muddy. Spray the moss patches, then gently press them into the wet gaps. You can carefully stretch the moss to fit the gaps, then fill any remaining open places with soil.

Moss has no roots or veins (it must absorb water from where it grows), so be sure to water it lightly but frequently until it's established. You won't need to mulch it in the winter, but you might want to apply a solution of one part dried skim milk or buttermilk and seven parts water twice a day for two weeks in the spring to repair any winter damage and help acidify the soil.

ornamental gravel and pebble floors

Gravel and pebbles—the least complicated of paving materials—are also among the most venerable. The ancient Greeks used pebble paving for both indoor and outdoor floors. The Japanese raked gravel into symbolic patterns in meditation gardens and paved the banks of their pond gardens with round pebbles. And the Moors used small stones in shades of gray, white, and purplish blue to create mosaic floors featuring intricate patterns. What a relief to have all that tradition to back you up! You can confidently use gravel or pebbles today, whether you want a formal floor to frame your parterre garden or a comfy patch of paved ground near your herb beds.

design options

When you're planning a floor of gravel or pebbles, much of the design work is in the choosing of the material. With options including dark polished river stones, honey-colored gravel, stark-white angular chippings, and many other variations, gravel and pebbles become the raw ingredients for looks ranging from rustic to urban, old-world to contemporary. Gravel and pebbles also blend easily with other paving materials and landscaping elements, whether you want to wrap your gravel floor around an existing tree or fill extra-large joints between pavers with colored pebbles. Edge restraints are a good idea with gravel or small stones that might otherwise migrate from the garden floor to the grass beyond; consider incorporating the edging into your overall design. Though simple steel edging, which is nearly unnoticeable, will do the job, other materials, such as brick, stone, and timber, keep your gravel in place while adding to the floor's character.

BELOW: For centuries, small stones have been used to create floor mosaics and other interesting patterns for outdoor floor designs. For details on embedding pebbles in concrete, see page 130.

IMAGINE

installation

Foundation

On a site that drains well, you can use a simpler, modified version of the flexible foundation (Option 1) described on page 46. Excavate the foundation to a depth of 3 inches, and add a trench around the foundation for your edging material. Fill the foundation with 2 inches of road bond, the unscreened gravel described on page 42, featuring lots of granite dust and small particles that compact into a strong yet flexible base. Compact the road bond well. You may need to add additional road bond after compacting, to bring your foundation layer up to its full 2 inches. Once your foundation is set, install your edging material.

If drainage is a problem, excavate your foundation 7 to 8 inches, lay a 1-inch layer of crushed rock, then install a 4-inch perforated PVC pipe, holes facing down, and direct it to a low area where it can release water. Wrap the pipe with landscape fabric

BELOW: **A simple gravel floor is an unobtrusive backdrop for this serene garden setting.**

FACING PAGE: **This imaginative patterned floor is made of alternating blocks of river stone and brick.**

ABOVE: **Often, gravel doesn't have to take center stage to add interesting texture to a garden floor.**

or a specially designed landscape sock, to keep it from getting clogged with sediment. Finally, fill the rest of the foundation with another 6 to 7 inches of crushed rock.

Adding the Gravel or Pebbles

Simply add your top layer of paving material to the remaining 1 inch of space in your foundation. Shovel it onto the foundation, rake it, spray it lightly with water, then tamp it to settle it. Once tamped, your gravel or pebble layer should sit about 1 inch below the top edge of the surrounding ground, so it won't be likely to spill out past your floor's borders.

B E L O W :   Gravel
provides the perfect
floor for this outdoor
living room.

maintenance

You may want to rake your gravel or pebble floor occasionally to neaten it up. Every once in awhile, you'll also want to hoe out weeds and pick out any debris, such as fallen leaves from surrounding trees. Unless your new floor gets heavy use, it will likely be years before you need to replenish the surface layer.

ABOVE: **Add it to a carefully planned garden design, and gravel can become the most formal of paving materials.**

RIGHT: **Gravel floors must be contained with an edging. Here, cobbles do the job.**

BELOW: **In this Japanese-style garden gravel makes a natural bed for rough stones.**

purchasing tip

If you want the ease and low cost of a gravel or pebble floor, but you also want your surface to be accessible to wheels (whether in the form of strollers or wheelchairs), consider using granite fines, also called rock dust, instead of gravel. Granite fines create a smooth, stable surface that is both handicap accessible and easier for someone wearing high heels to negotiate. If you go with granite fines, use a power compactor to prepare your foundation and to compact the fines, so you're sure your floor is as firm as possible. It's best to use fines on a flatter or only slightly sloped site, otherwise gullies will form in your floor surface when it rains.

flagstone
and fieldstone
floors

With their delightful assortment of bumps, nicks, irregularities, and ragged edges, these unpretentious stones can create garden floors that look as if they grew up—slowly and comfortably—right out of their surroundings. Most accessible and affordable (not to mention most appealing if you're after a natural look) will be stones that have been gathered or quarried in your local area, whether that means indigenous limestone or quarried rough marble. Their subtle, changing shades and distinctive textures will reflect the character of your region and gently link your garden with the larger landscape.

special tools and supplies

When laying flagstone or fieldstone, you've often got to do some trimming here and there, shaping the pieces so they fit together. To do so, you'll need the following:

▪ Pencil or chalk for marking cuts

▪ Mason's chisel and hammer

▪ Eye protection

design options

With flagstone and fieldstone, you won't be able to plot your paving pattern exactly, as you can with brick, for example. But you can make some design choices in advance, starting with the stones you pick. Think about whether you want stones that are relatively similar in size and shape: all smallish fieldstones with rounded edges, maybe, or huge flagstones in rough rectangular shapes. Or, maybe you'd rather your look be more random, with a mix of sizes, shapes, and even colors of stones.

ABOVE: **Mortared brick makes a tidy edge for flagstone floors that you want to look a bit less casual. This one makes space for a central focal point surrounded by plantings.**

FACING PAGE: **Broken units of lilac bluestone blend artfully with the stacked-stone wall that borders the floor.**

Consider, too, the option of combining the stones with other paving materials; brick and gravel are two of the most common companions. What you use to fill the joints between the stones will also affect your floor's character. Mortar will make it neater and more polished, sand or soil will look less formal, and plantings in the joints will give your floor an always-been-there air. Edging isn't necessary for the uneven edges of these stone floors, but you can add it as a purely decorative element if you want your floor to look a bit more finished.

installation:
flexible foundation

Foundation

Clear and grade your site, mark your floor layout, and prepare one of the two flexible foundation options described on page 46. If you're laying a very informal floor and using only large and thick stones, you can get by with the simpler, sand-only foundation (Option 2) or even lay the stones directly on the ground—just excavate a small amount

planting in the gaps:
full sun

A starter list of tolerant, hardy plants you can incorporate into soil-filled gaps of a garden floor that gets a lot of light:

Creeping Baby's Breath (*Gypsophilia repens*). Clusters of small pink or white flowers on thin stems.

Harebell (*Campanula rotundifolia*). Broad, bell-shaped blue flowers in late summer.

Lady's Mantle (*Alchemilla mollis*). Gray-green leaves, chartreuse flowers in the summer.

Moss Phlox (*Phlox subulata*). Creeping stems with needle-like evergreen leaves. Early summer flowers range from white, pink, and rose to lavender blue.

Sandwort (*Arenaria montana*). Blooms white from late spring to early summer. Needs moist soil in full sun.

Sedum, dwarf types. Low, drought-tolerant plants with carpet-like foliage and flowers. They're not as resilient as others, though. Plant them on the edges of floors; they won't survive heavy traffic.

Snow-in-Summer (*Cerastium tomentosum*). Gray leaves with white flowers in early summer. Needs soil that drains well.

Thyme, albus and wooly (*Thymus pseudolanuginosus* and *Thymus praecox*). Wooly thyme features silver-gray mats and lavender flowers. With albus thyme, you'll have emerald green mats and white flowers.

ABOVE: **The wider-than-usual gaps between stones in this picturesque floor break traditional paving rules—let's hear it for rebellion!**

of soil to make a spot for them, and let grass or other plants grow in between the pavers. For most other flagstone and field-stone floors, you'll want the sturdier foundation of rock and sand (Option 1). If you're paving your floor with small stones only, use road bond in place of the rock in the foundation for added stability (this alternative is described on page 46), or prepare a concrete foundation (see page 103).

Setting Bed

The top layer of leveled sand in the foundation serves as your setting bed.

---

tip

Use topsoil instead of sand between the joints if you want to set in creeping plants.

ABOVE: **A casual outdoor carpet of broken flagstone and baby's tears**

LEFT: **Fieldstones creating a drainage channel in a flagstone floor**

tip

If the surfaces of your stones are rough and uneven, you may have to rely on a trained eye rather than a level for checking slope. Bend down so your eyes are at nearly ground level, and gauge your floor's slope as best you can.

Laying the Stone

The fun of laying irregular stone is that it's much more like piecing together a puzzle than following a formula. There's an added challenge, though: these puzzle pieces are often heavy. The process will flow more smoothly as you develop an eye for which stones will fit best where, without having to move each one in and out of place multiple times.

Begin at one of your floor's outer edges. If your stones vary in size, place larger ones here and at door thresholds and where paths lead away from the floor, so they can provide added stability. Lay several stones, shaping them with the chisel as necessary, and leaving a gap of about ¼ to ¾ inch between them (or larger if you want to plant between the gaps). Once you have several in place where you want them, work each one into the sand, then tap it with a rubber mallet to settle it. Fieldstones, especially, will have uneven thicknesses, so you'll need to adjust the setting bed to help the stones sit level by digging out spots or by filling them in.

Continue laying the rest of your floor the same way, stepping back every now and then to see how it's looking. Always kneel in the sand behind where you're working, so you won't dislodge the stones you've

making a fit

You'll often need to chip, trim, and make outright cuts to get all the pieces of a flagstone floor to fit together just right. With most types of stone, you can make the adjustments yourself with a mason's chisel. Simply nick off small pieces or, for bigger cuts, follow these steps. First, mark your cut line with a pencil or chalk. Then, slip on some eye protection and score the line with the chisel itself or by hitting the chisel with a hammer. Once you've scored the stone, place it on a piece of wood or on another rock, letting the score line and the portion you want to remove overhang, and strike one sharp blow to split it along the score line.

Dense stones such as slate are in danger of shattering if you cut them with a chisel; they respond better to a water-cooled mason's saw (also known as a wet saw) or a circular saw fitted with a diamond blade. If these aren't tools you keep on hand in your own shed, enlist the help of a stonemason for your cutting jobs.

just set in place. And check your work occasionally with a level to make sure you're maintaining the slope you established when you graded your site.

Joints

After laying all the stone, sprinkle clean, fine, dry sand across the surface of your floor, sweep it into the joints with a stiff push broom, and use a hose to sprinkle the floor lightly with water to settle the sand. Repeat the sweeping-and-watering process until the sand is well packed (about ¼ inch below the surface of the stones) and the stones don't wobble.

Variation

If you've laid your floor on a sturdy foundation of at least 4 inches of crushed rock, rather than sweeping sand into the joints between your stones, you can sweep in dry mortar mix. Once the mortar is evenly distributed, spray the floor with water to soak the mix, wait approximately 15 minutes, then spray it again. After the floor is dry and the mortar has hardened, you may need to repeat the process to firmly set all of your stones. (A note of caution: though this method is much easier than installing a concrete foundation and laying stones in mortar on top of it, it's also not as durable, and your mortar may eventually crack.)

BELOW: **This tiny flagstone seating area is an extension of the surrounding garden.**

maintenance

If you've dry laid your stones on a flexible foundation, some of them may occasionally shift out of place as the floor gets more and more use. Simply adjust the sand setting bed, as necessary, to resettle or level them again. You'll probably also need to add more sand between the joints every year or so and do some weeding in the joints now and then. If you'll be shoveling snow from your floor during its off season, make sure your shovel is rubber tipped, so you avoid chipping or scratching the stone.

installation:
concrete foundation

A concrete foundation provides maximum stability for any garden floor. If that's what you're after for your flagstone or fieldstone floor, the procedure is the same as the one for installing cut stone on a concrete foundation, outlined on page 103.

ABOVE: Filling the joints between the flagstone with crushed rock of a similar shade gives this floor a neat, somewhat polished appearance.

RIGHT: Flagstone floors can wrap easily around other garden features.

cut stone floors

Cut stone, also called ashlar, is the city cousin of flagstone and fieldstone. It's the branch of the family that favors precise forms, uniform sizes, and refined paving patterns. If you want your terrace, poolside patio, or courtyard floor to feature a dash of elegance and formality, this handsome paving material, which includes sandstone, limestone, bluestone, slate, granite, and marble, has the pedigree to pull it off.

PREVIOUS PAGE: Unmortared stone slabs mingled with plants for an informal floor

Cut stone is an obvious choice for crisp, formal-looking floors; mortar the pavers together with tight joints for ultimate polish (LEFT). If, however, you want a slightly softer look, widen the joints and fill them with groundcover instead (LOWER LEFT).

special tools and supplies

You may need to trim your stones to help them conform to the edges of your floor, especially if the edges curve or if you're setting the stones on a diagonal. You can either hire a masonry professional to help, or use the following tools to make the cuts yourself.

- Pencil or chalk for marking stone
- Circular saw with masonry blade
- Sturdy piece of lumber to use as a cutting guide
- Eye and ear protection

In addition, if you're installing a flexible base with crushed rock, you may want to rent a power compactor. It'll help you create a firmer base, which you may want if you're laying a thin, brittle paving stone.

ABOVE: **A quiet retreat area paved with granite blocks laid with an informal, curved edge. A circular opening in the floor makes room for plantings.**

design options

Predictability has its advantages. Once you've settled on the shape and size of the cut stone you'll be using, you can plot your floor design on graph paper rather than by moving actual stones around. Simply make a scaled drawing of your patio area, with 1 inch on your paper representing 1 foot on the ground. Then, make copies of the drawing (or lay tracing paper on top of it), and play with paving patterns.

Just because individual types of cut stone are uniform in size and shape doesn't mean your design has to be routine. Consider mingling several different forms and even different shades of stone—or eliminating stones altogether in key places and adding other paving materials or plantings. Creeping plants incorporated within the surface or along the edges of a cut stone floor can help soften the design if it becomes too austere. The look of your cut stone floor will also be affected by how tight you make the joints between stones,

FACING PAGE: Cut stone was dry laid on a flexible base to create these steps and the casual waterside seating area.

RIGHT: Cut stone doesn't have to look serious. Here, non-mortared joints and a pocket for plantings create a casual floor for a rustic seating area.

whether you line them up or offset them (offsetting them makes for a stronger floor), and whether you seed the joints with grass, fill them with a light mortar, or choose something else altogether. Finally, though edging isn't necessary as a restraining edge, you may want to add it for aesthetic appeal.

installation:
flexible foundation

Foundation

Clear and grade your site, mark your floor layout, and prepare the sturdier foundation of rock and sand (Option 1) described on page 46. If the paving stones you've chosen are on the thin side, use road bond in place of the rock in the foundation for added stability (this alternative is described on page 46), or prepare a concrete foundation (see page 103).

Setting Bed

The top layer of leveled sand in the foundation serves as your setting bed.

---

planting in the gaps:
full or partial shade

A starter list of floor plants that can handle a bit of abuse (such as foot traffic), but not full sun:

Bruce's White or Blue Ridge (*Phlox stolonifera*). Low, creeping, woodland plant with white or blue flowers.

Bugleweed (*Ajuga reptans*). Low-to-the-ground plant. Blue, white, or pink flowers in spring.

Bunchberry (*Chamaepericlymenum canadensis*). Formerly known as Cornus canadensis. Tiny clusters of white blossoms in spring followed by red berries. Leaves become burgundy red in the fall.

Foamflower (*Tiarella cordifolia*). Creeping stems, heart-shaped leaves, and white flowers in the spring.

Partridgeberry (*Mitchella repens*). Small evergreen leaves and light pink flowers. Red berries in the fall.

Periwinkle or Myrtle (*Vinca minor*). Trailing, evergreen ground cover with blue or white flowers.

Wintergreen (*Gaultheria procumbens*). Creeping plant with shiny leaves and tiny white flowers followed by scarlet berries.

Strawberry Geranium (*Saxifraga stolonifera*). Creeping plant with white-veined leaves and white flowers that makes runners like strawberries.

Laying the Stone

With your graph-paper design in hand, temporarily lay out a portion of your floor to make sure you're happy with your plan. Once you're satisfied, begin by stretching level string lines across your floor area to use as guides for keeping your pattern lines straight and your surface level (see page 54).

Start at one of your floor's outer edges, and lay several stones. The size of the joints between the stones can vary according to your design, but for a traditional floor, you'll want a gap of about ¼ to ¾ inch. Adjust the sand setting bed underneath, as necessary, to make sure the tops of the stones are up against the string level. Once you have several stones in place where you want them, tap each with a rubber mallet to settle it.

Continue laying the rest of your floor the same way. Always kneel in the sand behind where you're working, so you won't dislodge the stones you've just set in place. And check your work occasionally with a level to make sure you're maintaining the slope you established when you graded your site.

Joints

After laying all the stone, sprinkle clean, fine, dry sand across the surface of your floor, sweep it into the joints with a stiff push broom, and use a hose to sprinkle the floor lightly with water to settle the sand. Repeat the sweeping-and-watering process until the sand is well packed (about ¼ inch below the surface of the stones) and the stones don't wobble.

ABOVE: **Random cuts of bluestone combined with flagstone and pea gravel**

Variation

If you've laid your floor on a sturdy foundation of at least 4 inches of crushed rock, rather than sweeping sand into the joints between your stones, you can sweep in dry mortar mix. Once the mortar is evenly distributed, spray the floor with water to soak the mix, wait approximately 15 minutes, then spray it again. After the floor is dry and the mortar has hardened, you may need to repeat the process to firmly set all of your stones. (A note of caution: though this method is much easier than installing a concrete foundation and laying stones in mortar on top of it, it's also not as durable, and your mortar may eventually crack.)

installation:
concrete foundation

The process is more expensive—and it's more work—but mortaring your cut stones in place on top of a concrete foundation gives you a stronger, longer-lasting, and more finished-looking floor.

Foundation

Clear and grade your site, mark your floor layout, and prepare the concrete foundation (Option 3) described on page 51. Finish it with a rough texture, using a screed or a float, and let it cure for at least seven days before adding the stone.

BELOW: **Large cut stone pavers are substantial enough to hold their own when combined with a stout rock wall and sturdy furniture.**

Setting Bed

With a mason's trowel, spread a ¾- to 1-inch layer of mortar over one workable section of the foundation at a time (about 5 square feet). Mortar sets quickly, so you don't want to apply it to the entire foundation at once. Screed the mortar to level it.

Laying the Stone

Begin pressing stones into the mortar according to your design, and tap each with a mallet. If you want the joints between the stones to be uniform, use spacers between each. After you've laid several stones, place a level or a long, straight board over them to make sure they're flat. Adjust any that aren't by tapping them into place. It's a good idea to keep a bucket of water and a sponge nearby, so you can quickly sponge off any mortar that makes its way to the surface of a stone before the mortar stains it. Continue laying the rest of your stones, then let the floor rest overnight.

Joints

Use a small pointed trowel or a grout bag to fill the joints between the stones with mortar. (This is another good time to keep

BELOW: Brick edging keeps this unmortared table support made of marble slabs in place.

a sponge and water handy, to immediately clean any misplaced mortar from the surfaces of your stones.) Once the mortar begins to set (you can tell because it will hold the impression of your finger), finish it off by pulling a jointing tool across it to compact and shape it.

---

trimming cut stone

Wearing eye protection, use a circular saw with a masonry blade to score the stone where you want to make your cut, lining up a sturdy piece of lumber as your cutting guide. Score to a depth of about ½ inch. Next, lay the stone on top of the wood, lining up the score line with the edge of the lumber. Strike the section of stone you want to trim away with a hammer, and it should easily snap off.

---

maintenance

If you've dry laid your stones on a flexible foundation, you may need to occasionally rework them to keep the surface smooth and level. You'll probably also need to add more sand between the joints every year or so and do some weeding in the joints now and then. Mortared stone on a concrete foundation should require no more maintenance than periodic sweeping. If you'll be using a snow shovel on either during the off season, make it one that's rubber tipped, so you don't scratch the stone.

concrete
paver
floors

L ittle wonder that concrete pavers have
been winning popularity contests with home
landscapers lately. When a material is inexpensive, easy to install, highly durable, and available
in a huge range of multipurpose styles, it tends to
become a crowd pleaser. To meet the demand, paver
suppliers are rapidly expanding their lines. At nearly
any home improvement center today, you can find
pavers in a wide selection of colors, textures, shapes,
and patterns, including concrete pavers that link
together in a sturdy interlocking design.

special tools and supplies

If you're laying your pavers according to a pattern, you may need to trim them here and there to help them conform to the edges of your floor. You can either hire a masonry professional to help, or use the following tools (and the same process you'd use for cutting brick, page 64) to make the cuts yourself.

▪ Pencil or chalk for marking cuts

▪ Power masonry saw (if you've got lots of cuts to make) or a mechanical paver splitter (if you need to trim only a few pavers)

You'll also need a power compactor (a compact base is essential for this material) and eye and ear protection (for using power equipment).

PREVIOUS PAGE: **Leaving extra-wide gaps for planting between these concrete pavers allows the distinction between garden and floor to blur.**

TOP: **Close-up of a hexagonal paver stamped with an intricate pattern and laid with tight joints**

MIDDLE: **Pavers made to mimic cut limestone**

BOTTOM: **A standard style of interlocking concrete pavers**

TOP: **Irregular cuts allow these concrete pavers to conform to a circular design.**

MIDDLE: **Brick-like concrete pavers are available in an array of colors.**

BOTTOM: **Pigmented pavers stamped with a wave-like pattern**

design options

Concrete pavers lend themselves to three general types of paving designs.

▨ Interlocking pavers, made to fit together snugly and create a very sturdy surface, are a good choice for large floor areas such as drives and parking pads that need to be strong enough to bear heavy loads. The result is neat and orderly, but definitely manufactured; if you want a natural effect, interlocking pavers won't suit you.

▨ If you want to imitate the look of nearly any other paving material—cut bluestone, granite block, brick, you name it—there's likely a look-alike concrete paver on the market to help you do it. When you've got a lot of ground to cover, concrete is often far less expensive, more accessible, and easier to work with than the real thing, and good imitations are quite convincing.

▨ On the other hand, you may choose concrete pavers simply because they can look appealingly fabricated. If you want to pave your floor with fun geometric shapes, a collection of colors, or personalized pieces (such as pavers that have been painted, stamped, or embedded with designs), you can choose from a delightful selection of commercial pavers—or even make your own.

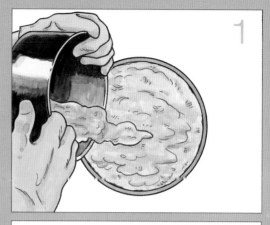

making concrete pavers

Okay, it's not the quickest route to paving your garden floor. But making your own pavers, even if you create only a few to place here and there among dozens of other commercial pavers, is one of the best ways to make your floor one of a kind.

1 Start with a cement mixture of 3 parts sand and 1 part cement, then mix in approximately 1 part water, until the cement is a pouring consistency. (You can also add dye at this point, if you want to color your pavers.) Choose or make a plastic mold that's about 2 to 3 inches deep and bottomless. The top rim of a large flowerpot works well for round pavers. Home-and-garden stores sell other molds in various shapes. Lubricate the inside of the mold with oil, set it on a sheet of plastic, then fill it to the top with the concrete mixture.

2 Drag a straight edge across the top of the mold to even and level the surface.

3 Decorate the paver by embedding the wet concrete with nearly any durable material you like, from tile fragments and glass nuggets to marbles and pieces of broken ceramic pots. Wearing rubber gloves, press the pieces into place, then push each piece in with a float, so about two-thirds of its depth is embedded. This is a wonderful way to incorporate mementoes from travels (maybe oyster shells from last summer's beach trip), sentimental bits (perhaps the remnants of a shattered piece of your grandmother's china), and other meaningful tokens.

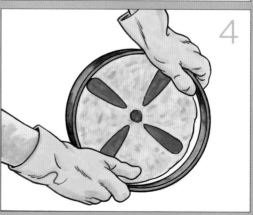

4 When the concrete is dry and fully set (about three days after pouring it), remove the mold by applying pressure and pulling outward around the edge. Finally, use a stiff-bristled brush to remove any excess concrete from the paver's surface, then clean it off with a fine spray of water.

LEFT: **Laying a floor doesn't have to be a huge undertaking. Here, a small section of concrete pavers creates a snug seating area just off a gravel path.**

BELOW: **Concrete pavers come in a multitude of shapes—and can be simply laid in a bed of decorative stone.**

installation

Foundation

Clear and grade your site, mark your floor layout, and prepare the sturdier foundation of rock and sand (Option 1) described on page 46. Use at least 4 inches of crushed rock in the foundation if you're building a floor that will bear light pedestrian traffic, 6 inches for a floor that will be traveled heavily, and 8 inches for a driveway. Add the 1-inch layer of sand, then wet (but don't saturate) the foundation material with a sprinkler and compact it well.

In most cases, concrete pavers, especially those you'll be laying in a tight or interlocking design, require an edge restraint to hold the floor firmly in place. Be sure to dig a trench around your floor foundation that is deep and wide enough to hold the edging you've chosen.

LEFT: **A pool surround featuring interlocking pavers that create a scalloped pattern**

Setting Bed

The 1-inch layer of leveled sand in the foundation serves as your setting bed. Be sure to use clean, washed, coarse concrete sand and not fine mason's sand or silica sand. Screed the sand to level the surface.

Laying the Pavers

How you lay your concrete pavers will depend on which type you've chosen. If you're working with brick-like pavers or those that have an interlocking design, proceed as if you were laying a brick floor. Begin by stretching level string lines across your floor area to use as guides for keeping your pattern lines straight and your surface level (see page 54). Start at one of your floor's outer edges, and lay a small section of pavers (about 4 to 5 feet square), following your pattern. If you want a floor with maximum strength, it's best to lay the pavers so the joints are as tight as possible; try to make them no larger than ⅛ inch. If you're working with larger pavers, lay them as you would cut stone. You'll still want level string lines as

---

hidden metal or plastic edging

Metal and PVC edging, which work especially well with interlocking concrete pavers, aren't designed to be a visible part of your floor design. Their main purpose is to strengthen your floor by providing horizontal resistance to the pavement, helping to maintain the interlock and load-spreading capabilities of the units. You also install these edging variations after laying your floor surface (rather than before, as you do with most other edging types). Metal edging is very durable and designed to curve easily. You simply position the wedge-shaped restraint in place, then nail it through the foundation base using 10-inch nails. PVC edging isn't quite as strong as metal, but if your floor won't have to accommodate vehicle traffic, it'll do its job just fine, as long as you're sure to buy PVC edging that's specified for paving and not for landscape edges.

guides, but you have much more leeway in terms of spacing between the pavers.

Whichever approach you're taking, adjust the sand setting bed underneath the pavers, as necessary, to make sure the tops of the pavers are up against the string level. After laying each row, lay a short length of 2 x 4 across the pavers, and tap it to level them. Use a rubber mallet to level individual pavers, if necessary. Always kneel in the sand behind where you're working, so you won't dislodge the pavers

planting in the gaps:
for fragrance

A starter list of aromatic plants that will release their fragrance (and survive) when they're stepped on:

Chamomile (*Chamaemelum nobile*). Lacy leaves, tiny yellow flowers, the scent of apples.

Cranesbill (*Geranium macrorrhizum*). Perennial with pink flowers and highly fragrant leaves.

Creeping Mint (*Mentha requientii*). Bright green leaves and light purple flowers. Creates a mossy effect. Best in partial shade and evenly moist soil. Minty, sage-like scent.

Lemon Thyme (*Thymus citriodorus*). Variegated gold and green leaves and lavender flowers in late spring. Lemon scented.

Snowbank (*Dianthus gratianopolitanus*). Shaggy plant, white flowers, highly perfumed.

you've just set in place. And check your work occasionally with a level to make sure you're maintaining the slope you established when you graded your site.

Compaction

If you've laid interlocking pavers, before you finish the joints, set the pavers in place firmly by making at least two passes over the entire surface with a power compactor.

Joints

Sprinkle clean, fine, dry sand across the surface of your floor, sweep it into the joints with a stiff push broom, and use a hose to sprinkle the floor lightly with water to settle the sand. Repeat the sweep-ing-and-watering process until the sand is well packed, the joints are full, and the pavers don't wobble. If you're working with interlocking pavers, before sweeping sand into the joints and wetting it, vibrate a layer of sand into the joints with the power compactor.

Finishing Work

Clean the surface of your floor with a cleaner specifically made for concrete pavers. After the surface is completely dry, you can spray or roll on a concrete paver sealer to protect the surface, if you like. Use a sealant that is made specifically for concrete pavers, not a general, all-purpose solution. And don't seal pavers around a pool deck; the chemicals can leach into the water.

RIGHT: In some cases, interlocking pavers that create patterns (like the fan-shaped one shown here) are sold in pre-formed slabs of connected pavers.

BELOW: In this small herb and cutting garden, pavers that simulate cut stone create a casual and practical little floor.

ABOVE: **Pavers of various colors and cuts resemble an elaborate tiled floor.**

maintenance

Over time, individual pavers may dislodge or settle in too deeply. Use a flat-headed screwdriver to remove problem pavers, adjust (and in many cases add to) the sand underneath, then position the pavers back into place. Occasionally, you'll also need to replace washed out sand in the joints between pavers and do a bit of weeding.

Efflorescence, the same whitish mineral that leaches out of bricks, creating stains or streaks, can also plague concrete pavers. If it doesn't disappear with normal weathering, choose a warm, dry day to wash it off with water and a rag or to brush it away with a stiff, dry brush. In addition, you can reapply sealant over the pavers every two to five years to prevent efflorescence, help the pavers resist other stains, and enhance the color of the pavers.

poured concrete floors

Poor concrete, it gets such a bad rap. Probably because most of us think of it as a wide, unimaginative expanse of glaring white, best reserved for city sidewalks and office-park entranceways. Think again. When you combine the growing number of ways to texturize, tint, and otherwise treat concrete with its marvelous flexibility (you work with it wet, so it conforms to any design you choose), you've got a sturdy paving material you can customize to suit a wide range of garden settings.

PREVIOUS PAGE:
This poured and stamped concrete floor connects to precast steppingstones beyond.

LEFT: The joints in this concrete floor were embedded with brick to add interest and connect it visually with the path beyond.

LOWER LEFT: The jointing in this poured-concrete terrace adds to the design. Precast pavers set in turf carry the floor into the yard.

special tools and supplies

Concrete sets up quickly. Prior to starting to work, make sure you have everything you need, so you don't spend precious time searching for tools.

- Heavy gloves

- Rubber boots

- Power compactor

- Rectangular concrete trowel

- Edger (also called an edging trowel, for cutting a rounded edge between the concrete and the form)

- Groover or jointer (for cutting smooth, straight control joints in the floor to prevent cracking)

- Bull float or darby float (These tools smooth out depressions or ridges after you've roughly leveled the cement with a screed. The bull float has a long handle for larger jobs; the darby is best for smaller jobs.)

the good news and the bad news

A concrete floor is one of the most durable types you can install; a well-constructed concrete slab can last up to 30 years, which is exactly the problem if you change your mind once your floor is in place. Altering your design will probably require breaking the floor to pieces and starting over. Concrete also sets up quickly, so there's little time for tweaking your design once you've started to pour.

▓ Wood float (optional) (for giving your floor a rougher finish to improve its traction)

▓ Contractor-quality wheelbarrow (if you are doing the mixing yourself)

▓ Hammer, nails, stakes, and 2 x 4 lumber for constructing forms

▓ Expansion material for filling control joints (You can buy either asphalt-impregnated felt or ½-inch molded fiber at home-improvement stores.)

▓ Plastic sheeting or tarp to cover the slab during the curing process (in case of rain).

design options

Because this most durable of paving options is the only one that is soft and flowing when you lay it, you can easily wrap it around a fountain, wind it along the curved edge of a pond, or adapt it to the shape of your space in nearly any other way.

A B O V E : **Here, tinted and stamped concrete takes on the look of stone.**

You can also alter the color and texture, whether you want your floor to blend naturally with other landscaping elements, provide a dramatic contrast, or resemble some other paving material altogether. Both tinting agents (available in powder form) and texturizing materials such as decorative gravel will alter the concrete before you pour it. Once you've poured your floor, you can stamp or stencil the still-wet surface with textured patterns to give it the appearance of cobblestone, brick, or other paving materials, or you can embed the surface with anything from stones, seashells, and cut glass to tile

installation

fragments and leaves. Various finishing tools, from stiff brooms to specialized floats, will also alter the surface of your poured floor. Or, wait until the floor has cured, and you can embellish it with concrete stains and paints.

Often, the trick to making concrete look less utilitarian is to use it sparingly and combine it with other materials, from bands of brick to randomly embedded pavers. Decorative edging can also add interest to a concrete floor in danger of seeming static.

The process for installing a concrete floor and pouring a concrete foundation as a firm base for another paving material is essentially the same. You can follow the process below for either situation. If you're simply pouring a foundation, you won't need to finish the surface. However, you will need to dig your foundation deep enough so that there's space to add a setting bed and your pavers on top of the concrete.

BELOW AND FACING PAGE: Poured concrete is ideal for floors with layouts that flow rather than adhere to straight lines and careful corners. Here, the surfaces have been stamped.

quick-glance glossary

The terms concrete and cement fly about interchangeably (with mortar tossed in every now and then, too). It can all be confusing to newcomers who need to know the difference. Here's how the definitions break down.

Cement: Also called Portland cement, this is the limey powder you combine with water and aggregate (sand and/or gravel) to create a durable surface. Premixed cement is Portland cement already mixed with aggregate; it's usually sold by the bag. With premixed cement, you simply add the water.

Concrete: When the cement mixture hardens, it forms concrete.

Mortar: Use a slightly different recipe of cement, aggregate, and water, and you create this mixture that is used as a bonding agent to lay brick, tile, and stone.

Foundation

Clear and grade your site, and mark your floor layout as described on page 42, placing your marking material about 1½ inches outside of where you want your floor's concrete edge, to allow enough room for wooden forms. Remove the sod, excavate the foundation, and compact the subgrade well, making sure it's free of tree roots, large rocks, and any other matter.

For a concrete floor, your foundation should be deep enough to accommodate 2 to 4 inches of crushed rock and 3 inches of concrete. (You'll usually pour 4 inches of concrete, but the final inch will sit above ground level.) If you're pouring a concrete foundation for another paving material (rather than a concrete floor), increase the depth of your excavation, so

ABOVE: **You can tint your wet cement before pouring it or paint or stain your cured concrete floor.**

About the Foundation's Crushed Rock

 Crushed rock as the first layer of your foundation makes your floor stronger and minimizes settling and cracking. However, if you have a dry, solid subgrade that is not clay, you can eliminate the crushed-rock layer without tremendous risk if your floor won't have to accommodate vehicles.

 If your soil drains poorly, err on the high side of the range for crushed rock, adding 3 to 4 inches.

 If your floor will have to accommodate vehicles as well as people, increase the amount of crushed rock in the foundation to 6 inches.

Forms

Wooden forms, typically made by setting 2 x 4 lumber vertically into the ground, hold the concrete in place until it dries. Once the concrete is set, you can do one of three things: rip out the forms, cover them with dirt or sod, or use them as decorative edging.

1 Begin by pounding 12-inch wooden stakes into the ground, leaving the tops of the stakes 1 inch above the ground. Place the stakes every 3 or 4 feet.

2 Use double-headed nails (which will be easy to pull out later) to nail the forms to the stakes (figure 1). Nail from the outside of the stakes through the forms (again, this makes it easier to pull out the nails later). As you work, make sure the forms maintain the slope you established when you graded your site. (To protect

you have room for your paving material on top of the concrete.

Along any area where the floor you're building will abut a foundation wall or existing concrete, install asphalt-impregnated expansion joints or ½-inch molded fiber, extending down the entire depth of the foundation. These strips, which you set in place so they'll be flush with the surface of your floor, will absorb any fluctuation in the concrete from temperature changes and will help prevent cracking.

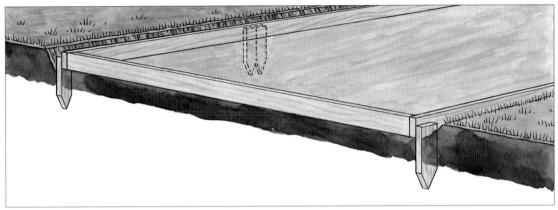

FIGURE 1. **Nail form boards to the stakes.**

forms that you want to use as decorative edging when your floor is finished, cover the top edges of the wood with masking tape. If you plan to leave the forms in place and cover them when your floor is finished, use cedar or redwood stakes, and position the stakes and the forms 1 inch below the ground rather than above it.)

If the floor you're building features curved edges, use 3½-inch-wide hardwood that is ¼ inch thick for your forms. Nail one end of the board to a stake, curve it to the shape you want, cut it, and nail the other end to another stake. You may need to cut slits that go halfway through the board every inch or so to help the wood bend.

Mixing the Cement

Premixed bags of cement have everything you need but water, but they're more expensive and primarily suitable for very small jobs. In most cases, you'll need Portland cement and aggregate (sand and gravel) that you'll mix together yourself in a wheelbarrow or a large plastic tub.

A good mix for a concrete floor is 1 part Portland cement, 2½ parts clean sand (not

---

let someone else do the mixing

For quantities greater than 1 cubic yard, you may want to have a concrete supplier mix the cement for you, deliver it to your site, and pour it directly from the truck to your floor, using a swinging chute. Keep in mind that this option may include unexpected costs (for pumping the cement to the pour area if it's not reachable by a large truck, for example) and added complications (such as ruts from the delivery truck on your lawn). On the other hand, it will save you tremendous time and labor and will reduce the chance for mixing error.

---

mason's sand or ocean sand; the salt will prevent proper curing), 2¾ parts clean, washed gravel (ranging from ¼ to 1 inch in size), and ½ part clean, potable water. The proportions may vary depending on where you live and the dampness of your sand; it's a good idea to also ask for advice on proportions from a local concrete supplier. Getting the right mix of ingredients is critical. If your cement mixture is too watery, your concrete will be weak and prone to cracking. If it's too dry, it will be hard to spread evenly, and you could end up with air pockets as a result.

When mixing cement for use in colder climates, you'll want to also include an additive that creates evenly distributed tiny bubbles in the mix. The enhanced mixture, called air-entrained cement, hardens into concrete that better withstands the expansion of freezing. Air-entrained cement must be mixed with a power mixer, rather than by hand. You can order it already mixed from a ready-mix supplier or add an air-entraining admixture to regular cement and mix it with a rented power mixer.

It's always a good idea to mix a small batch of your cement and test it before you pour your floor. When you spread it out with a trowel, the trowel should leave a smooth, wet surface in the cement. If water puddles where your trowel was, the mix needs more dry cement. If the mix is rough and crumbly, carefully and slowly add more water. (The water content of the sand and your area's humidity levels will also affect the moisture of your mixed cement.) A good mixture should feel smooth and creamy, but not soupy or crumbly.

Reinforcement

Adding reinforcement to the foundation in the form of wire mesh or steel rebar isn't necessary for small floors in a residential setting, as long as your cement mix includes strengthening fibers. Most concrete manufacturers are now adding fiberglass to their mix as a strengthener and a replacement for the reinforcing. You can also buy bags of fiberglass from concrete-supply stores. If you're ordering your cement already mixed, specify that the supplier add fiberglass.

tip

Don't plan to pour cement unless the air temperature is at least 40°F (4°C) at the coldest part of the day. You'll have the best luck if you install your floor when you expect a month or two of weather in that range or warmer. The temperature will help your floor cure and dry properly.

Pouring the Floor

When pouring your floor, work in small sections of 3 or 4 feet at a time, completing all the steps listed before you move on to another section.

1. Lightly moisten the forms with a hose.

2. Pour the cement in small patches throughout the section rather than dumping large piles and then dragging it long distances with a rake. Rake the cement to roughly level, using a hard rake (not a leaf rake). If you have your cement

FIGURE 2. **Screed the wet cement.**

FIGURES 3 AND 4. **Use either a darby float** (LEFT) **or a bull float** (RIGHT) **to smooth the surface.**

BELOW:
Concrete floors are stable enough that they don't require edging, though you can choose to add it for aesthetic appeal.

delivered, make sure you pour it within 90 minutes of the time it was loaded in the truck. After pouring, move a shovel or hoe up and down in the mixture to remove air bubbles, especially near the edges, but be careful not to overwork it.

3 With the help of a partner, screed or level the raked cement with a 2 x 4 board that's long enough to rest on the forms on both sides of the floor. Shimmy the screed horizontally across the slab twice (figure 2). Screeding the cement is the first stage of leveling it.

4 Use either the darby float or the bull float to further smooth the surface and push the larger aggregate pieces to the bottom of the slab (figures 3 and 4). Push the float away from you with the front edge slightly raised, and then pull it back again with the blade lying flat. Continue this process until water stops rising to the surface. Don't overwork the cement, though, or you'll bring too much fine material to the surface, which makes it weaker.

5 When there is no water visible on the surface, begin edging the perimeter of the floor, moving the edger along the surface with the front tilted up slightly, so it glides smoothly (figure 5).

6 Use the groover or jointer to create grooves along the surface at regular intervals to prevent cracking. Guide the tool against a long plank (figure 6). If you like, the grooves can be integral to the surface design of your floor. A good rule of thumb is to place your grooves the same distance apart as your floor is wide. For floors that are wider than 10 feet, run a joint down the center of the floor, as well. Control joints should run about 1 inch deep for a 4-inch-deep floor or 1½ inches deep for a 6-inch-deep floor (such as a driveway). (If you like, you can cut your joints in later with a circular saw.)

If you're pouring a concrete foundation for another paving material, you can stop at this point, cover the foundation with a sheet of polyethylene plastic, and let the concrete cure for a week, then add a setting bed and your pavers.

If you're creating a concrete floor, move on to finishing it.

FIGURE 5. **Edge the perimeter of the floor.**

FIGURE 6. **Create grooves along the surface to prevent cracking.**

finishing
the floor

1 Texturize your surface, so your floor will have some traction and be skid resistant. A wood float will give you a rough surface. So will sweeping a stiff broom across the floor surface. (Be sure not to use a steel float, though; it will create a surface that's too slick.) Now is also the time to enhance your floor by stamping, stenciling, or embedding the surface (see Enhancing the Surface, below). If you're adding quite a bit of texturizing surface decoration, you don't need to texturize the surface with a float or a broom beforehand.

2 Cover your floor with a sheet of polyethylene plastic for a week to hold in the moisture and prevent it from drying too quickly. This curing process allows the concrete to bond properly.

3 Two days after removing the plastic, you can pull off the form boards. Don't walk on the floor for four days after removing the plastic, and don't drive on it for seven days.

4 Backfill any areas around the edge of the floor that might be tripping hazards, and add plantings along the edges, if you like.

enhancing
the surface

Once your floor is poured, you have about an hour to work on the surface before the concrete is too stiff. You can add a retardant to the concrete mix to slow the hardening process. Even so, if you're adding an intricate surface design (a mosaic, for example), you'll probably want to pour and complete only small sections of your floor at a time.

TOP AND BOTTOM: Pieces of this floor, such as the central green circle, were poured in place with pigmented concrete, then surrounded by precast concrete pavers. Pavers set on end create the floor's edging. The design complements the home's art deco interior.

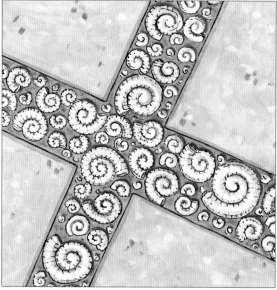

Concrete embedded with glazed tiles, brick, and tile shards (UPPER LEFT); **lines of stone paving blocks and black and white pebbles** (BOTTOM); **and shells in the joints between pavers** (UPPER RIGHT)

Embedding Materials

Glazed tiles, pottery shards, interesting found objects (see the horseshoe embedding on page 139), colored glass, leaves, and countless other materials can personalize the surface of your concrete floor, whether you place the pieces randomly, position them inside decorative edges, or create an elaborate mosaic. The basics for embedding are the same; you simply change the material and design to suit your style.

1 Pour only as much wet cement as you can embed in about an hour (or less if the weather is hot and dry). After that time, it will be too hard to work with. You may even want to add a retardant, which you can buy at a hardware store, to slow the cement's hardening.

2 With your mapped-out design and the objects to be embedded close at hand, slip on some rubber gloves and press the pieces in place. You may want to rest a long, sturdy board across the forms on either side of your floor, so you can kneel on it as you work.

3 After you finish a section, lay a thin piece of plywood over the embedded surface and apply light pressure to firmly embed the objects, tamping them to about even with the concrete.

4 When the concrete is hard, typically after about 36 to 48 hours, sweep the embedded surface clean with a stiff broom.

Coloring the Concrete

Concrete paints and stains are both available at home improvement stores. The paint (choose water-based latex paint) simply coats the surface, while the stain infiltrates the concrete. Check the manufacturer's instructions on whether you need to apply a primer first. Typically, you won't, but if your concrete floor is freshly installed, make sure it's completely cured before you apply the paint or stain. You may also need to etch the surface first with muriatic acid to roughen it up. If your concrete floor has been in place for awhile, wash it and let it dry completely before adding color. Finally, look for an inconspicuous spot where you can test the paint or stain you've chosen to make sure it's what you had in mind before you bathe your floor in it. You may need to apply several coats of your coloring agent to achieve the look you want. Both paint and stain will weather over time, so you'll have to freshen the color occasionally.

Stamping

Stamping concrete floors is becoming an increasingly popular technique. Stamps come in patterns ranging from brick and tile to quarried stone, and they're often used in conjunction with coloring agents to create a quite natural look. Most home landscapers hire a contractor with imprinting tools to help with the stamping, which can be a complex process, especially on a large floor.

TOP: **Hand-painted concrete**

BOTTOM: **A simple stamping job, this pigmented concrete was stamped with the frond of a yucca plant**

On a much simpler level, you can stamp small sections with purchased or home-made stamps that make impressions of everything from animal tracks to letters of the alphabet.

Texturizing

Different floats and brooms can give the surface of your concrete floor various subtle textures, but if you want something more dramatic, add extra aggregate to your cement mix, then expose it. For best effect, use an aggregate (decorative pebbles, for example) that contrasts in color with the concrete. Once you've finished the wet surface of your floor with a float, let it dry for about 6 hours, then remove a thin layer of concrete with a stiff-bristled brush followed by a fine spray of water, until the aggregate is exposed. (Careful not to expose too much, though. About two-thirds of each piece of aggregate should remain embedded.) Let your floor set for another 36 to 48 hours, then

ABOVE: **An aggregate of pea gravel was added to this pigmented mix, then exposed.**

UPPER LEFT: **Poured concrete featuring exposed aggregate and embedded with a design of pre-cast pavers**

LOWER LEFT: **Quartzite aggregate was added to this concrete before it was poured to give it a sparkling effect. It was finished with a broom.**

clean any remaining concrete from the aggregate with a high-pressure water jet.

Another way to achieve a similar look is to sprinkle small stones into the surface of the concrete before it dries. In warm climates that don't experience winter freezes, you can also create a pitted surface by evenly scattering ordinary rock salt across the surface of your wet concrete, using about 3 to 6 pounds of salt per 200 square feet of surface area. Roll a piece of plastic pipe over the salt to embed it in the concrete, allow the concrete to cure for seven days, then wash and brush the surface.

maintenance

Though concrete floors need very little care and attention, you can do a few things to keep yours in shape.

▪ Protect your new floor from draining water (the kind that might run out of downspouts).

▪ Don't use salt or other de-icers during the first winter. After that, use de-icers that contain only sodium chloride or calcium chloride.

▪ Water-repellent sealers can help reduce damage from freeze-thaw cycles and from salt, but some may slightly darken your floor. Follow your sealer's instructions regarding how long to wait after the concrete has been poured before you can seal it. Most sealers are effective for about two years.

exposing decorative aggregate

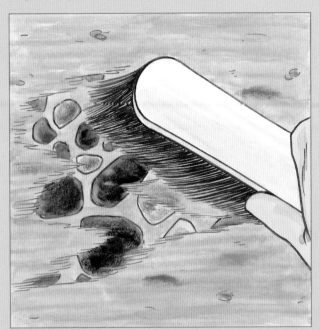

Remove a thin layer of concrete to expose about one-third of the aggregate.

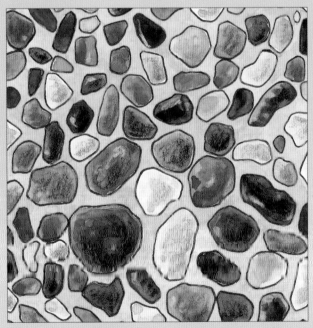

After another 36 to 48 hours, clean any remaining concrete residue with a high-pressure water jet.

floors of recycled and nontraditional materials

Some gardens—and, more to the point, some gardeners—simply aren't cut out for tidy rows of new, neatly mortared bricks or perfectly molded concrete pavers. If tried and true approaches have always been a bit too predictable for you, you've probably got your suspicions that standard paving materials are only a starting point. Here's a sampling of one-of-a-kind floors—from funky to modern to highly personalized—that proves you're exactly right.

FACING PAGE:
These recycled railroad tracks and ties were laid on compacted gravel over compacted earth. (Note: One of the reasons wooden railroad ties are available for recycling is that they've been treated with creosote to keep them from rotting. This gooey, tar-like substance can stain clothes. And it makes the ties best for floors that don't incorporate ground cover; it can be toxic to plants.)

RIGHT: Manhole covers and machinery parts in a setting bed of mulch create a quirky garden floor outside an artist's warehouse studio.

BELOW: A millstone whose days of grinding grain are long gone creates a focal point in a tiny brick terrace.

industrial cast-offs

Gone is the time when recycling meant grudgingly making do with already used leftovers. Today, salvage yards and flea markets have become hot shopping spots, as more and more of us seek out pieces that feature the nicks, chips, and other imperfections that prove they've got some history.

recycled paving

Ironic, but often you can end up with great paving material by snatching up what some-one else decides is no longer good enough.

LEFT AND ABOVE:
When the city of Easley, South Carolina, ripped out its streets' granite curbstones, the landscapers at J. Dabney Peeples Design Associates, Inc., transformed the decades-old material into their firm's front entranceway.

natural materials

Some of the most obvious materials you can recycle into paving for your floor are those that already make themselves comfortably at home in your yard: pine needles, bark mulches, leaves, and the like. They create soft, welcoming surfaces that blend seamlessly with their surroundings. They're also some of the easiest and least expensive materials to work with.

If your soil drains well, you can probably get away with simply clearing the surface you've marked out for your floor, adding some simple edging, and spreading on several inches of your paving layer (did we mention that these are casual floors?). For better protection against a mud-filled floor after a heavy rain, go ahead and dig a foundation 4 to 6 inches deep and fill it with compacted crushed rock (see page 46 for details), then spread on your surface layer. You'll likely need to replenish natural paving materials frequently (at least once a year) as they pack down and decompose. Natural-material floors also require a bit of weeding now and then.

recycled wood rounds

Recycled wood rounds set in sand or mortar create a charmingly rustic floor. Cut the rounds with a chain saw (usually 8 to 10 inches thick), let them dry out, then soak them in a penetrating wood preservative before laying them. One word of caution: it's best to attempt this version of rustic charm in dry areas and on properly draining soil only. In soggy soil, even treated wood rounds will eventually become covered with moss, making for an extremely slippery surface.

nontraditional materials

Just as interesting as cleverly recycling a material is choosing a paving material that's entirely unexpected. Place something people typically associate with manufacturing plants beneath garden benches and pots of flowers, and your worries about coming up with good conversation starters for your garden parties are over.

ABOVE: In these city gardens, floors of industrial grating blend well with the contemporary, urban setting. In one, the grating is placed on crushed stone and edged with painted timbers (and topped with commercial-grade mixing bowls as planters). In the other, the grating is settled into black lava rock.

LEFT: With a nod to the notion that anything goes when you're adding personality to your garden, the creators of this small, informal seating area wedged chunks of their recently removed bathroom tile in among more traditional paving units.

BELOW: Embedding concrete is one of the most effective paving techniques for adding originality to an outdoor floor. A household of horse lovers used the technique to link their porch floor with the one in the room just beyond. (For details on embedding concrete, see page 130.)

personalized paving

Of course, the best way to create a garden floor that defies standard classification is to pave it with something all your own.

PATHS AND WALKWAYS

the big book of backyard projects

getting started

Should your path wind lazily along or follow a strong, straight line? Is it best to make it wide and roomy, or narrow and cozy? And how do you choose between bricks or pebbles, mulch or steppingstones? You'll be much better prepared to make these and other decisions if you start by thinking through the purpose of your path and studying the place where it will lie. We start with the key questions you should ask about purpose and place. Then we guide you in using your answers to design your path, prepare a strong base, choose appropriate paving materials, and build the path that truly gets you where you want to go.

PURPOSE: who will be traveling your path, and why?

Putting yourself in the place of those who will regularly use your path will help you make decisions about everything from layout to materials.

- Will your path's primary users be children with bare feet traveling from patio to pool? If so, you won't want to top it off with sharp gravel.

- Are you helping someone push a stroller to the back door or a wheelbarrow to the compost pile? Then brick or concrete will make better paving materials than decorative pebbles.

- Will a person taking out the trash regularly walk the path after dark? In that case, you'd be better off choosing a direct path of pine needles or earth rather than a meandering maze of steppingstones.

Decide whether travelers will be using your path to move efficiently from point A to point B or to take a leisurely stroll. If it's meant to be utilitarian, you'll want your path to be as direct and obstacle-free as possible.

- People juggling groceries on their way from the car to the door don't want to zigzag through a bed of perennials. In fact, they won't—they'll eventually forge a shortcut (and everyone from delivery people to guests carrying casseroles will follow).

- On the other hand, if people will be using your path to wander through your rose garden, they'll love graceful turns past trickling fountains and unexpected openings at benches and bird baths.

Heavy-use paths designed to get people to main entrances should be wide, very comfortable underfoot, inviting, and clearly marked, whether by a gate or potted plants at the entrance or hedges along the border. A path that offers a casual tour through the herb garden might be narrower and more subtle, and a purely practical path that veers off to the tool shed may be a simple earthen track that slips off nearly unnoticed.

OPPOSITE PAGE: **California orchard entrance**

BELOW: **A stone path set into a front lawn**

PLACE: what do you need to know about your path site?

Existing Structures and Objects

Decide whether your path will abut the foundation of a house, garage, shed, or other building. If so, before laying your path base, you'll need to check (and perhaps adjust) the site's slope to make sure water is directed away from the building foundation (see Adjusting the Slope, page 170).

Also, in the early planning stages consider whether there are shapes or lines you want your path to echo, from the curve of a pool to the geometric edge of a plant bed. As outlined in Choosing Your Path Material (page 148), some path materials lend themselves better to straight walks while others are best for winding trails.

Think, too, about the style and materials of existing structures. A wide, formal brick walkway would be out of place leading to a modest cabin in the woods; a three-story estate needs something more than stepping-stones for a front walk.

Finally, note whether there are nearby trees whose roots will grow and eventually cause your path to buckle (oaks and maples are notorious offenders). If so, you may want to use flexible material rather than concrete or brick as paving materials. The tree roots can crack concrete and reduce your brick walk to rubble. Other ways to deal with trees are to prune the tree roots or re-route the path.

Climate

Think through the seasonal range of weather in your region. If you live in an area with a lot of rain or snow, prepare your path for good drainage (see Improving Drainage, page 178) or it may settle into a muddy chain of puddles. If your ground freezes hard in the winter or if your soil expands during the wet season and contracts during the dry season, a

proper base is extra-important (see Laying a Base for Your Path, page 168). In Florida, the South, and southern and coastal California, on the other hand, soils are generally more stable and path bases need not be as deep.

Take climate into consideration when you select your path material as well. For example, concrete may crack and bricks may unsettle in deep freezes that cause the ground to heave; some cut stone and stepping-stone paths will be slippery when it's wet; grass paths need adequate moisture and sunlight; and tile may be too hot underfoot if it bakes in the sunshine. The Choosing Your Path Material chapter (page 148) addresses considerations like these for a full range of materials.

Drainage

Good drainage is essential to the long-term stability of your path. By determining how well your soil drains before you begin, you'll be prepared to correct poor drainage, if necessary, when you lay your path base.

The makeup of your soil will give you a good idea of how well it drains. If it's sandy or gravelly, chances are water will percolate easily through it. Clay and heavy topsoil, on the other hand, hold water and may create a muddy or spongy layer beneath your path if you don't improve the drainage.

To test your soil's drainage, follow these steps:

1 Dig a hole in the path site roughly 4 inches in diameter by 12 inches deep and fill it with water.

2 Let the hole drain completely, then refill it.

3 If it doesn't drain again within 12 hours, your soil's drainage is poor. You can improve it by excavating the path base at the deepest level suggested for the path type you're building and by laying a drainage pipe in your base (see Improving Drainage, page 178).

It's also important to know how water naturally drains on the site you've chosen for your path. Go outside during a heavy rain and study the movement of storm water across the ground. Or, if you'd rather stay dry, sprinkle a line of lime, pine bark chips, or anything else that will float down the center of your path site. After a rain, the material will show the water run-off pattern. When you prepare the ground for your path, you'll want to take advantage of natural drainage to direct water off and away from the path or to carry water along the run of the path and toward an existing drainage area.

Terrain

If the path site slopes steeply, consider how you'll adjust it to accommodate your path (see Adjusting the Slope, page 170). The terrain should also guide your choice of materials. Certain materials are better for paths that slope. Gravel, for instance, is less likely than mulch to wash downslope in a heavy rain, and it won't be as slippery as slate pavers when it's wet. Also, with a sloped path you'll want to take precautions against leaving low spots where puddles form.

Available Materials

Ask local suppliers (and other path builders) about paving materials that are available in your area. Are there native stones? Are pine needles so common that they are baled for sale each year? Is there a source of river gravel? Heavy paving materials, such as brick, stone, and ornamental gravel, are costly to transport, making local materials not only better suited to your climate, but also less expensive.

PERSONAL INVESTMENT: how much time, effort, and money do you want to spend?

Finally, before you order a load of paving materials and start digging, give some thought to the magnitude of the project you are willing to take on. Laying down a short steppingstone path from the back door to the tomato plants will be a considerably easier undertaking than building a concrete front walk with embedded tile designs. A casual garden path topped with straw will be far less expensive than an ornate, cut-stone promenade. Study Choosing Your Path Material beginning on page 148, which outlines everything from purchasing information to difficulty of construction for a range of materials. Then, beginning on page 182, we tell you how to lay various types of paths and help you gauge how involved a project you have in mind might be.

PREVIOUS PAGE: Native stone and other local materials will be much less expensive and more readily available than those that must be transported.

ABOVE: Existing beds of flowers determined the layout for these natural paths.

RIGHT: Gravel works well as a paving material for paths on gently sloping sites.

choosing
your path
material

very paving material has its pros and cons—characteristics you'll want to consider before deciding which one to use. In this chapter, we provide overviews of common paving materials so you can compare, contrast, and determine which one is best for the path you want to build.

natural material

EFFECT ACHIEVED:

Materials such as pine needles, bark mulches, straw, crushed shells, and earth create the most informal, natural-looking paths.

ADVANTAGES:

Natural material paths are among the least expensive and easiest to build, and they conform easily to areas with slight dips, rises, and curves.

DISADVANTAGES:

Natural material paths can become soggy and can break down or erode quickly. Weeds can invade them, and the materials can be tracked to inside environments if the path is near the house. All organic materials break down and need periodic refreshing, depending on climate and use. Bark and needles tend to wash away when it rains on sloping sites.

CLIMATE CONSIDERATIONS:

Specific materials such as pine needles may be readily available only in certain regions. Natural material paths in rainy areas might become too boggy. In windy areas, materials might blow away, and in most areas they are susceptible to invasion by weeds.

DURABILITY:

Varies. Dirt has good durability, unless the area becomes too muddy. Pine needles, bark mulches, and straw have poor durability under heavy use.

DIFFICULTY OF CONSTRUCTION:

Easy.

CALCULATING QUANTITY:

Multiply the length and width of your path by the depth you want for your surface layer to determine the volume of material needed. This will give you cubic feet or meters. Divide by 27 to convert cubic feet to cubic yards. Natural materials may be sold by the truckload or the bale—in bulk by the cubic yard and in bags by the cubic foot. Sellers will be happy to help you determine the amount you need, based on the area to be covered. For example, one bale of pine needles covers 40 square feet to a depth of 3 to 4 inches. For small projects, pine bark nuggets can be bought by the bag at home and building supply stores; refer to the bag for recommended coverage. Shredded hardwood bark is usually sold in bulk by the cubic yard (1 cubic yard of shredded hardwood usually covers 81 square feet 3 inches deep). It knits together well and doesn't erode as easily as pine bark, and it's more durable. A bare soil garden path is made by use the worn path but may need some grading or stepping-stones to keep it from becoming muddy.

WHERE TO PURCHASE:

Some materials you can collect yourself in the woods or other areas. Others can be purchased from garden centers, saw mills, farms, and other suppliers of regional materials. Bulk suppliers will generally load your truck for free or deliver for a small fee.

PRICING:

Most natural materials are priced by the cubic foot or meter and sold in bags. Or, they're priced in bulk and sold by the bale at home, garden, or building supply stores. The cost is relatively low; a natural material path is typically the least expensive type you can build.

gravel and ornamental stone

EFFECT ACHIEVED:

Gravel, crushed stone, and decorative pebbles add ribbons of texture, color, and sound (that nice crunching underfoot) to both formal and informal areas.

ADVANTAGES:

Gravel paths are among the least expensive path types you can build. If properly graded, they drain quickly, hold well on moderate slopes, and retain their shape if the ground heaves.

DISADVANTAGES:

Gravel paths can wash on steep slopes and weeds can invade them. The pebbly materials can also be tracked inside if the path is near a door, and gravel tracked onto stone or brick steps or patios can roll underfoot.

CLIMATE CONSIDERATIONS:

Grade for a cross slope or prepare a draining base if you're working in a wet climate.

DURABILITY:

Good. You may need to occasionally rake spillage back onto the path and replenish the gravel.

DIFFICULTY OF CONSTRUCTION:

Moderate.

CALCULATING QUANTITY:

Most bags of loose rock materials are sold by the cubic foot, while bulk purchases are usually made in cubic yards or tons. To calculate materials in cubic feet or meters, multiply the width and length of the path by the desired depth of the material, keeping all measurements in feet or meters. Divide cubic feet by 27 to convert to cubic yards.

WHERE TO PURCHASE:

Gravel and other loose rock paving materials can be purchased from sand and gravel suppliers, who sell by the cubic yard or the ton. You can cart loose rock and gravel home in a pickup truck or have your order delivered for a fee. Gravel or stone any larger than ¾ inch can be difficult to walk on. For best results, select ⅜-inch stones.

PRICING:

You'll get the best pricing on the quantity of loose rock usually needed to fill a path or walkway by buying in bulk at a quarry, a sand and gravel yard, or at another stone supplier. Bulk suppliers sell gravel and loose rock by the ton (2000 pounds). For smaller projects, bags of pebbles are available at home, garden, and building supply stores. Decorative stones are more expensive than pea gravel. A simple gravel path costs about the same or slightly more than a natural material path.

grass

Sod being cut at a sod farm.

EFFECT ACHIEVED:

These strips of natural green can be formal or informal, and they present handsome foregrounds for flower beds, herbaceous borders, and shrub gardens.

ADVANTAGES:

Grass paths are cool under bare feet, they work well on sloping land, and they're among the least expensive paths you can build.

DISADVANTAGES:

Keeping a grass path green may be a challenge in drought-prone areas. If you're creating a grass path from seed rather than sod, you'll have to refrain from walking on it for several weeks after sowing the seeds. Weeds can be a problem, and newly seeded soil can erode on sloped areas. Excess traffic can wear bald spots in the path. Oh, and you'll be doing some mowing.

CLIMATE CONSIDERATIONS:

Grass paths do best in full sun, need plenty of water, and can turn to mud in snowy winter climates. Warm season grasses (Bermuda, zoysia, centipede) endure traffic best, but they go dormant in winter. (They do best in climate zones 8 and higher.) Cool season grasses (fescue, bluegrass, rye) are evergreen, but often need overseeding to stay thick. Use red fescue in areas of heavy shade.

DURABILITY:

Fair to good, depending on maintenance and traffic.

DIFFICULTY OF CONSTRUCTION:

Moderate in good soil, though laying sod is heavy work.

CALCULATING QUANTITY:

Sod is sold by the pallet and comes in strips 18 to 24 inches wide and 2 to 5 feet long. Grass seed is typically pre-bagged and sold by the pound at garden centers, where retailers can guide you on how much you need to cover your path. Note that seed sizes vary; for example, 5 to 6 pounds of fescue seed will cover the same 1000-square-foot area as 2 to 3 pounds of Bermuda seed. Multiply the length of your path by the width to get the total square feet or meters you need to cover with seed.

WHERE TO PURCHASE:

Sod can be purchased directly from a sod farm, which is typically less expensive than a garden center. If purchasing from a sod grower, calculate the square yardage of the area and order your sod in advance so it can be cut before you arrive. Most sod companies deliver for an extra charge for minimum orders of 4 pallets, or 240 square yards.

PRICING:

Sod strips are priced by the square yard. Seed costs vary according to type and from year to year, but seed will be a fraction of the cost of sod.

cut stone

Cut stone refers to any stone paving material that has been cut into a uniform shape, usually a square or rectangle ranging in size from about 1 square foot to 4 square feet. Types of cut stone will vary by region and include limestone, sandstone, bluestone, slate, and granite.

EFFECT ACHIEVED:

Cut stone provides a formal, stately look.

ADVANTAGES:

Especially handsome (and formal) when laid in mortar on a cement base. Large stones on a flexible base are striking, too. Cut stone is nearly permanent and can provide a smooth surface.

DISADVANTAGES:

Slate and marble pavers are very smooth and become slick when wet. They're especially dangerous when used for sloping walks or ramps.

CLIMATE CONSIDERATIONS:

Cut stone can be susceptible to cracking in harsh winter climates.

DURABILITY:

Excellent, though limestone will wear down with years of weathering and use.

DIFFICULTY OF CONSTRUCTION:

A cut stone walkway is one of the most labor-intensive path types. However, cut stones may also be placed informally to form simple steppingstone paths.

CALCULATING QUANTITY:

Multiply the length of your path by its width to get the square feet or meters of stone needed.

WHERE TO PURCHASE:

Purchase from masonry suppliers, stone yards, and tile companies. Cut stones can be transported in a pick-up truck or delivered to your site for a fee (many suppliers charge a flat local delivery rate and sometimes add mileage costs, depending on the distance.)

PRICING:

Cut stone is sold by the square foot or meter, and prices vary by size and color. Cut stone is more expensive than most materials, with rare colors such as desert rose or oak being the most costly.

natural stone

Naturally occurring or quarried flat stones of various sizes, colors, shapes, and thicknesses make charming paths that are less formal looking than cut stone paths. Fieldstone, collected from fields or old stone walls, is often rough and weathered. Quarried stone, dynamited or pried from large rock masses in the earth, can have a cleaner look. Common types of quarried stone include sandstone, granite, and limestone. Large, 3- to 4-inch-thick pieces make the most stable paths.

EFFECT ACHIEVED:

The random shapes and aged surfaces of natural stone create a rustic, informal look. Natural stones also lend themselves to imaginative patterns, and their irregular gaps leave perfect spots for planting. Some have very attractive colors.

ADVANTAGES:

Stone walks can be laid on level and gently sloping surfaces, and the stones can be broken and shaped for a good fit. Locally available materials can often be used to build a stone pathway.

DISADVANTAGES:

Stones with irregular surfaces will collect puddles when it rains.

CLIMATE CONSIDERATIONS:

Puddles that collect on the surface of concave stones will form pools of ice in winter climates. Small, dry-laid stones will be subject to frost heave in cold winters. Poorly mixed or thin mortar joints between natural stones will tend to crumble.

DURABILITY:

Good to excellent.

DIFFICULTY OF CONSTRUCTION:

Laying stone is a bit like doing a very heavy jigsaw puzzle. Every piece is different, so you may end up spending a good deal of time fitting each to your liking. Simply laying stones one after the other in a steppingstone fashion is far less labor-intensive.

CALCULATING QUANTITY:

Multiply the length of the path by the width to get square feet or meters needed. Though stone is generally sold by the ton, the square foot or meter figure will allow your supplier to roughly calculate the amount needed.

WHERE TO PURCHASE:

If you don't have access to fieldstones, purchase flagstone from stone yards. They will load your truck or car with small amounts. Delivery costs extra and depends on the size of the truck and the distance.

PRICING:

Because stone is sold by the ton, prices vary greatly according to the thickness and type of stone. Other factors affect price, too. Some colors are more expensive than others. Fieldstone, which is labor-intensive to gather, is more costly than quarried stone. And you'll pay more if you want to handpick your stones at a quarry.

brick

EFFECT ACHIEVED:

Because bricks come in various colors and textures and can be combined in many different patterns, they can be used to create everything from regal walkways to homey paths with plant or moss-filled gaps. Be sure to use paving bricks rather than facing bricks, which are intended for walls.

ADVANTAGES:

Their standard size makes bricks easy to quantify and to lay. They usually mix well with other materials. For example, brick makes an excellent edging for gravel paths.

DISADVANTAGES:

Growing tree roots can cause brick paths to buckle. Batches of bricks can be difficult to match if you're trying to connect a new walk to an existing structure, such as a patio. Also, old brick, which looks charming, may not hold up well.

CLIMATE CONSIDERATIONS:

Old bricks may crack or crumble in winter climates. Bricks tend to grow mossy and slick in rainy climates, and to get hot underfoot in sunny areas.

DURABILITY:

Good, depending on the quality; old brick doesn't weather well.

DIFFICULTY OF CONSTRUCTION:

Requires great attention to detail, especially if you're laying intricate patterns, and needs a firm base to maintain a smooth surface.

CALCULATING QUANTITY:

Brick pavers are typically 2 inches thick, 3½ inches wide, and 7¾ inches long. It takes approximately five bricks to pave a square foot. Multiply the length of your path by the width to get the total square feet or meters (the area). Keep in mind that bricks come in different sizes—brick pavers come in thin or thick shapes (1 to 2 inches)—and brick laid on edge will cover less area.

WHERE TO PURCHASE:

Bricks can be purchased through brick suppliers, tile companies, and home and building supply centers. A full-sized pick-up truck with good suspension can normally haul about 1000 pounds or more of bricks, but most suppliers will deliver for a fee. Renting a load-and-go vehicle is another option available at some home and building suppliers—they load the vehicle, you drive it home and unload it.

PRICING:

Bricks are sold individually, so the cost will depend on how many bricks you need and what style of brick you choose. The three common colors of brick—red, tan, and gray—sell for the same price, but the price of brick in other styles and other colors may vary.

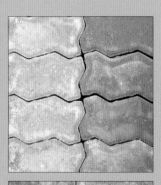

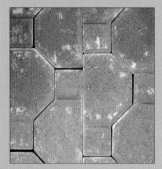

concrete

EFFECT ACHIEVED:

Because of concrete's versatility, it can be used to achieve almost any effect. It can be poured into curved forms or symmetrical molds to make pavers; it can be colored; it can be stamped with brick or rock patterns; or it can be decorated with embedded materials, such as pebbles, shells, brick, and crushed tile. Concrete can also be textured with brooms, leaf imprints, or burlap, and different floats can be used to vary the smoothness.

ADVANTAGES:

Usually needs no base. Durable and easy to clean.

DISADVANTAGES:

A bit tricky for beginners, and unforgiving of mistakes. It loses durability if it's mixed too long. Once the concrete has hardened, chances are you'll have to break your path to pieces and start over if you want to make changes. And it may be hard to match patchwork to the original.

CLIMATE CONSIDERATIONS:

Harsh winter climates and growing tree roots can cause concrete to crack. It gets hot underfoot in summer and cold and icy in winter.

DURABILITY:

Good, if mixed and poured correctly.

DIFFICULTY OF CONSTRUCTION:

Concrete paths require more careful planning and more equipment than other path types. A concrete path should be poured in sections that can be finished before the concrete sets. Expansion joints are needed every 12 feet and at abutments to existing buildings or patios. Extremes of heat and cold can cause damage during concrete "curing."

CALCULATING QUANTITY:

Generally, a bag of pre-mixed concrete (to which you add only water) will say how much coverage it will provide. Multiply the length by the width and depth of the walkway to determine how many bags you will need. For a concrete path 20 feet long, 4 inches thick, and 4 feet wide, buy materials for approximately 29 cubic feet of concrete (20 x .33 x 4, plus 10 percent for spillage or waste). Divide by 27 to convert cubic feet to cubic yards, and you get just over 1 cubic yard. For large jobs, buy in bulk (Portland cement, sand, and aggregate) and rent a power cement mixer, or order ready-to-pour concrete by the cubic yard.

WHERE TO PURCHASE:

Bags of concrete can be purchased at home and building supply centers. Most will deliver for a fee.

PRICING:

Concrete mix is priced per bag (with bags usually weighing about 60 pounds). A walkway that measures 48 square feet and 4 inches deep will require approximately 32 bags of concrete mix.

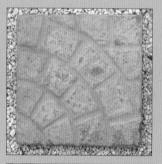

Concrete pavers provide an alternative to pouring a concrete path. Calculate quantity as you would for cut stone.

tools
and equipment

The basic list of tools and equipment needed to make a path is surprisingly brief. If you spend time digging in the garden and/or doing easy projects around the house and yard, chances are you already have much of what's required.

You can probably borrow anything you're missing, or purchase what you need for a modest price. In a few cases we recommend that you rent non-standard items; these are easy to find at a local equipment rental service. Also, at the beginning of each section on specific kinds of paths (starting on page 182) there's a short list of additional tools or pieces of equipment you might need for that project. Once you begin using the tools, you'll gain a feel for how to make substitutions (you might be more comfortable with a different digging tool than the one we've recommended, for example) and where to add to the list (it's common to have favorite tools for specific jobs).

general tools and equipment

4-FOOT LEVEL AND/OR STRING LEVEL. Levels are essential for building a path. You'll use them when you first grade your site, when you set the final paving stones in place, and at several stages in between. Techniques for using levels are described in detail beginning on page 47.

String level

SCREED. You'll want to make this special leveling tool (which you drag over base or surface materials) yourself so the size is exactly right. Simply cut notches out of a 2 x 6 board so it fits over your path edging and can be used to level the material underneath it.

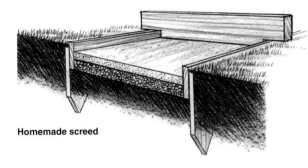

Homemade screed

HARD IRON RAKE. A rake is handy for spreading piles of gravel, sand, or decorative stone.

HAMMER, SAW, AND HEAVY-DUTY WORK GLOVES. These standbys will come in handy for a variety of activities, from cutting and pounding stakes to cutting drainpipe to carrying rough paving materials.

WHEELBARROW. You'll need a wheelbarrow for hauling out dirt and hauling in materials to fill the path.

TROWELS. A pointing trowel is best for mortaring brick and stone; a finishing trowel works for smoothing surfaces.

Pointing trowel and finishing trowel

TAMPING TOOL. As you make your path, you'll need to compact the layers. Hand tampers with metal plates typically measure 8 x 8 inches or 10 x 10 inches and are available at supply stores. Or, you can make your own tamper by nailing a solid, 8-inch square piece of thick lumber to one end of a 5-foot-long 4 x 4-inch piece of lumber (or any similar scrap material you can find).   For a large site (200 square feet or more), you may want to rent a drum roller you can fill with water.

200-pound (90 kilogram) drum roller

tools for laying out your path

■ **PIN FLAGS AND INVERTED MARKING PAINT.**
The easiest way to lay out a path is to use pin flags and inverted marking paint. Tying string between wooden stakes is another option. For a curving path, you might want to experiment with the layout first using a hose or a rope, then mark the borders with pin flags or stakes.

digging tools

MATTOCK. A mattock has a broad, slightly curved digging blade at one end and a small, chopping blade or pick at the other, making one end useful for loosening packed earth and embedded rocks and the other just right for cutting out roots.

SQUARE-BLADED SHOVEL. Square-bladed shovels are good for leveling rough spots, skimming grass, and later scooping gravel to fill the path base.

ROUND-NOSE SHOVEL. This all-purpose tool is helpful for digging and for spreading material into the path base.

LOPPING SHEARS OR PRUNING SAW. If you need to cut back small roots, these will come in handy; for larger roots you'll need an axe.

FOOT ADZ HOE. This tool is preferred for some digging jobs and perfect for skimming a layer of grass off the surface grade or for breaking up clay.

ABOVE: **Metal tamp, mattocks, foot adz hoe, shovels, metal rake**

TOP LEFT: **Pin flags, measuring tape, inverted marking paint, level**

BOTTOM LEFT: **A path site layed out with pin flags and marking paint**

equipment for laying the base

LANDSCAPE FABRIC. A protective layer can help retard the growth of weeds through your path and keep sediment from seeping into a perforated drainpipe.

4-INCH PERFORATED DRAINPIPE. This plastic pipe, used in a path base to improve drainage, is sold at home and building supply centers in various lengths that you can shorten with a saw or lengthen by joining pieces together. Sometimes, the pipe is already fitted with a "sock" that prevents sediment from seeping in. Other times you may have to purchase the sock separately and fit it around the pipe yourself.

finishing tools

BROOM. A broom is helpful for sweeping sand into cracks and cleaning up.

RUBBER MALLET. This tool can be used for tapping paving stones or brick into place.

LENGTH OF REBAR. Use a length of rebar as a pry bar when rearranging paving material.

STONE MASON'S HAMMER. With a head that is broad and flat at one end and tapers to a wedge at the other, a stone mason's hammer is just right for breaking and trimming stone.

LEFT: **Landscape fabric, pipe sock, perforated drainage pipe**

BELOW: **Stone mason's hammer, rubber mallet, rebar, broom**

laying a base for your path

Though you may think first of surface materials such as pebbles and wood chips when you picture a path, the unseen, unheralded layer underneath is what keeps a path stable and firm. To lay a standard, flexible (as opposed to concrete) path base, simply follow the procedures and how-to photos in this chapter. With certain paving materials, the base "recipe" will change slightly. Those changes are explained within the individual sections on making paths, beginning on page 182.

We've also included details for pouring a concrete base, beginning on page 176. This alternative is more labor intensive and more expensive than a standard, flexible base, but it provides a more solid, durable foundation, which you may want if you're building a brick or stone path. You can dry-lay brick or stone in sand on a concrete base or, for maximum durability, you can mortar the materials into place on a thin layer of wet cement.

clearing and smoothing the ground

Clear your path site by removing any stumps, old concrete, or sod. If you're building a path on a completely flat surface, you'll have little smoothing to do. Likewise, if the ground gently rises and falls and you're planning a path of grass, steppingstones, or loose materials such as gravel or wood chips, your path can follow the contours of the land with little problem. Your job might be as simple as leveling prominent bumps and filling potholes.

If you intend to lay a path of stone, concrete, or brick on an uneven or undulating area, however, you'll need to smooth the ground first. To do so, use a mattock to loosen the earth, a square-blade shovel to skim off soil from high spots, and a wheelbarrow to carry soil to places you need to build up. When filling in deep areas, add soil in 6-inch layers and compact it well using a hand-held tamping tool. If your site is 200 square feet or more, you may want to rent a gasoline-powered tamper (and purchase a set of earplugs to wear when using it!).

what percentage of slope tells you

0%–1.5%
The site is fairly flat and will need cross-slope drainage or drainage through the walk surface to get rid of standing rainwater.

1.5%–5%
The site is prime walk slope.

5%–8%
The site is technically considered a "ramp," and you should consider adding steps or even a handrail.

8%–15%
The site is steep. Mulches and gravel will wash, and your path will be slippery when it's icy.

adjusting the slope

FIGURE 1. **A two-percent slope**

When you're laying out your path, study the way it slopes. If the slope is gentle, take advantage of it to help direct water off or away from the path surface. If it's too steep to walk on comfortably, you'll want to adjust the slope, with options ranging from cutting the path across the slope to building in landings and/or steps. (A brief description of adding steps to a path appears on page 172. For more complicated situations you may want to consult a landscape architect or builder.)

House sites should already be graded to direct water away from the foundation; make sure your path takes advantage of this slope, especially if it abuts the foundation of the house (such as a path that meets the front door) or if it runs alongside the house or another structure. For example, a path from the front door to the street should slope away from the house at ¼ inch per foot for a two-percent slope (see figure 1). A path running parallel to a tool shed might slope the same percentage, but do so across its width (a cross slope) (see figure 2). A standard two-percent slope is nearly imperceptible to a walker, but it's enough to direct water off the path and away from buildings.

To monitor the slope of a path site as you're grading it, use a level that has double lines on the level's vial; a 4-foot-long model is most useful. First, set it on any level surface, then lift up one end to the slope position you're trying to achieve. Say, for example, you want a two-percent slope. With a 4-foot-long level, lift one end 1 inch; raise a 2-foot-long level ½ inch. With the level supported in this position, the air bubble inside should rest against the outer line on the level's vial, which marks a two-percent slope. As you grade the site, periodically rest the level on the ground and adjust the soil, as necessary, to maintain a two-percent slope.

For long runs of path, you may want to use a string level. You can use it to determine the slope of your entire path site, so you know whether you need to add or remove soil from certain areas to improve drainage.

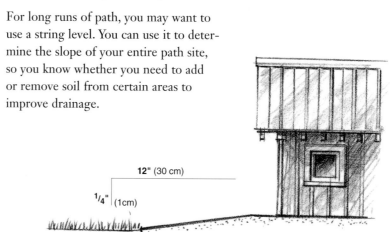

12" (30 cm)

¹/₄" (1cm)

FIGURE 2. **A two-percent cross slope (illustration not to scale)**

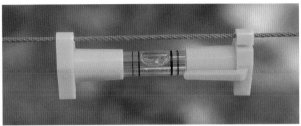

PHOTO 1

Here's how. A string level attaches to the middle of a taut string tied to two stakes, one at the high end of your path (at the door of the house, for example), the other at the low end. To determine the slope of such a run or a section of a run, adjust the string until the air bubble rests in the center of the vial, meaning the string is level (photo 1). (It's best to have someone help you with this, so one person can watch the air bubble while the other adjusts the string.) Once the string is level, measure the distance from string to ground at each end of your path (or at each end of the section for which you're determining the slope). Calculate the difference between those two measurements, and divide that number by the length of your path or of the section you're working with. The resulting figure is your percentage of slope. Say, for example, you have a 50-foot path. The distance from string to ground at one end is 1 foot; at the other end it's 2 feet. Divide the difference (1 foot) by the length of the path (50 feet) and you get .02, or two percent. This means your path has a two-percent slope (see figure 3).

If you plan to build your path on a steeper slope, keep in mind that a rise or descent of any more than 1 foot in 12 feet of path is generally too steep for comfortable walking over much distance. To grade a slope that is steeper than that, lay your path out so that it weaves back and forth across the slope, or add steps at various intervals.

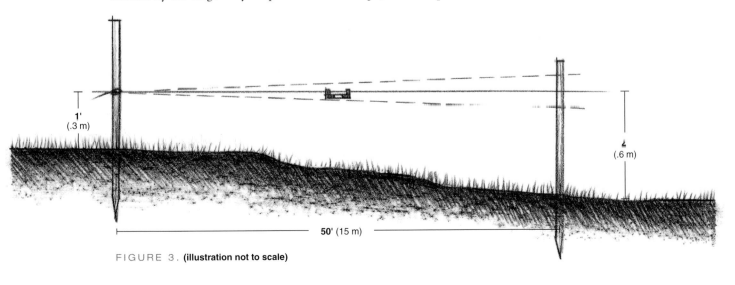

1'
(.3 m)

(.6 m)

50' (15 m)

FIGURE 3. **(illustration not to scale)**

when you need a step up (or down)

If your path must cross a steep area, you may want to simply add a few steps rather than doing a lot of digging to alter the slope. Here's an easy way to make spaced-landing timber steps. First, clear the step area of plants, leaves, and topsoil. Then, measure the distance in height between the spots where you want the top and bottom steps. Divide the measurement by the step height (the width of your timbers) to get the number of steps you need. Space your timbers evenly, working from the bottom of the slope to the top, compacting the soil behind each timber as you go. Before anchoring the timbers, walk the steps to make sure the layout is comfortable. Finally, drill two ⅝-inch holes through the center of each timber about 6 inches in from each end. Drive 24-inch pieces of #5 rebar down through the holes into the ground below until they're flush with the top of the timber. For another version of informal steps, you can place pieces of natural stone at similar intervals. If you're interested in more elaborate steps, *The Art and Craft of Stonescaping*, by David Reed (Lark Books, 1998) provides a thorough overview of stone steps and terraces. In addition, numerous gardening and landscaping books cover step building in detail.

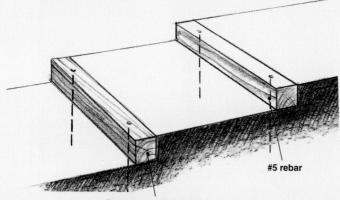

#5 rebar

Pressure-treated timber

laying out your path

Use pin flags (available at home and building supply centers and some hardware stores) or stakes every two paces (approximately 6 feet) to define the borders of your path, then spray the borders with inverted marking paint (photo 2). Garden hoses or rope can be used to lay out a path that winds and curves. Once you're satisfied with the design, leave the hose or rope in place and set pin flags or stakes again, every two paces—to mark the edges, then remove the hose or rope and spray the outline.

Don't forget to make sure the width of your path remains constant. The standard walking-surface width for a path is 2 feet per person, so if you want your path to accommodate two people walking side by side, plan for it to be a minimum of 4 feet wide. For one person plus an object (such as a wheelbarrow or a trash can), the standard width is 3 feet. If you plan to hollow out space in the base for edging, add the necessary inches (depending on the thickness of your edging material) to your path width before marking it.

If you are building the path into a steep slope and plan to add steps to portions of the route, mark off that area at this stage or when you dig out the path base.

PHOTO 2

PHOTO 3

digging out the base

You'll need to hollow out a trench approximately 6 to 7 inches deep to hold your path (depending on the thickness of your paving material). Plus, if you plan to add edging, you should dig out "shelves" for the edging at this point as well (see Edging, page 180). Increase the depth of your base by 4 inches if you also plan to add a drainage pipe (see Improving Drainage, page 178) and/or if you live in a climate where hard freezes are common or where the soil expands during a wet season.

A mattock or a foot adz hoe is good for loosening and carving out packed earth, removing rocks that are embedded in the ground, and cutting out small roots (photo 3). Use a shovel to toss your loosened soil into a wheelbarrow and, at the same time, to smooth the sides of the trench and edging shelves and to level the bottom (photo 4). You may use some of the soil to level the base. The rest you can move to a storage spot and use later to fill low spots in the lawn, transplant plants, or build up the compost pile. Use a level to check the slope of your base as you work (photo 5).

PHOTO 4

PHOTO 5

adding materials

standard path base

1 Fill your hollowed-out trench with 3 inches of ½- to ¾-inch washed gravel (photo 6) and use a shovel to level it (or to achieve a two-percent cross slope if you're sloping the path for drainage; see Improving Drainage, page 178). Walk back and forth over this gravel layer to pack it down (a lawn roller or big-footed friends would be helpful here). If you're working on a slope, begin at the low end and work your way up so you keep packing the base materials firmly against each other as you go.

ALTERNATIVE: If drainage is not a problem at your path site, you may want to substitute "crusher run" gravel (also known as "road bond") for washed gravel. Because it compacts so well, this inexpensive material, commonly used in road building, has the character of a fixed, solid base (almost like concrete), yet it's still flexible enough to accommodate shifts underneath the path, such as growing tree roots. A word of caution: this base is so stable that it doesn't allow water to drain quickly through it. If you need good drainage, stick with washed gravel for this base layer.

PHOTO 6

PHOTO 7

2 Next, you may want to lay a landscape cloth to filter sediment out of draining storm water and to serve as a weed barrier. (A landscape cloth isn't necessary to filter sediment if you've used crusher run instead of gravel in your base.) You can purchase landscape cloth at garden centers in 3-, 4-, and 6-foot widths and cut it with scissors. (Make sure you get cloth wide enough to both cover your path and to be held in place under your edging stones if you're using them [photo 7].) Non-woven landscape cloth is best; it's not as slick as the woven cloth, and it doesn't break down as quickly.

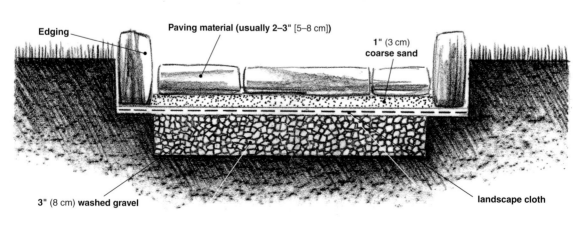

FIGURE 4.

A standard, flexible path base on well-draining soil

Edging

Paving material (usually 2–3" [5–8 cm])

1" (3 cm) coarse sand

3" (8 cm) **washed gravel**

landscape cloth

3 Finish your base by smoothing in a 1-inch settling bed of sand (photo 8). This leaves several inches for paving materials. (Your finished surface should be slightly above the surrounding ground.) Be sure to check the level of your path base at this final stage (photo 9).

4 At this point, the base is ready, and you can begin laying the paving material (photo 10).

Figure 4 on previous page shows a cross-section of a standard, flexible path base.

PHOTO 8

PHOTO 9

PHOTO 10

ordering base materials

You can order base materials from a sand and gravel yard. To figure out how much you'll need, there are two different formulas.

1 When figuring the amount of sand or gravel to cover the width and length of the path, multiply the length of the path times its width, and multiply the result by the depth of the sand or gravel (in feet). This will give you the amount you need in cubic feet. Divide the number of cubic feet by 27 to determine how many cubic yards you need. Sand and gravel suppliers typically sell by the cubic yard, cubic foot, or the ton, and they'll be glad to help you calculate the amount you need.

EXAMPLE
Calculating amount of sand needed
Path length: **30 feet**
Path width: **4 feet**
Sand depth: **1 inch or .08 feet**
30 x 4 x .08 = 9.6 cubic feet

2 When figuring the amount of gravel for a path base prepared with a drainpipe (which fills a "V" shaped trough the length and half the width of the path, see figure 9, page 179), multiply the length of the path times half the width, and multiply the result by the depth of the layer (in feet). This will give you the material amounts you need in cubic feet. Again, divide the number by 27 to determine how many cubic yards you need.

EXAMPLE
Calculating amount of gravel needed
for a base with a drainpipe
Path length: **30 feet**
Path width: **4 feet**
Sand depth: **3 inch or .25 feet**
30 x 2 (half the width) x .25 = 15 cubic feet

ALTERNATIVE
concrete path base

A concrete base is more labor intensive, but it ensures an even, finished surface that won't settle or shift.

You'll need the following special tools and equipment.

▪ Bagged (dry) pre-mixed concrete or Portland cement (a bonding agent) plus sand and/or gravel for mixing your own concrete

▪ Tub or wheelbarrow and hoe to mix cement or a rented power cement mixer (An electric cement mixer is easiest for most work. Gas mixers are an option for large jobs and remote locations without power.)

▪ Mason's float (a small, flat tool much like a trowel) for smoothing wet concrete

▪ Hammer, nails, stakes, and framing lumber for making form boards

▪ Hose with an adjustable spray nozzle

▪ Plastic sheeting to protect the curing concrete from rain or other inclement weather while it sets

Dig out a bed approximately 8 inches deep, depending on the thickness of your paving material. On each side of the bed, remove approximately 4 to 6 inches of additional dirt about 3 to 4 inches deep for setting the form boards. Tamp the base well. A hand tamping tool is usually best; powered tampers can drop the grade an inch or more. If the soil is firm, you'll be able to pour the concrete directly onto it (after making any necessary adjustments for a cross slope, if desired).

If the soil is unstable, you'll need to reinforce the base as follows:

1 To reinforce the base by adding strength to the concrete, use either wire mesh or rods of #4 steel rebar (both should be set up on rocks or brick chunks so the cement will flow around them). You can also mix fiberglass into the wet concrete to make it stronger.

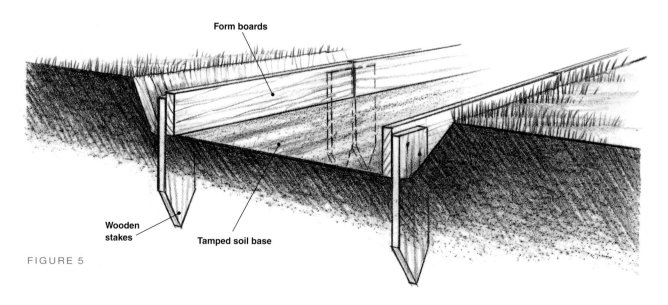

Form boards

Wooden stakes

Tamped soil base

FIGURE 5

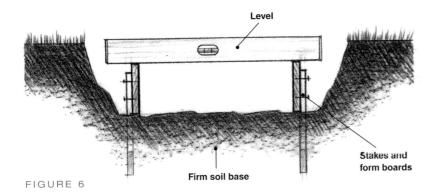

FIGURE 6

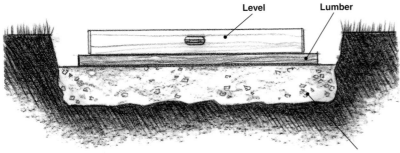

FIGURE 7

2 On the sides, put in form boards to hold the concrete when it's poured. You can make these from pieces of scrap lumber held in place every 3 to 4 feet by wooden stakes driven into the ground against the outside of the boards and nailed in place. Strips of 4-inch-wide particleboard work well as form boards on curves. On flat slopes, you can pre-nail the stakes to the form boards. On rolling grades, it's easier to set the form boards in the bed, drive stakes in behind the boards, and nail the boards to the stakes (supporting the stake behind with a stone mason's hammer). These forms help establish a strong edge and can be checked with a level to monitor the grade of the concrete base. Once the concrete is set, the forms can be ripped out and discarded (or reused). You can also leave them in place and cover them with dirt.

Figure 5 on previous page shows a path base prepared with form boards.

A good concrete mix for this base would be 1 part Portland cement, 2 parts clean river sand, and 3 parts gravel. You can either mix the cement with a hoe, rent a cement mixer, or call a company that delivers ready-mixed cement, depending on how ambitious you are and how much ground you have to cover. The surface of a concrete base need not be very smooth, but if you want your path to have a cross slope, the concrete base should have one as well. Rest a level on the form boards, if you're using them (see figure 6), and adjust their height as necessary to maintain the desired cross slope. If you're not using form boards, place the level on a piece of lumber laid flat across the wet cement (see figure 7).

Allow the concrete to set overnight. On the concrete base, you can either dry-lay stones or bricks on a settling bed of sand or, for maximum stability, mortar them in place. Figure 8 shows a cross section of dry-laid stone on a concrete base.

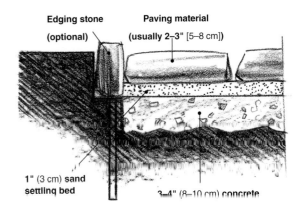

FIGURE 8. Dry-laid stone on a concrete base

improving drainage

Correcting drainage is a site-specific job. If your soil drains poorly but your path is sloped to drain or carry water, you might not have any problems. If your path slopes steeply, you may find it best to build in water break troughs at various intervals to help water drain during heavy rains. Following are some general guidelines for improving drainage. If you have specific concerns or live in an area where drainage is poor, you may want to consult other references, including books geared toward site grading and site engineering, and/or consult a landscape architect or a civil engineer.

PHOTO 11. **Drainpipe**

PHOTO 12. **Drainpipe and sock**

Adding a Drainpipe

If the soil test (outlined on page 146 of the Getting Started chapter) indicates poor drainage, you can compensate for it by adding a drainpipe when filling in your base materials.

Lay down just 1 inch of gravel; then place a perforated, 4-inch plastic drainpipe along the center of the base. The drainpipe should run the length of the path and continue away from the low point to a ditch or low spot where water naturally runs off. To prevent sediment from filling the pipe, you can wrap it with a landscape cloth, use a sock designed to cover the pipe (some pipes come with the sock already surrounding it), or cover the gravel base with a landscape cloth (photos 11 and 12 and figure 9). After laying the drainpipe, fill the trench with 6 inches of gravel and 1 inch of sand, again leaving several inches for paving material. (In this case, rather than making the finished surface just above the surrounding ground, it should be flush with the ground.)

Figure 9 shows a cross-section of a path base prepared with a drainpipe.

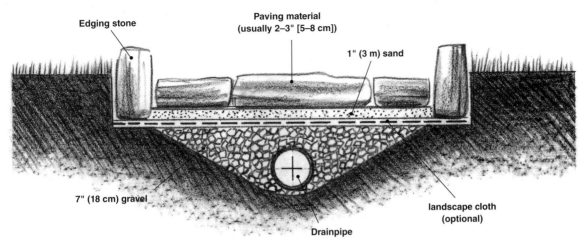

Edging stone

Paving material
(usually 2–3" [5–8 cm])

1" (3 m) sand

7" (18 cm) gravel

Drainpipe

landscape cloth
(optional)

FIGURE 9. **Standard, flexible path base with a drainpipe**

Adding a Water Break Trough

If your path slopes steeply, you may want to add a water break trough to assist with drainage and reduce erosion of a gravel or natural material path. This trough is a two-sided ditch that runs across the path at intervals along a steep slope.

Dig a trench 5 inches deep by slightly more than 8 inches wide. Build the trough by nailing two 8-foot-long pressure-treated 2 x 4 boards to an 8-foot-long pressure-treated 2 x 8 board. Connect the 2 x 4 boards with two galvanized bolts that are approximately ⅜-inch in diameter and spaced at even intervals with nuts and washers on each side of the boards. The trough should be set into the trench at a slope of at least two percent (it may slope more, depending on the downward angle of the trough across the path); see figure 10.

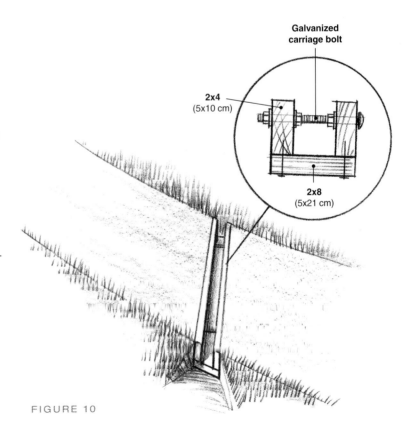

Galvanized
carriage bolt

2x4
(5x10 cm)

2x8
(5x21 cm)

FIGURE 10

setting edging

Edging helps contain your path, keeping soil, grass, and weeds from creeping in and loose paving material from spilling out. Though you may decide it's unnecessary for informal paths, edging enhances durability and adds detail and style.

Usually, it's easiest to dig a shelf in the base and set the edging during the excavation of your path base before you add paving material. However, if you plan to simply line the edges of your path with field stones set on top of the ground or accent it with a creeping perennial, you can add the edging after you've completed the path surface.

Figure 11 shows various edging materials and designs.

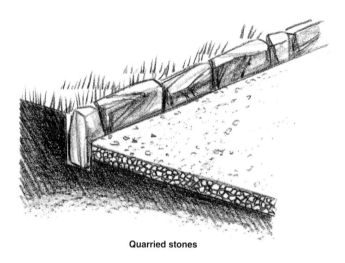

Quarried stones

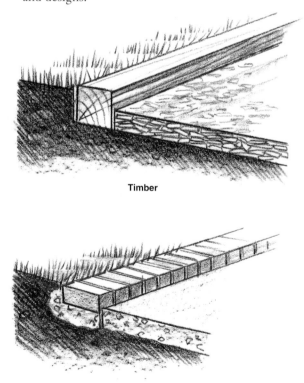

Timber

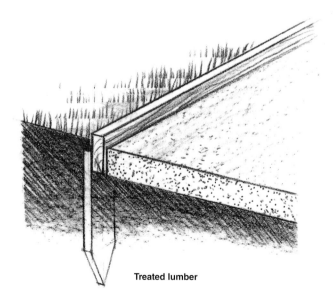

Treated lumber

Mortared brick edging

FIGURE 11. **Various edging materials and designs**

If you're edging with stone, brick, or another material in a lawn area, set the upper surfaces of the edging just at or not more than ½ inch above ground level so it won't be an obstacle to lawn mowers. If you're using a landscape cloth, set the edging on top of it to hold it in place (photo 13).

PHOTO 13

common edging materials:

◼ **Wood,** such as 2 x 4 or 2 x 6-inch boards. (Most woods rot quickly in soil, so use pressure-treated wood.)

◼ **Pre-formed plastic or metal edging,** available at gardening and landscape centers. (Opt for ¼-inch commercial-grade metal edging, which is much more durable than the thinner, residential-grade edging. These forms of edging usually come with loops attached at the base through which you drive stakes to hold the edging in place.)

◼ **Stone or brick** that is identical or complementary to your paving material.

◼ **Myriad other materials.** Be creative; everything from ornamental tiles and concrete blocks to cockle shells can make appropriate edging in the right setting.

To use timber as edging, dig a shelf along your path that is deep enough to bury half the timber. Then drill ⅝-inch-diameter holes through each timber, spacing the holes 3 or 4 feet apart. Position the drilled timbers on the gravel base (or on the landscape cloth that covers the gravel). Then, using a sledge hammer, drive 2-foot lengths of #5 rebar through each hole into the ground, sinking the lengths of rebar until they're flush with the tops of the timbers.

creating
paths and walkways

natural material paths

Natural materials—pine needles, bark, sawdust, leaves, the earth itself—make paths that look as inviting as weathered forest trails. They welcome travelers with soft, comfortable surfaces and pungent, earthy scents. These most informal of paths are also among the easiest to build. For details on using natural materials for path surfaces, see page 150.

Base

If your soil drains well, you may be able to create a natural material path with no more preparation than clearing the surface of the soil and spreading on several inches of path material.

However, if you want to guard against a mud-filled path after a rain, prepare a deeper base. Dig a bed of 6 inches and cover the bottom with 3 inches of ½-inch to ¾-inch clean gravel or "crusher run." Rake the stone level and stomp back and forth on it to pack it, then finish your base with approximately 2 inches of bark mulch, which will provide a soft, springy foundation for the path's 1-inch surface layer.

A natural path on a gently sloping site

This quiet mulch path curves toward a resting spot.

If the drainage of your path area is especially poor, dig a base of approximately 10 inches. Fill it with 1 inch of clean gravel, lay a 4-inch drainage pipe, then cover it with more gravel and a landscape cloth to serve as a sediment barrier. Finish the base with 2 inches of bark mulch—again, to provide a springy foundation underneath the path's top layer. (See page 178 for details on adding a drainage pipe to your path base.) Be aware that natural materials are fairly easy to kick through or lose to erosion, and nothing looks worse than a "bald spot" of landscape cloth peeking through a natural material path. If you use a landscape cloth, watch for this potential problem, and add more surface material when it occurs.

Design

Designs for these unassuming paths should be as simple as their materials the more natural-looking the better. Let them follow routes where people are already wearing a trail—to the boat dock, the neighbor's fence, or the climbing tree at the back of the yard.

drainage for earth paths

Earth paths are familiar and welcoming, and they often "create themselves" as the product of human and animal traffic. They also share the disadvantages of natural landscape features, such as forming puddles after a rain and sinking below ground level under the weight of repeated footsteps. One way to improve drainage on an existing earth path is to add dirt to raise the grade. If the extra dirt doesn't improve the natural storm water flow, you may want to bridge any troublesome swales in the path with logs, field stones, or simple wooden boardwalks.

Adding the Top Layer

After laying the base, spread the surface material on top of the bark mulch. If you're creating a bark-mulch path, just add 1 to 2 inches of additional mulch as surface material (this means you will have a total of approximately 4 inches of bark mulch, including the base layer). If you're adding another surface material such as pine straw or leaves, add 4 to 6 inches, since the material will compact.

This pine-needle path is impossible to resist, as it curves out of sight in the distance.

Maintenance

Materials such as pine needles and leaves will have to be replenished each year, and you may even have to add some as the year goes along. Other material, such as bark mulch, can simply be replenished as it decomposes.

LEFT: **A short stretch of a pine-needle path leads to a tiny retreat amid concrete and a city street.**

BELOW: **This natural path blends perfectly with the wooden landings and steps.**

gravel and ornamental stone paths

Gravel, crushed stone, and decorative pebbles can be used to add texture, color, and comforting crunching sounds to paths in both formal and informal settings. These materials work especially well on curving paths and areas with slight slopes. For details on gravel and ornamental stone as path materials, see page 152.

Base

The standard path base described on page 174 can be simplified for a gravel or ornamental stone path.

Simply excavate a bed 3 inches deep, and fill it with 2 inches of "crusher run" (also called "road bond"—an unscreened gravel with lots of granite dust and small particles that compact into a strong yet flexible base).

However, if the drainage of your path area is especially poor, dig a base of approximately 7 inches. Fill it with 1 inch of clean gravel, lay a 4-inch drainage pipe, then cover it with more gravel and finish with a landscape cloth. (See page 178 for details on adding a drainage pipe to your path base.)

Add an edging material (see page 180) before filling in the top layer. Edging is essential to keep gravel or ornamental stone in place.

Design

Gravel and loose rock can be used to create everything from straight, neat walks to formal pleasure gardens or narrow connector paths that wind through trees or behind tool sheds. Along with the path layout, the color and texture of the gravel or pebbles will affect the look you achieve. For example, as angular pieces of fine-textured crushed stone settle into a path, it will begin to look more natural and pleasantly timeworn. Rounded, decorative pebbles on a path lined with a boxwood hedge, on the other hand, will create a much more manicured look. Colors that blend well with other landscape features near the path and that complement the colors of surrounding flowers and plants will add to the serenity and natural quality of your path site. And though contrasting colors—say, cool-colored gravel against a rich green lawn—can create a striking appearance, bright white gravel or marble chips tend to be too stark a contrast in most settings.

FROM LEFT TO RIGHT:

Fieldstone edging adds charm to this gravel path.

"Granite gravel," or decomposed granite, is a popular paving material in the Austin, Texas, area.

At the Austin Area Garden Center, they've used pieces of limestone for edging; this gravel path provides a comfortable transition from a grassy area—and is welcoming to travelers of all kinds.

Adding the Top Layer

After compacting the base materials, you should be 1 inch below the surface of the surrounding ground. Add your top layer of gravel or ornamental stone, bringing it just to or slightly above grade level. Rake the path smooth, water it, then tamp it or go over it with a lawn roller.

Maintenance

If you're after a neat, well-groomed look, rake the path regularly. On a sloping path, you'll need to rake the gravel upward, since gravity and rain will tend to work it downhill. Weeds hoe out easily in loose gravel, and your surface layer shouldn't need to be replenished for several years unless the path gets lots of heavy traffic.

LEFT: **Mortared brick provides formal edging for a path that leads to an ornate iron gate.**

RIGHT: **As you plant along the borders, remember that you may eventually share your walking space with blooming trees and flourishing plants.**

grass paths

A grass path is one of the easiest and least expensive types of path to build. Ribbons of natural green that run between beds of flowers, shrubs, hedges, and ornamental grasses and merge with surrounding lawn and countryside can be created in several ways, as described here. For details on grass as a path material, see page 154.

A plush grass path at a South Carolina residence

base

To create a grass path, there's no need to lay the standard path base described on page 174. For the first two approaches outlined below, simply shape a path out of the existing grass or field. For the second two approaches, prepare the soil for either sod or seed by breaking up the top 1 inch or so for good root contact or a good seedbed.

It's best to set edging before you make the grass path, but you can install it afterwards, or cut a 2 to 3 inch ditch along the path edge and fill it with mulch once you've finished.

you will need

In addition to the basic tools and equipment outlined ion page 164, you'll need the following.

If you're creating a grass path by mowing an existing field or lawn:

- Lawn mower or tractor-mounted mower
- Edger, used to cut sod back from flower beds or other edges

If you're using sod to lay a grass path:

- Hatchet for cutting sod
- Rototiller (optional; can be rented)
- High-phosphate or super-phosphate fertilizer
- Kneeling board
- Sod staples (These heavy, wire staples, available at garden supply centers or made out of coat hangers, keep newly laid sod in place on steep slopes or on drainage swales.)
- Hose with sprinkler

If you're seeding a grass path on bare earth:

- Rototiller (optional)
- High-phosphate or super-phosphate fertilizer
- Drop-seeder (This rolling seeder, available for rent from equipment supply centers, will distribute your seed better than a "broadcast" seeder that hangs around your neck.)
- Hose with sprinkler
- Hay or straw for mulch

Dry-laid bluestone stepping stones lead to a grass path beyond.

This path begins at a bench (LEFT), then winds uphill and joins a year-round garden (RIGHT).

Mowing a Grass Path out of a Field

Once you've decided how you want your path to flow (perhaps following a fence line or curving gracefully toward a gate), mark the centerline by wrapping marking tape around bunches of tall grass or wild-flower stalks. You can let the width of the mower determine the path width—one pass wide for a tractor-mounted mower, two passes for a riding lawn mower. Set the blades on your mower to low and mow the course you've marked, then remove the grass clippings from the path. That's it! This easiest of paths is most appealing when it flows with the gentle roll of the land, and it's perfect for linking lawns with surrounding countryside. To keep it healthy and green, mow it once or twice a month. You can let the grass bordering the path grow as high as 3 feet or more, mowing it only seasonally or even yearly.

A mown grass path

Making a Grass Path in an Existing Lawn

Tired of that plain, boring lawn? Try converting it to a grass path that winds between beds of plants. Begin by marking the outline of the path. Then, use an edger or shovel to slice into the turf and define the borders of the path. Remove the sod from areas that are to be flower beds, using a foot adz, mattock, flat shovel, or, if the area is large, a rented sod cutter. (The sod can be transplanted to worn spots in the yard or used to re-shape plant beds.) Place edging along the path to add definition and to prevent grass from creeping into the surrounding flowerbeds. (For details on types of edging, see page 180.) The edging should be less than 1 inch above with the grade if you want to avoid hand trimming each time you mow. Finally, prepare the soil in the beds for planting and fill them with herbs or flowering plants. This is an easy path to create if your site is already full of beds that can simply be re-shaped, extended, or joined to form grass walkways between them.

A perennial border was renovated to create this path.

Laying a Sod Path
or Sowing a Grass Path

There are several reasons why you might choose to lay a sod path rather than sow grass seed. First, sod paths are ready to view and use soon after you've finished laying them; grass seeds need three or four weeks of undisturbed time and good weather to germinate and grow. Plus, seasonal sod can be laid anytime of year other than deep winter (and even winter may be fine for growth if you're in a southern climate). Seeds, on the other hand, do best when they're sown in fall or in early spring. (If they're sown in the summer, they'll require persistent watering.) Also, sod does well on sloping path sites, where seeds can wash away in a heavy rain, and certain hybrid grasses are available only as sod. Finally, while weeds will sprout along with grass seed, sod smothers potential weeds underneath it.

So why would anyone plant seed? Laying sod is more expensive, and it's much heavier work.

preparing the soil

Regardless of whether you use sod or seed, begin by sending a soil sample from your path area to the local agricultural extension office or testing lab. The results of the soil test will tell you how to treat your soil to produce a healthy lawn. Next, after marking the borders of your path, clear the site completely, removing all rocks, roots, weeds, and unwanted grass. Cut out grass with a flat-nosed shovel or a foot adz (or a rented sod cutter if you're clearing a large area). If the soil is heavy, break it up with a hard rake or mattock or till it with a rototiller so that the roots of your new sod will be able to penetrate it.

The results of the soil sample test will tell you whether you need to spread lime (to raise your soil's pH level) and/or add a high-phosphate starter fertilizer that will promote root growth (0-20-0, for example). After treating the soil, break it up with a hard rake to a depth of a couple of inches, then use the rake to smooth the surface.

laying sod

Timing is important when laying sod. Don't pick it up or have it delivered until you're ready to use it. In hot weather, it may begin to yellow and die if it isn't laid within about 12 hours of being harvested. In cooler weather, it will keep for several days.

If the soil is very dry, water the path area lightly (so the moisture in the sod rootlets isn't pulled into the soil), but not so much that your workspace turns to mud. Then begin laying. Your sod will come in strips, usually 1½ to 2 feet wide and several feet long. Use a spade or a hatchet to cut it as necessary. Generally, it's best to begin at one end of your path and work toward the other. If your path is on a slope, laying the sod strips lengthwise across the slope will help prevent erosion. Where it's likely that the sod could wash downslope, you can use heavy wire sod staples to hold the uphill-side pieces in place (or all pieces on a diagonal slope). Remove the staples after the roots have taken hold (usually two weeks, or after the first mowing). Use a small piece of plywood as a kneeling board when laying the sod so that your knees aren't pressing directly into the sod you've just laid.

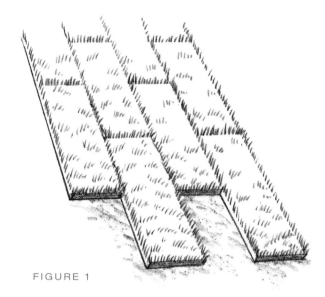

FIGURE 1

Be sure the individual pieces of sod are set tightly against each other to keep the edges from drying out. Also, to retain moisture, it's important that the joints between strips of sod alternate rather than meet from one row to the next. So, if your first row begins with a whole piece of sod, start your second row with a half piece, followed by a whole piece, and so on (see figure 1).

When you've finished laying the path, use a lawn roller to press the grass roots into the soil and even out the bumps. This is very important; roots can dry out if air pockets are left between the sod and the earth. Sprinkle damp topsoil into any gaps between pieces of sod and the grass will quickly fill those areas in. Finally, set up a sprinkler to water the entire path deeply. In hot weather, water two or three times a week or more while the sod is getting established. At the same time, keep in mind that excessive watering can cause disease; your local agricultural extension office can provide guidance on how often to water in your area.

sowing grass seed

Check with a feed and seed store about the best turf grass seed to meet your needs; different seeds have different qualities.

Check the instructions that accompany your grass seed for recommended distribution (usually calculated in pounds according to square footage). A drop-seeder, which allows you to set a distribution rate, will help you sow seeds more evenly than you can by hand.

After spreading your seed, rake the entire path area lightly to mix the seed into the top ¼ inch of soil then roll it with a roller half-filled with water. Establishing good contact between the seeds and the soil will help ensure germination. Mulch the area lightly with marsh hay or straw to help retain moisture as the seeds germinate and the seedlings grow.

Don't mow your new grass path until the seedlings are 2 to 3 inches high. When you do, be sure the soil is not too wet and your mower blades are sharp so you don't uproot the seedlings. After about five weeks, the root systems will be established and the path will be ready for foot traffic.

Maintenance

Care for a grass path just as you would care for a lawn.

steppingstone paths

When imagining a quaint steppingstone path ambling through a vegetable patch or winding into the woods, most people picture rough, randomly shaped natural stones. Rough stones do make a marvelous material for these casual walks, but you can also use decorative concrete pavers, more formal cut stones, or even wood rounds to create different versions of this easy-to-build path.

ABOVE: An enchanting route through a bed of ivy

LEFT: Don't create overly artistic patterns that require people to hop crossways from one stone to the next. Simple designs like this one attract many types of travelers.

Base

In most cases, each steppingstone is set directly onto a patch of ground that has been excavated, sometimes with 1 or 2 inches of sand underneath to create a level base.

If you're concerned that harsh winters with deep freezes will heave your steppingstone path, however, you can prepare the standard path base described on page 174. Lay your stones on top of it, then fill in around them with the soil you removed to create the base.

Bluestone dry-laid in an irregular pattern

wood rounds

Cross sections of trees, usually cut 8- to 10-inches thick, make especially picturesque stepping-stone paths. You can cut the rounds yourself with a chain saw. Let them dry out, then soak them in a penetrating wood preservative before laying them. One warning: wood rounds aren't the best choice for wet climates or areas with poor drainage. In soggy soil, even treated wood rounds will eventually become covered with moss, making them extremely slippery.

Design

Rigid design rules don't apply to steppingstone paths, but there are a few general guidelines that will make your path more comfortable, functional, and pleasant to walk on.

▨ Because people have different strides at different speeds, steppingstones should be spaced with easy-to-cross gaps—1 to 4 inches—between them. If the path is to be primarily utilitarian, make the stones and gaps uniform. Stick with large, similar-size stones and space them close together. If the path is more ornamental, the design can be more creative, but don't stagger the path back and forth without a reason for doing so. A good rule of thumb to remember: If the path looks too difficult to walk on, the visual impression will be disturbing. Figure 2 shows a number of designs for steppingstone paths.

▨ Typically, path builders lay steppingstones so that they cross the path route lengthwise rather than run parallel to it.

▨ Steppingstone paths are traveled by one person at a time, so your stones don't have to be huge—and might look out of scale if they are.

▨ Use larger, more identifiable "threshold" stones at the beginning of your path and at any transition point, such as where a separate path veers off.

▨ When choosing your stones, avoid concave shapes that will collect water. Also, stay away from smooth-surface stones (especially marble and slate) that will get slick in the rain. Precast geometric pavers are better for straight, formal steppingstone routes.

▨ Before you set your stones for good, lay them out and have a look, paying attention to how well the shapes and sizes work together. Ideally, you want them to form a harmonious pattern, looking a bit like drifted continents that were once connected.

FIGURE 2.
Designs for steppingstone paths

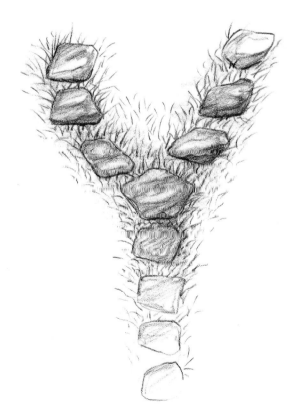

TOP LEFT: **Weathered wall stone laid in a setting of natural rock outcrops**

Steppingstones work well in beds of gravel or ornamental stone.
LEFT: **A whimsical trail of round river rocks meanders through a wide gravel pathway.** ABOVE: **Flat stones rest level in a bed of gray gravel.**

Laying Steppingstones

Once you've developed the layout for your path and test-walked it to your satisfaction, set the stones one by one. Cut around the outline of the first stone with a garden trowel or a straight-nosed spade. Move the stone aside (leaving it in the same orientation it will lie in), and shave enough soil and/or grass from the space you outlined so that the stone will be flush with the ground when you set it in place. You may also want to excavate enough soil to allow for a 1- or 2-inch bed of sand, especially if the bottoms of your stones are uneven and won't balance firmly on flat earth. Set the stone and tamp it firmly in place with a rubber mallet. Repeat this process to set each stone in your path.

Maintenance

Steppingstone paths that run across a lawn may require regular trimming around the edges. The string blade of a "weed-eater" is a handy tool for this.

Colored concrete pavers were used for this short crossing to a cut stone entranceway.

adding moss to your path

Moss matches the mood of steppingstone paths especially well. Though you don't want it to make the surface of the path slick, it adds a wonderful, fairy-tale quality when used in the gaps between stones or as a ground cover around a shady path.

Propagating moss is a bit of a challenge, but you can transplant sections by hand from wherever you find them. (Nearby construction sites, drainage ditches, or any place where high-acid soil has been compacted and neglected are ideal; take no more than a palm-size cut out of a patch). Prepare the places where you want the moss to grow by pulling up all existing growth and watering until the ground is muddy. Gently water the moss patches, then press them onto the wet ground, water them again, and walk on them.

Moss has no roots or veins, so it must absorb its water from where it grows (meaning you'll need to water it lightly but frequently until it's established). Various mosses have evolved to survive in different environments. Sphagnum moss thrives in wet bogs, for example, while cushion moss lives on dry rocks. Be sure to match the moss you collect with the transplant environment. Wet, streamside mosses won't survive on a dry rock path, and vice versa.

cut stone walkways

Typically shaped in squares or rectangles, cut stone is a handsome and time-honored paving material. Cut stone is most often used to create paths and walkways that are formal and neatly kept, and it's best for straight paths or for paths with gentle arcs or curves. Types of cut stone vary by region; limestone, sandstone, bluestone, and granite are most common. For details on cut stone as a path material, see page 156.

you will need

In addition to the basic tools and equipment outlined on page 164, you'll need the following.

- ■ Circular saw with a masonry blade, a sturdy piece of lumber to use as a cutting guide, and eye and ear protection if you need to cut your stone.
- ■ Hose with adjustable spray nozzle

See page 176 for additional tools you'll need if you opt for a concrete base.

Chinese pink slate is used for this formal walk. Note how the bordering shrubs are trimmed to mimic the paving pattern.

Base

The standard path base described on page 174 works well for a dry-laid cut stone walkway. However, if your stone is thin, brittle, or especially small, you'll want more stability. You can either replace the gravel in the standard base with "crusher run," or pour the concrete base alternative (see page 176) and mortar your stones in place.

RIGHT: Offsetting the seams between stones increases the strength of a walkway—and adds visual appeal.

BELOW: This handsome cut stone walk features bluestone.

Design

It's far easier to design a cut stone walkway by sketching possibilities rather than by moving around actual stones. Start by familiarizing yourself with the sizes and shapes of available stones. Then, using graph paper and pencil, make a scaled drawing of your path layout, copy it several times on a copy machine, and experiment with paving patterns. Graph paper you find in the school supplies section of the grocery or drug store is all you need.

It commonly features a grid of squares measuring $1/4$ inch on each side. If you're playing with paving patterns for a small path area, let 1 inch on the graph paper equal 1 foot; for areas that are larger, let $1/2$ inch or $1/4$ inch equal 1 foot.

Consider laying repeating patterns using stones of similar size, alternating square and rectangular stones, juxtaposing large and small stones, or setting stones on a

FIGURE 3. **Cut stone paving patterns**

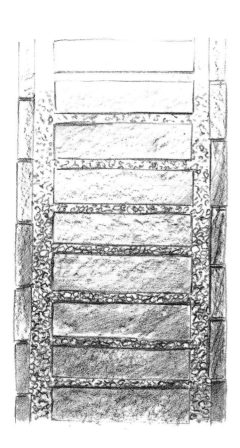

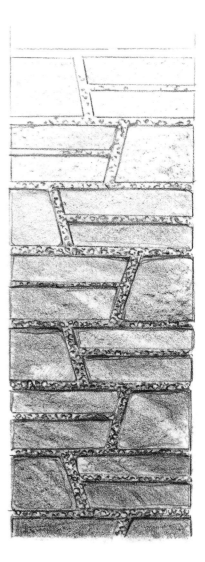

diagonal. You can also combine cut stone with other materials, from bricks and tile to crushed gravel, or leave open spaces within the walkway design for planting a creeping thyme or another path herb.

If you're creating a random pattern with stones of different sizes, be sure to use one of your largest stones as a threshold to stabilize the beginning of the path. Smaller stones can dislodge if they're used along the edge of a cut stone path; save them for the interior, and use larger stones on the edges. Various cut stone paving patterns are shown in figure 3. Once you've settled on your design, it will help you determine the number and dimensions of the stones you need to order.

Bluestone dry-laid on sand with an irregular border

Cutting Stone

You may want to trim some of your cut stones to smooth their shapes or to adjust the shape to the edges of your design (especially if you are setting them on a diagonal). If you find you have a lot of cutting or need to cut curves into some of your stones, you may want to hire a masonry professional. If you're comfortable using a circular saw, you can make straight cuts yourself.

Here's how: Wearing eye and ear protection, use a circular saw equipped with a masonry blade to score the stone where you want to make the cut. As a cutting guide, use a sturdy piece of lumber. If you are only cutting off an inch or so, go ahead and cut all the way through the stone. Otherwise, score it to a depth of about ½ inch. Lay the stone on top of the wood, setting the scored line just above the edge of the board. Press or tap with a hammer on the center of the section to be removed, and it should snap off easily.

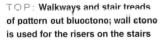

TOP: Walkways and stair treads of pattern cut bluestone; wall stone is used for the risers on the stairs

RIGHT: Bluestone is used for a short steppingstone path leading to a main walk of cut stone, all surrounded by blue chip gravel.

These cut stone steps blend with the adjoining path.

Laying Cut Stone on a Dry Sand Base

If you're building a path on a slope, start at the low end of the slope and work uphill; stones settle naturally downhill. If the path leads from a house or another building, start at the structure and work toward the other end. If the path runs from one structure to another, work from both ends toward the middle so that you're sure to place the best stones near the buildings.

Begin laying the stones on the sand, according to your paving pattern design. You can set them tightly against each other, but stones are rarely cut identically in the manufacturing process, and trying for neat, stone-by-stone fits may require much more additional cutting.

If you want to avoid that, leave gaps of ¼ to ¾ inch between each stone. These spaces give you room for adjusting the stones and help with drainage.

After setting four or five stones, work them back and forth into the sand until they are situated where you want them, then tap each one several times with a rubber mallet to set it. Don't step on thin stones (stones less than 1 inch thick) until you've set them; they may snap if they're not evenly supported. Each time you set a series of stones into place, use a level to make sure the stones are even and the surface of your path is flat (or appropriately sloped, according to how you've graded your path). Placing your level on top of a 6-foot 2 x 4 laid across several stones will ensure that crooked stones don't become inaccurate reference points for the entire path.

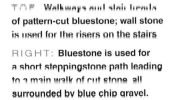

When your path is laid, spread sand over it and sweep the sand into the gaps between the stones. Spray water across the surface for several minutes, walking back and forth on the stones until the sand feels thoroughly wet and settled. You may need to add more sand to the gaps to bring them to about ¼ inch below the tops of the stones. The ¼ inch will keep the sand from spilling onto the path surface.

Laying Cut Stone on a Concrete Base

If you're mortaring your cut stone path surface (rather than dry-laying it on sand) you won't be able to easily change your mind about stone placement, so be sure you're happy with your pattern before beginning. After allowing your concrete base to set overnight, use a trowel to spread a thin, ¾- to 1-inch layer of mortar on top of it and set your stones according to the pattern. Add more mortar to the gaps between the stones, using a trowel to

drop it into the gaps and the edge of the trowel to smooth them. Neatness counts; wipe off any cement mixture that spills onto the stones with a damp sponge.

A standard mortar recipe is one part dry cement to three or four parts sand. You can tint the mortar you use to fill the gaps with coloring agents (sold where cement is sold) so that it blends well with the color of the stone.

Maintenance

Dry-laid stone may need occasional reworking to keep the surface smooth. Tree roots may need to be cut out and the surrounding stones reset from time to time. If the sand in the gaps between stones washes out or settles in too deeply, you may need to add more. Finally, you'll want to weed the cracks between the stones as needed.

Mortared stone on a concrete base should require no more maintenance than occasional sweeping.

Cut stone pavers with plantings in between

natural stone paths

Randomly shaped stones of all kinds make charming, informal paving material for paths. Fieldstone, collected from fields or old dry-laid walls, often has an appealing rough or weathered look. Quarried stone, dynamited or pried from large veins in the earth, can have a jagged, stark, or clean appearance. Common types of quarried stone include sandstone, granite, and limestone. For details on natural stone as a path material, see page 158.

For details on natural stone as a path material, see page 158.

you will need

In addition to the basic tools and equipment outlined on page 164, you will need the following.

- Mason's chisel for breaking stone
- Hose with adjustable spray nozzle

Base

The standard path base described on page 174 works well for a dry-laid stone walk. However, if you plan to use only small stones for your walk, you'll want more stability. You can either replace the gravel in the standard base with "crusher run" or pour the concrete base alternative (see page 176) and mortar your stones in place.

OPPOSITE PAGE: Spicata grass makes a striking edging for natural stone paths.
BELOW: Natural stones can create a more formal look.

Design

Because the shapes of natural stones are so variable, you won't be able to plot your path design at the kitchen table as you could for a cut stone walk. You'll have to design it on-site, and you'll have a number of interesting choices: you can use stones that have a similar size, outline the path with large stones and fill the center with smaller ones, develop a pattern of alternating shapes, or set the stones in a gravel path. Figure 4 suggests a number of paving patterns for stone walks.

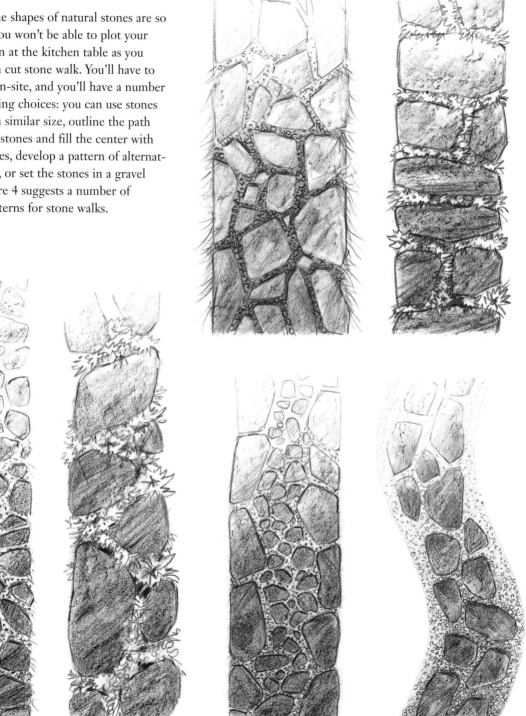

FIGURE 4. **A selection of paving patterns for natural stone paths**

Laying Natural Stone on a Dry Sand Base

Begin by laying several stones along the outer edges of your path. Don't settle the stones permanently at this point—just set them on top of the sand. Next, fill in between the outer stones according to your design, shaping stones with a mason's chisel and/or hammer so that they fit together well. It's best to set the stones about ¾ inch apart, using larger stones on the edges and saving smaller ones for the center of the path.

Once you have several feet of path laid out the way you want it, set the stones more firmly. First, settle them in place by hand, working them back and forth in the sand. (If you set the stones approximately ½ inch above the adjacent soil, the path will drain better.) Then, tap each stone with a rubber mallet several times to set it in place. If your stones have rough surfaces, a level won't always be accurate in making sure your path is flat or appropriately sloped; you'll learn to use your eye as well. If the surfaces of your stones are flat, however, use a level to check your path as you finish each section.

Natural stone paths often entice travelers to stay awhile.

shaping stone

Use a mason's chisel to score stones where you need to trim them and a heavy hammer to do the actual breaking, chipping, and shaping.

After laying the stone, fill the gaps with sand to within ½ inch of their tops and spray the path thoroughly with water to allow it to settle. The path will continue to settle as people begin to use it, so you may have to repeat the filling and watering process a time or two. If you want to plant creeping plants or herbs or place bits of moss in the gaps between the stones, substitute topsoil for sand when filling the gaps.

Laying Stone on a Concrete Base

If you're looking for maximum stability, the process for laying cut stone on a concrete base (page 211) can also be used for laying and mortaring a natural stone path.

Maintenance

On an annual basis, at most, you may need to level some of your stones if you've laid them on a flexible base. You'll also need to weed the gaps and/or water any growth you're encouraging. Moss, especially, should be watered often, though lightly, until it's established.

TOP OF PAGE: **A simple stone path leading through a garden gate**

ABOVE: **Wide gaps between the stones and border plantings of purple thrift create a path that looks as if it might wind to a country cottage.**

Brick Paths

Bricks are available in an array of colors and textures, making them a versatile material for everything from a front walkway laid in a formal design to a rustic path through a patch of wild-flowers. For details on brick as a path material, see page 160.

you will need

In addition to the basic tools and equipment outlined on page 164, you will need the following.

■ Brick sett (wide-bladed chisel) and hammer for cutting bricks, plus safety glasses. (If you have a lot of cutting to do, you may want to rent a brick saw, which you should use only with gloves, safety glasses, and ear protection.)
■ Kneeling pad (Insulation board or a piece of plywood will do.)

Base

The standard path base described on page 174 works well for brick paths. However, you may want to consider two minor adjustments.

1 Your brick path will drain better if it is at least ½ inch above the surrounding grade (ground level), rather than flush with the grade. To achieve the slight elevation, increase the amount of crushed stone fill in the bottom of the base.

2 If you live in a region with hard-freezing winters and slow-draining soil, use a deeper base to avoid the danger of frost heaving, which can cause bricks to unsettle, by digging your path base several inches deeper and filling it with extra crushed stone.

For added stability, use a concrete base (see Concrete Path Base, page 176).

Design

Patterns for laying bricks for a walk range from simple and symmetrical, such as running bond, to more elaborate and ornamental, such as herringbone and basket weave. You can lay bricks flat or stacked on edge, use them whole or in halves (halves are usually alternated with whole bricks in the design), or alternate bricks with sections of other materials, such as gravel or concrete. Figure 5 illustrates some popular brick-laying patterns.

How wide a gap you leave between your bricks will affect your design tone. Tightly laid bricks create formal-looking paths. Gaps of about ⅜ inch between bricks create a more relaxed feel. What you fill those gaps with makes a difference, too. If you dry-lay your bricks and fill the gaps with sand, your path will look less formal than bricks joined by mortar. (If the mortar is a whitish contrast to the bricks, your path may look not only formal, but insti-

Basketweave   **Brick and tile**

Brick and pebbles

FIGURE 5. **A selection of paving patterns for brick**

tutional. Think about softening the color of the mortar with a powdered tinting agent that can be mixed with the cement.) To add life and color to a dry-laid brick path, leave gaps by omitting entire bricks from your design, then fill the gaps with topsoil and plant them with creeping herbs or perennials.

Finally, consider an edging material when developing your overall design. Edging is critical for brick paths laid on sand (see Edging, page 180) to keep the outermost bricks in place. The edging material can range from upturned bricks identical to your paving bricks, which looks somewhat formal, to weathered railroad ties, which are rough and informal.

Brick and pebbles

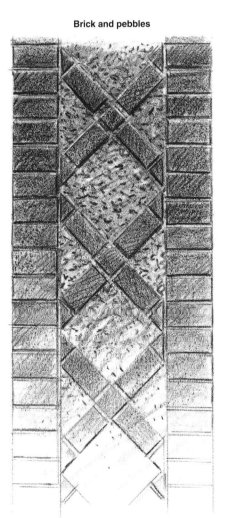

Herringbone

Diagonal running bond

RIGHT: **Bricks can be used to create gracefully arching entranceways.**

BELOW: **Moss was used to fill the gaps in this brick and stone mosaic.**

Cutting Brick

To make a straight cut on a brick (such as cutting a brick in half), use a brick sett (a wide-bladed chisel) and a hammer. Place the blade of the sett along the cut line. With the hammer, tap it there and on the other three sides, then strike it more sharply (beveled edge away from you) along one of the scored lines. The brick should snap apart. If you plan to cut a lot of brick, you can make the job easier and faster by renting a brick saw, which is like a table saw with a water spray that keeps the blade cool. Always wear goggles and heavy gloves when cutting brick. Add ear protection if using a brick saw.

Edging

If you're laying a brick path on sand, use sturdy edging, such as treated 2 x 4 boards, to hold the paving bricks in place. Set the edging before laying the brick surface. Brick paths mortared on concrete don't require edging for stability, but most of them look better with an edge. For detailed information on edging types and procedures, refer to page 180.

Laying Brick on Sand

One method of building a brick path is to lay the brick directly on the 1-inch layer of sand that tops the standard flexible path base. Wet the sand first with a hose, using a fine spray, then drag a screed over the sand (see page 165) to level the surface.

Both of these walks feature the popular "running bond" brick-laying pattern, but the end results are quite different.

Begin laying bricks according to the pattern you've chosen. Work from a kneeling position, using a kneepad (such as a scrap piece of board or insulation) in the sand just ahead of where you're laying brick. As you lay each one, tap it with a rubber mallet to settle it. Use a level frequently to make sure the bricks are even and the surface of your path is flat (or appropriately sloped, according to how you've graded your path).

After laying several feet, spread sand over the completed section, sweep it into the gaps between the bricks, and water the section to settle it. You may need to repeat this process several times, until the sand fills the gaps almost to the tops of the bricks. (If the sand is too far below the surface of the bricks, the gaps may trap weed seeds and debris.)

Mortaring Brick on Concrete

It's a good bit more work, but you'll get more stability and durability by mortaring on a concrete base. Because it will be a bigger job to change the path after you've finished mortaring, be extra-sure you're happy with your path layout and your surface design before beginning.

THIS PAGE:
A brick path being mortared on a concrete base

OPPOSITE:
The finished brick walkway

After allowing your 3-inch layer of concrete base to set (at least overnight), spread a ¾-inch layer of mortar mix on top of it and begin laying bricks according to your pattern. Use a trowel to drop mortar into the gaps between each brick, and smooth the gaps with the edge of the trowel. Neatness counts; wipe off any mortar that spills onto the bricks with a damp sponge or rag. As described in the sections on mortaring stone, use a level frequently to make sure the bricks are even and the surface of your path is flat or appropriately sloped.

A standard mortar recipe is one part cement to three or four parts sand. Consider tinting the mortar you use to fill the gaps with coloring agents (sold where cement is sold) so that it blends well with the bricks and/or the path surroundings. Let the mortar set for at least a day before walking on the path.

Maintenance

Dry-laid brick may need occasional reworking to keep the bricks level. Tree roots may need to be cut out and the surrounding bricks reset from time to time. If the sand in the gaps washes out or settles in too deep, you may need to add more. Finally, you'll want to weed the cracks between the bricks as needed.

ABOVE: **These bricks were laid with tight gaps on a bed of sand, creating a neat, formal look.**

RIGHT: **Brick paired with bluestone**

concrete paths

Because you work with concrete in its soft (cement mix) form, you can use it to create almost any look you want. Concrete can be curved and formed into myriad shapes, used on steep slopes, poured into molds to create pavers, textured, colored, even decorated with anything from embedded crushed tile to shells. In just a day or so after pouring, it hardens into a durable walkway that will last for many years (depending on such variables as the weather, the firmness of the base, and the kind of traffic it has to bear). One caveat: once the concrete is set, there isn't much you can do to change the design without breaking the path to pieces and starting over. For details on concrete as a path material, see page 162.

LEFT: **Colored concrete was used to create walkways through the Rainbow Garden at University of Michigan's 4-H Children's Garden.**

BELOW: **Personalized concrete walk leading to a sundial**

you will need

In addition to the basic tools and equipment outlined on page 164, you'll need the following.

- Hammer, nails, stakes, and lumber for making form boards

- Expansion material for filling control joints in the path (This material, sold at concrete supply stores, is typically an asphalt-impregnated felt.)

- Bagged (dry) pre-mixed cement or Portland cement (a common bonding agent) and sand and/or gravel for mixing with Portland

- Tub or wheelbarrow and hoe to mix cement with water, or a rented power cement mixer (An electric cement mixer is best for most work. Gas mixers are an option for large jobs and remote locations that lack electricity.)

- Float: a flat, rectangular tool with a handle (similar to a finishing trowel) used for spreading and smoothing wet cement

- Edging tool (see figure 8, page 230)

- Hose with adjustable spray nozzle

- Plastic sheeting to the cover the "curing" concrete during rain or other inclement weather

Base

A concrete path can be poured directly into an excavated, compacted path bed approximately 4 inches deep. Follow the process outlined on pages 176 and 177 for preparing the soil and making form boards. Note that since you won't be laying a material on top of the concrete (your base and your path are one and the same), your form boards should come up to the "surface grade" (where you want your path surface). For added support, you may also want to nail in splice boards (small pieces of wood) where the ends of the form boards meet (to hold the form boards together). Be sure to nail the splice boards from the outside of the form boards—not from inside, where the cement will be poured—so they can be removed.

When warm concrete expands, internal pressure can cause cracking, buckling, or surface chipping. Expansion joints—gaps between sections of concrete filled with compressible material—help prevent this. Create them by placing expansion material anywhere your path abuts a structure such as a porch and every 12 to 20 feet along the path, as well as any place where sharp turns or path intersections make cracking likely.

ABOVE: **Concrete pavers are used here with crushed limestone for steps in a path.**

LEFT: **The concrete for this play-area pathway was stained and, while still in wet cement form, stamped with treasures including leaves, feathers, and shells.**

Concrete steps edged with brick lead to intersecting concrete and brick walks

planning ahead

What if you need to run a utility line underneath your concrete path sometime in the future irrigation lines to the garden, lighting wires to the patio by the pool, or electrical lines to the work shed? You can save lots of time and money by planning ahead. Purchase a 2- to 4-inch plastic pipe, or "sleeve." Cut a section long enough to span the width of your path, plus an extra 6 inches on either side. Cover the ends with duct tape and lay the sleeve in the ground underneath your path bed. If you decide you need it some day, this easily accessible channel will be a welcome alternative to tearing out a section of path.

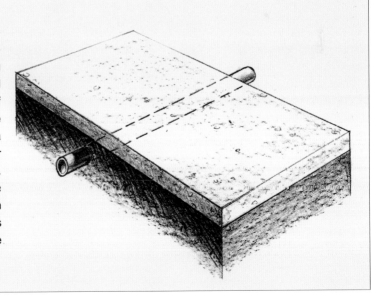

Design

The most important thing to know about using concrete for your path is that you can't change the design once the concrete sets. Consider all design possibilities carefully before you begin. If your first image of a concrete path is a uniform, institutional walk beside a city street, you'll be delighted to know that many other options exist. Tinting agents (available in powder form at home and building supply centers, in colors ranging from brick-red to green

or gold) can be added to the cement mix, as can materials that add texture, such as decorative gravel. You can enhance the surface of a concrete path by sprinkling it when wet with colored sand or by embedding it with materials ranging from colored rock or pieces of brick to crushed tile. Parts of the path can also be reserved (blocked off by boards) for other materials such as gravel, brick, or stone. See figure 6 for a variety of concrete path designs.

texturizing the surface

To create an exposed aggregate look and feel for the surface of your path, mix decorative gravel with the wet cement, then wash away the finished surface of concrete with a stiff spray of water a day or two after pouring it. Timing the wash-off is critical; test boxes like the one described on page 232 should be used for experimenting first. If you spray the surface too early, too much concrete will wash out, leaving a pitted look. If you wait too long, the concrete will not wash out, leaving an unattractive surface of concrete covering most of the decorative gravel.

As another option, rock salt can be pressed into wet cement, then dissolved with the hose a couple of days after the concrete is set.

FIGURE 6. **Some designs for concrete walkways**

Mixing the Concrete

A standard recipe for concrete mix for a path is one part cement, two and a half parts sand, and four parts gravel.

Mixing concrete is a bit tricky. If it's too wet, the ingredients can separate, which will cause cracking or uneven color. If the mix isn't wet enough, it may be too stiff to spread into the corners and air may be trapped along the edges. If that happens, you'll find gaps in the concrete when you remove the forms. To get the mix just right, pour a small amount in a test location before you pour your entire path. Pass your trowel across it; it should leave a smooth, glistening surface. If free water fills in where the trowel has passed, add more dry cement to your mix. If the surface is rough, add water, a small amount at a time.

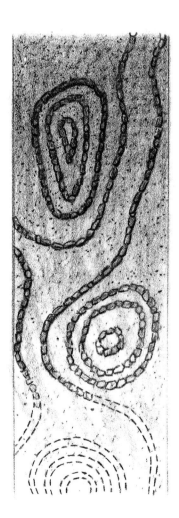
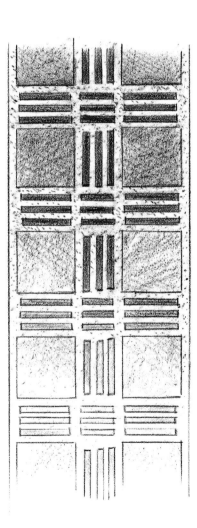

Pouring the Path

If you're covering a small area or plan to work in stages, you can mix your concrete with a hoe in a tub or a wheelbarrow, then shovel or pour it onto the path. For larger jobs, you may want to rent a commercial cement mixer, which does the hard work of mixing for you and allows you to mix bigger batches and pour it from the mixer into a wheelbarrow and then to your path. If your path site is accessible to a large vehicle, you can have the cement delivered by a cement truck. The driver can pour the cement directly from the truck onto your path by using a swinging chute. But be aware that the weight of the truck can leave deep ruts in a healthy lawn.

Once the cement is poured, push it into place with a shovel or a hard rake (not a leaf rake). Then, shimmy a screed back and forth as you pull it along the top of the form boards to distribute the concrete evenly (see figure 7). It's best to have one person on each side of the screed for this job.

Next, you need to smooth the surface with a float. You may want to use various floats, since different ones create different textures. Timing is important; you should work with the concrete as soon as possible after pouring.

FIGURE 8

If you're not embedding the path with decorative materials, a common finish that provides a coarse texture is a "broom finish," created by working a stiff-bristled broom across slightly set concrete.

Finally, work around the edges with an edging tool (see figure 8); shimmy it back and forth as you pull it along to create a smooth finish. Use this same tool to create 1-inch-deep impressions across the width of the path every 3 to 6 feet or so (using a board as a guide). These "control joints" (like the lines you see in sidewalks) will help control cracking.

Cover the finished walk with plastic if it rains within one and a half days of pouring the cement. Also, mud can stain fresh concrete permanently; be sure to wash any off immediately. After about two days, you can pull out the form boards. The walk should be ready for your feet in three to four days.

A warning: Cement will harden on everything, from clothing to shovels, and its lime content is irritating to skin. Be sure to wear gloves, long sleeves, pants, and old or rubber boots when working with cement, and wash your tools as soon as you're finished. As you work, wash yourself often with a hose. Washing skin with vinegar helps balance cement's drying effect.

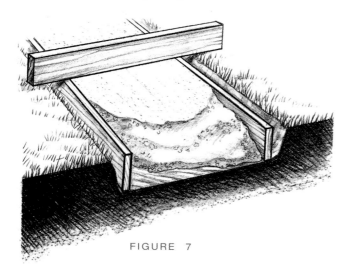

FIGURE 7

Embedding Materials

Adding designs of embedded materials, from tiles to glass to shards of pottery, is a creative way to personalize a concrete path (see figure 9). You'll need to work pretty fast; after about an hour (less if the weather is hot and dry) the concrete will become too hard for you to embed anything.

Have the materials you plan to add within reach, and mix and pour only enough cement to cover a few feet of the walk at a time. If you're embedding an elaborate design of many small pieces you may want to add a retardant, which you can buy at the hardware store, to slow hardening. Wear rubber gloves while pressing design elements into the surface. You'll probably also want to lay a sturdy board over the form boards on the edges of your path so that you can kneel on it while you work.

After you finish a section, lay a thin board or piece of plywood over the embedded

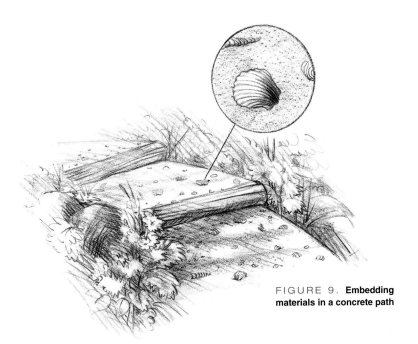

FIGURE 9. **Embedding materials in a concrete path**

Embedded concrete walk

building a test box

When embedding materials, it's important not to overwork the hardening cement. Too much agitation causes a physical separation of the hardening agent and the aggregate. The overworked surface will start to look watery, which means that it may be weak and vulnerable to chipping (especially in freezing temperatures).

It's a simple matter to create a sample slab for practicing your embedding technique before trying it out on the actual path. Nail together four boards (each approximately 1 foot long) to create a frame. Place it on a piece of plywood, plastic sheeting, or a large trash bag on a flat piece of ground or driveway. Pour in a small batch of cement, which you can mix in a five-gallon plastic bucket or a wheelbarrow, and experiment away.

materials and use it to gently tamp them level with the surface of the concrete. Once the concrete has hardened (probably the following day), you can sweep the surface clean with a stiff broom.

another option:
Concrete Pavers

Concrete pavers have gained popularity as a surface material for paths. You can make your own using commercially available forms or you can purchase pre-cast pavers. Both forms and pavers are widely available at home and building supply centers. Pre-cast pavers are approximately 2½ to 3½ inches thick and come in various sizes and shapes, ranging from rounds and hexagons to brick-patterned squares or interlocking designs. Color choices are numerous too, from tan and black to weathered red, gray, and white.

Pre-cast concrete pavers can be dry-laid in sand over a standard path base. They can also be laid on cement and mortared like cut stone. If you want to soften the uniform look of a path of concrete pavers laid on a sand base, leave out a paver here and there, fill the spaces with topsoil, and plant them with a perennial such as creeping thyme.

Maintenance

Concrete paths are the most labor intensive to build, but the easiest to maintain. Occasional sweeping is usually all that's required.

LEFT: **A concrete "yellow brick" road**

LEFT AND BELOW:
Pre-cast concrete was used to create these pavers of simulated keystone.

BOTTOM LEFT:
Moss-covered concrete meets broken tile mortared in place.

WALLS AND FENCES

the big book of backyard projects

function
and
design

Those of us who enjoy working in our yards and gardens are usually habitual rearrangers. One year we want the purple iris smack dab in front of the pink peony. Two years later we start to wonder how that iris's upright, swordlike foliage would look beside the hosta's heart-shaped leaves. We also tend to be just a bit impulsive. Admit it: how many unopened seed packets do you have lying around the house? But moving a 5-foot-high brick wall just a tad to the left is not the same as transplanting a clump of asters, and figuring out what to do with fifteen 1-gallon boxwoods is not the same as squeezing in one more variety of daylily.

A border—whether it's a wall or fence—usually requires a sizable investment in time and money. Chances are, your choice will still be standing when it's time to sell your home. Build one with care, and it may still be standing long after you no longer can! So it's important to clarify in advance exactly why and where you want a border. Then you'll need to consider the conditions of your specific site, any legal restrictions, and the costs (both long- and short-term).

functions

Perhaps you already know exactly why you want a border. You'd like to block the noise and pollution from a busy street, or you're tired of watching your neighbor's compulsive Saturday afternoon car washing (who can enjoy a good snooze in the hammock with all that work going on?). Maybe you're trying to prevent intruders from breaking into your property or your golden retriever with wanderlust from breaking out. Or perhaps your goal is less practical: you crave climbing roses intertwined with clematis, and you need a structure for them to scramble up and over.

Before you rush out and build the wall or fence that suits your purpose, stop and think. Most borders can (and will) serve more than one function. Often this is a bonus: the fence that provides security could, if designed right, create the perfect microclimate for growing plants that normally won't survive in your zone. Sometimes, though, this creates a problem-the tall, solid wall that provides absolute privacy might also cast shade and funnel wind gusts right onto your patio.

Right now, leaving a 6-inch gap at the bottom of a fence might be perfectly fine. But if, in the future, you adopt a dog that can use that space to squeeze (or dig) its way out, you'll have a fence that can't fulfill its function. This is why you need to get out your crystal ball and try to look into the future well before you start to build or wall or fence. Right now you may not mind gazing over a picket fence at the cute little boy riding his tricycle next door. But a few years down the road when he turns 16 and trades in the trike for a motorcycle, you may wish you'd chosen a more sight- and soundproof barrier.

Dividing and Defining Space

Marking a boundary is perhaps the most common function of a wall or fence. We place them around the perimeter of properties to show, both physically and psychologically, what "belongs" to us—to separate private space from public space. On a more practical level, a boundary can establish where your yard ends and the neighbor's begins, or it can encourage visitors to use the path instead of shortcutting across your grass.

But walls and fences also play important roles within a yard or garden. Here they can create outdoor rooms—distinct areas with separate functions, not unlike the rooms in your home. Again, this can be largely psychological (a brick wall around a patio might lend a feeling of peace and seclusion) or practical (a metal fence can make a swimming pool safer).

Enclosing a large yard will help give it definition and make it feel cozier. Surprisingly, enclosing a small yard can make it feel larger (especially if you take care not to use a very high border that leaves the space feeling claustrophobic). Divide a small space so that every aspect can't be taken in with a single glance, and it will suddenly feel more expansive. Screening off sections of a small garden creates a sense of mystery that invites people to explore what's around the next corner.

ABOVE: **Picket fences can keep children out of flowerbeds but still safely in sight.**

LEFT: **This brick wall creates a cozy private enclave yet offers an enticing view of the gardens beyond.**

Privacy

How comfortable would you feel inside your home if it had no walls? Dining outside with family and friends, lounging on the chaise, and even assuming those unflattering weeding positions are all more relaxing when you feel a sense of privacy. Unfortunately, many houses in the suburbs, on city lots, or in new developments have yards that run right up against each other. No matter how fond you are of your neighbors, you probably don't want them to witness your every successful (or unsuccessful) flip of a burger.

This doesn't mean that you need to surround yourself with solid, 10-foot-high walls just to feel at ease in your yard or garden. In fact, most communities have zoning or building regulations that restrict the height of fences and walls. Structures that aren't completely solid can pro-vide a sense of privacy while maintaining the feeling of openness that brings us outdoors in the first place. Consider using a tall, freestanding section of a fairly solid wall or fence where privacy is most desired—beside a patio or hot tub, for example—while choosing a more open design to enclose the rest of your yard.

As a general rule, your border will give you the greatest sense of privacy if it is eye level or higher, so you can't see over it. But remember, the farther away from the structure you get, the easier it will be to see over it, so go to the far edge of your yard to determine an adequate border height. If privacy is your top priority, you may also want to situate your border to block views into your house from the street or from the neighbors' yards.

BELOW: **Privacy fences need not be completely solid.**

Security

Deterrence and containment were the original functions of walls and fences. Keeping invaders and wild animals out and preventing domestic animals from wandering off or destroying crops were once crucial to human survival. Even if marauders and hungry beasts no longer pose a threat, keeping your family safe may still be a priority.

For a structure to provide security, it must be tall, solid, and difficult to climb over or under. A wall or fence that is 6 feet high or higher will usually discourage all but the most determined climbers. Choosing a design that eliminates handholds and footholds is also important. Fences made from stakes and palings are descendants of early palisade walls, and their design principles still hold true: pointed tops, such as pickets or the spikes of an iron fence, make scaling a structure difficult. (More drastic measures—such as razor wire, embedded glass, or electric wire—are illegal in many communities.) If the top of a fence is not pointed, then make sure it has an extra wide cap on top so it doesn't provide an easy handgrip.

Of course, the most secure fence or wall is useless against intruders if its gate or door is easy to break through, so these features also must be designed with security in mind. Padlocks, inside latches, and

This brick wall enhances the appearance of the yard it surrounds, but it also presents a formidable barrier to intruders.

remote-control locks are all options, depending on where the gate or door is located and how it's typically used.

If the main function of your boundary is keeping four-legged intruders out of your garden, make it tall and hard to squeeze through or burrow under. (Boards, such as 2 x 8s or thin walls of concrete, set 2 inches from a fence bottom, should discourage burrowing. But don't allow contact between the boards or concrete and the bottom of a wooden fence or the fence may begin to rot.)

All sorts of borders have been erected in attempts to keep deer out of gardens—most have been unsuccessful. Deer can jump fences that are 10 feet high, but their favored method is to push through or under fencing. Electrical fencing is an option not covered in this book; otherwise, you might try a wire fence at least 8 feet tall, with the wires in the bottom 4 feet of fence no more than 10 inches apart.

If your goal is not keeping wild animals out, but rather keeping pets and wild children in, your wall or fence design will depend on your specific needs. To confine a dog, a wall or fence needs to be at least 5 feet high (higher for a very large dog). Metal fences are often preferred by dog owners since they are not as easily scratched or chewed as wood. Cats can usually be kept in by a solid barrier that is at least 4 feet high, but it must be one they can't climb up and over. Walls and fences built to keep children in the yard should be 5 to 6 feet tall, with no footholds or handholds to offer temptation.

Requirements for fences or walls surrounding swimming pools are often mandated by local zoning regulations and insurance policies. Check these carefully, so you can be sure the design you have in mind will be in full compliance.

TOP: The wire mesh added to this post-and-rail fence would be enough to keep toddlers or some small pets safely contained.

BOTTOM: Securely enclosing a swimming pool is not only common sense—in most places it's required by law.

Tempering the Environment

Perhaps your favorite plant thrives in just one USDA zone to the south, but your spouse can't see the logic of relocating the entire family for the sake of a tender perennial. Or you positioned your patio to catch the evening breeze, but now all your outdoor meals have turned into a game of "catch the paper plates." Or maybe that steady swish of traffic the realtor swore "you could hardly hear" has begun to make relaxing outside feel more like torture. Properly designed and located walls and fences can create microclimates con-

ducive to the plants you wish to grow, add both sun and shade to your garden, buffer strong winds, and muffle noise.

Garden dividers almost always have one sunny side and one shady side. Take advantage of this to grow a variety of plants. Plants that languish in the glare of the afternoon sun will welcome the shade cast by a nearby wall or fence. Full-sun plants that prefer a milder climate than your garden normally provides should be planted on the south side of walls or

An open brick wall can buffer winds and create a more temperate microclimate for plants.

fences that you've painted a light color and oriented east to west. The structure will absorb solar heat throughout the day and then release it during the night.

If your yard or garden is battered by winds, you might be tempted to erect a solid barrier to serve as a windbreak, but this will actually exacerbate the problem. As shown in figure 1, the lee side of a solid structure often suffers from downdrafts and strong gusts, since the wind vaults right up and over the fence or wall. Open designs (such as figure 2), which allow the wind to permeate the barrier, do a much better job of slowing down the wind while providing air circulation that will benefit both you and your plants.

Solid barriers, on the other hand, are most effective at buffering noise. The best sound barrier is a thick wall at least 6 feet tall; sound waves will bounce off the structure most readily if it has a smooth surface. Alternatively, fairly solid, rough-textured fences can absorb sound if they are tall enough. What should you do if you live near a noisy street but also have a windy yard? Then you should consider a wall or fence with a fairly open design. Simply obstructing the view to the source of the noise can help make it less noticeable.

FIGURE 1

FIGURE 2

A sloped section of yard can be transformed into useful space with the help of a stone retaining wall.

Creating Level Areas

Mowing a steep lawn can be dangerous, lounging or dining on one is inconvenient, and playing croquet up and down one, just about impossible. Sloped ground is difficult to garden because the soil (which is subject to erosion) tends to be dry and to lack nutrients. But a retaining wall can change all that. With a wall to hold back the earth, you can create level areas in your yard for a flowerbed, a small patio, and—if not a croquet court—maybe at least a place to play fetch with something other than a billy goat.

The forces on retaining walls are considerable, and adequate drainage is essential, so careful design and construction are of vital importance here. Walls more than 3- to 4-feet high are usually subject to building codes and should be built by a professional. Materials suitable for a retaining wall—depending on the wall's height and the amount of soil it will be retaining—include stone, brick, concrete block, interlocking concrete blocks, and landscape timbers.

Decoration

Just as with people, there are borders among us that do not actually have to work for a living; they just need to look good. Nobody asks them to keep the dog out of the traffic, no one demands that they block an unsightly view or buffer the wind or create a microclimate. Staying gorgeous—maintaining an erect, uncracked, and unblistered appearance—is their full-time job.

Of course, what most of us want is a wall or fence that performs a function or two and looks good at the same time. Getting this is really just a matter of keeping aesthetics in mind when determining the design, height, and placement of your border. Be sure the wall surface that deflects sound is also attractive. Make certain fence you erect for privacy matches the style of your house. Compromises will have to be made, but a quick look through this book should assure you of the many hardworking borders out there that manage to do their jobs and still look beautiful.

Beauty and function have found the perfect balance in this garden's decorative border.

evaluating your site

Now that you know what you want your border to do, it's time to decide where to locate it. This will depend in part on the functions the border will serve, but it will also depend on the specifics of your particular site.

Step Outside

The time has come to step outside and look around. As you examine your site, keep the following factors in mind; they will all play a role in determining the type of border you choose and where to locate it.

▪ How you currently use the different parts of your yard; how you hope to use them in the future. The current flow of foot traffic. Where openings in a wall or fence need to be located and how wide those openings should be.

▪ Views out from your property you'd like to conceal and views you'd like to retain and perhaps even emphasize.

▪ Views into your property you'd like to block (remember this may include windows or doors that afford a view into your house) and features you'd like to have remain in view or perhaps even emphasize.

▪ The source of any bothersome noise you'd like to muffle.

▪ Obstacles (trees, rock outcrops, buildings, etc.) that may be in the way of your wall or fence. (Remember that borders do not have to be designed in straight lines and can often be built around such obstacles.)

▪ The prevailing wind direction on your site.

▪ The path of the sun across your property (this will, of course, vary throughout the year). The sections of yard or garden you'd like to have remain sunny and those where you could use more shade.

▪ The topography of your site. How steep are the slopes? Any low-lying areas?

▪ The current drainage patterns and any drainage problems.

▪ The soil types in various parts of your yard or garden. (This affects how you build the foundations for walls and set the posts for fences.)

other considerations

Once you've determined the specific needs of your particular site, you still have a few more important questions to ask before you start mixing mortar or digging postholes-questions such as "is it legal?" and "can I afford it?"

Legal Aspects

In many communities, zoning regulations or subdivision bylaws restrict the size, placement, and even the style of a wall or fence, so be sure to check these thoroughly before getting started. Depending on your project, local building codes may also apply to the design and construction of your fence or wall.

Good fences may make good neighbors, but if the location of your fence is off by even an inch or two, you may be too good of a neighbor—you will have just built a fence that doesn't belong to you! You must know the exact location of your property lines before you begin work on a fence or wall. The cost of hiring a surveyor to find and mark the property lines and file an official record will certainly be cheaper than tearing down and rebuilding a structure. If the original survey stakes are still in place, get your neighbors to sign a document agreeing to their location.

If your fence or wall straddles the property line, then your neighbors legally own the half that is in their yard and are entitled to do whatever they like with it. They could paint their side of a fence hot pink if they like. You could get your neighbors to sign a document that states that each neighbor agrees to maintain the wall or fence in a certain manner, but remember, new owners may not agree to the arrangement. Your safest bet is to build your border at least

Check on setback requirements and easements before building or planting beside a road.

6 inches in from the property line. Remember, too, it is sometimes the law and usually the custom to build fences so that the "good side" (the board side) faces your neighbor's property while the frame side faces in. You can avoid this by choosing a "good neighbor" design that is finished on both sides.

Another legal consideration is the issue of easements. Sometimes utility companies have easements that allow them access to your yard. If this is the case, you may still be able to enclose your property, but you will have to provide a gate for access. Information about these should be on your deed, but you'll have to check with local utility companies to be certain. If you're building beside a road, check with the highway department to find out about any setback requirements.

Underground Utilities

Never, ever dig a hole in your yard without being certain of the exact location and depth of any underground utilities. Severing a power or gas line could be extremely costly or even fatal. Most local utility companies are happy to locate underground lines on your property for free. You can also hire a company that specializes in finding underground utilities (listed in your phone book's business section under "Utilities Underground Cable, Pipe & Wire Locating Service").

This fence and arbor harmonize perfectly with the house by borrowing architectural details from the structure.

Style and Scale

The style of your house or garden should influence the type of boundary you choose. A bamboo fence would appear out of place in front of a Victorian but be right at home with the simple lines of a contemporary house on the California coast. A formal brick wall could easily look pretentious in front of a ranch house where a split rail fence might better fit the bill, but that same wall would be just right enclosing the formal gardens of a Colonial brick home.

Scale also needs to be considered. A small bungalow can easily be dwarfed by a huge front wall, while a low fence will look silly surrounding a large property. Once you've decided on the dimensions you need your wall or fence to be in order to perform the jobs you've prioritized, then make sure its size will be in scale with its surroundings.

Cost

Somewhere along the line—hopefully sooner rather than later—you'll need to ask yourself what the project you have in mind will cost. When you do so, remember all the hidden expenses: gates, hardware, and finishes for fences, and foundation materials and mortar for walls.

If budget constraints keep you from erecting the wall or fence of your dreams right away, plan your project in stages. You might put up less costly chain-link fencing right now just to keep your pets and children safe while you save for that expensive wooden fence you covet, or you could start building a brick wall as time and finances allow.

In general, walls tend to be more expensive than fences to build initially, but they also, if constructed with care, can last longer and cost much less to maintain. Fences, especially wooden ones, while less expensive to build, usually require regular maintenance and eventually will need to be replaced. With both walls and fences, it only makes sound economic sense to use the strongest materials you can afford.

ABOVE: **Even inexpensive, temporary fencing can be cheerful.**

BELOW: **Chain-link fences can be made more attractive with plantings, such as this vigorous trumpet vine.**

walls

Think walls and you may envision the exotic, tiled structures enclosing Persian gardens or the humble but handsome stone walls crisscrossing New England. Despite the fact that walls come in so many different styles, they're generally divided into only three main categories, based on the material used: brick, stone, or concrete (timber is sometimes used for retaining walls).

Typically the most permanent of garden boundaries, freestanding walls are also usually the most expensive to build or have built. However, a well-constructed wall will last for many years and will require considerably less maintenance than most fences.

Walls are usually more solid than fences-if your main priority is blocking noise or creating privacy or security, a tall wall may be the right choice. No other border is as effective at making a garden feel separate from the world outside. Walls can also be the most versatile of borders. Features such as seating, barbecues, outdoor fireplaces, fountains, and planters can all be incorporated right into the structures. With the information from the first chapter in mind, let the guide that follows help you narrow your search for the best border for you.

dry stone

New England is home to many dry-stacked stone walls that are a couple of hundred years old, but in parts of Europe dry-stacked walls can be found that date back to the Bronze Age. Such permanence is only part of the appeal of stone walls. They are attractive, they are hardworking, and they bespeak the value of careful, time-consuming craftsmanship.

Extremely labor-intensive to build, dry stone walls rely on gravity rather than mortar to stay in place. Fitting the pieces together is something akin to completing a very challenging (and heavy!) jigsaw puzzle. But while they are time-consuming to build, these walls don't require a lot in the way of tools or materials. Unlike mortared walls, dry-stacked stone walls can shift slightly to accommodate the movement of the soil below, so they usually can be built with foundations of just hard-packed earth and gravel.

The natural look of stone makes it the perfect material for a garden wall.

Because these walls cannot be built very high, they provide little in the way of privacy or security. Dry-stacked stone retaining walls are excellent at holding back low banks and providing a microclimate for plants. Freestanding dry-stacked stone walls—built mainly for their good looks these days—are effective at defining boundaries.

mortared stone

When mortar is used to hold stone walls together, the wall can be built higher and so put to more uses. Mortared walls can vary widely in their appearance, depending on both their structure and the type of stone used. Stone that's been carefully cut to uniform shape and size is referred to as dressed stone or ashlar. Un-cut stone is called fieldstone or rubble. In general, mortared walls built from dressed stone will look more formal and will cost more than walls built from fieldstone. In either case, local stone will usually look best with your landscape and will cost less than stone that has to be transported from a distance. How the mortar holding the stones together is finished (or "pointed") will also affect the appearance of the wall.

Mortared walls require concrete footings and the careful construction that usually must be provided by a stonemason. These can be among the most expensive of all borders, but a well-built mortared stone wall is also apt to be the most permanent border money can buy. And you can get a lot for your money—this type of wall can, depending on its height, fulfill just about every function you could ask of a border. About the only thing a mortared stone wall can't do is provide a windscreen, but a structure consisting of stone columns with lattice infill can make an attractive border that will effectively buffer strong winds without creating downdrafts.

Although it is only a couple of years old, this mortared stone wall looks as though it could have been in place for centuries.

This beautifully pati-
naed wall shows
how gracefully brick
can age.

brick

Essentially baked blocks of pressed clay, bricks are one of our oldest construction materials. The fact that they are still in use is testimony to the way these low-tech blocks can be transformed into a diverse array of wall styles, from intimidating, fortress—like barriers to sensuously undulating serpentine structures to open, airy screens.

The color of clay, and thus the appearance of bricks, differs from one location to another; bricks manufactured locally are apt to fit in well with your landscape. Weathered bricks tend to blend in better with plants than new ones, and they have the added advantage of making your garden look as if it has been around for years. (Whatever bricks you use, make sure they are the correct grade for your climate.) The appearance of a brick wall will also be determined by the bond pattern used to lay the bricks, the thickness of the wall, the pointing of the mortar that holds the bricks together, and the method used to cap the wall to deflect rainwater.

A homeowner can tackle brick walls up to 3 feet high on fairly level ground; anything higher requires the design and construction expertise of a bricklayer. Although low brick walls can be built just one brick thick (these are referred to as single-wythe walls), a two-brick-thick (double-wythe) wall will be much stronger and will last much longer. Bricks themselves are fairly inexpensive, but the actual cost of a brick wall can vary, depending on the size of the structure, the design, and whether or not the services of an expert are required.

Low brick walls are useful as boundaries within a garden, as retaining walls on slopes, or as a divider at the edge of a patio. Tall brick walls are excellent for privacy and security, for reducing the noise and dirt from traffic, for creating warm microclimates for plants, and for keeping pets and children constrained. (Rumor has it that they can even keep big, bad wolves at bay.) Open brick walls can be effective as windscreens; tall, solid brick walls create downdrafts. A tall, solid brick wall will also cast shade in the garden, which may or may not be a benefit.

concrete

Concrete walls are valued because they're strong, relatively inexpensive, and they go up quickly. What many people don't realize is that concrete walls can also be beautiful. Finished with a coat of stucco, a concrete wall can mimic adobe or finely dressed stone. The flat surface of a concrete wall makes the perfect canvas for decorative touches such as mosaics or murals.

Concrete blocks are one of the most user-friendly materials for walls. The challenge is not in the building process, but rather in muscling the heavy blocks (which typically weigh 40 to 45 pounds each) into place. Cinder blocks, composed of lighter material, weigh (and cost) considerably less, but they are also not as strong as standard concrete block (their use is often restricted by local building codes).

A *poured* or *in situ* concrete wall, on the other hand, is *not* a project for a beginner. To make these walls (which may be curved

or straight), concrete with steel reinforcing wire is cast in a form, usually made from plywood. These walls can be especially striking with contemporary architecture and in urban gardens.

Depending on their height and construction, concrete walls, whether poured or constructed from blocks, can fulfill just about any function. As with all solid borders, though, they can create wind gusts. Unfortunately, most of the decorative concrete screen blocks available look dated and out of place in a garden setting.

ABOVE: **Even a ho-hum concrete wall can become a vibrant landscape accent with a coat of bright paint.**

BELOW: **With the right finish, concrete can fit in with almost any setting.**

interlocking concrete retaining systems

Concrete wall systems offer one of the easiest methods for building a retaining wall. These walls get their strength from modular blocks that use various mechanisms to interlock with one another without mortar. The blocks come in many different colors and shapes (some are hollow inside and can be planted) and can be stacked into straight or curved walls. These systems are for retaining walls, so while they work well for creating level areas, they usually won't provide privacy or security.

ABOVE: **Because they handle curves easily, interlocking concrete blocks are often used to edge planting beds.**

LEFT: **This long, steep slope is held in check with interlocking concrete blocks.**

timber

Landscape timber retaining walls are practical walls. They get the job done without a whole lot of fuss or expense. They won't last as long as a stone wall, but if you use pressure-treated timbers, they could, depending on soil conditions, last for a few decades. Railroad ties are not recommended; they're saturated with creosote (which is toxic), they're difficult to work with, and they're also usually ugly.

Most landscape timber walls consist of stacked timbers that use a system of deadmen (perpendicular timbers embedded in the bank) for stability. A concrete footing is usually unnecessary. These walls, like most retaining walls, are limited in the functions they can serve in your yard or garden.

Plants can help timber retaining walls blend in with their surroundings.

Building Wall Footings

The soil beneath a wall will sink and shift and (in areas with very cold winters) even heave. When this happens beneath a wall held rigid with mortar, the wall can crack or collapse. A concrete footing, which provides a solid barrier between the wall and the soil, helps prevent this from happening. Whether or not you need a footing (and the type of footing required) depends on the design and height of the wall and the climate and soil conditions of your site. Your local building inspections department can give you advice for your specific area—including whether or not a permit is required—but the following instructions should serve for most mortared walls 3 feet or less in height that are constructed on fairly level ground. Seek the advice of a professional if your wall will run on a slope; sloped walls require special stepped footings.

INSTRUCTIONS

1 First, determine the size footing your intended wall requires. Footings usually need to be twice as wide as the walls they support, with their length extending at least 4 inches beyond the ends of the wall. As a general rule, the footing's thickness should equal the wall's width. In severe winter climates, footing excavations need to extend below the frost line to prevent frost heave. When you check with your local building inspections department, you can find out how deep you need to dig footings in your area.

2 Drive 1 x 2 stakes into the ground to mark the four corners of the intended wall. Stretch mason's line between the stakes to outline the edges of the footing.

3 Unless the excavation is particularly deep because of frost concerns, you can dig the footing trench with a flat-bladed spade and, if needed, a mattock. The depth must take into account not only the thickness of the footing, but any

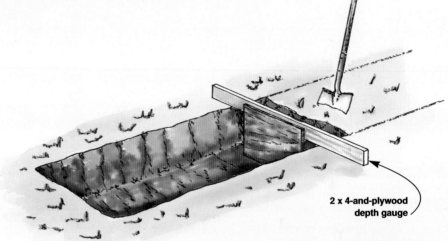

2 x 4-and-plywood depth gauge

FIGURE 1. **Digging the trench**

gravel you might use as a subbase in unstable soils. When digging, take care not to disturb any soil beyond what you need to remove to complete the trench. Square the sides and level the bottom of the trench with the spade.

4 To insure that the bottom is level, periodically lay a 2 x 4 across the trench opening and measure to the bottom with a measuring tape. Or you can nail a piece of plywood onto the 2 x 4 so

that the plywood extends to the correct trench depth. Then lay the 2 x 4 across the top of the trench, making sure the bottom of the plywood is snug against the trench bottom, as shown in figure 1. If you should collapse the side of the trench at any point, install temporary form boards against stable soil and secure them with stakes to prevent the concrete from slumping.

technique

Building Wall Footings

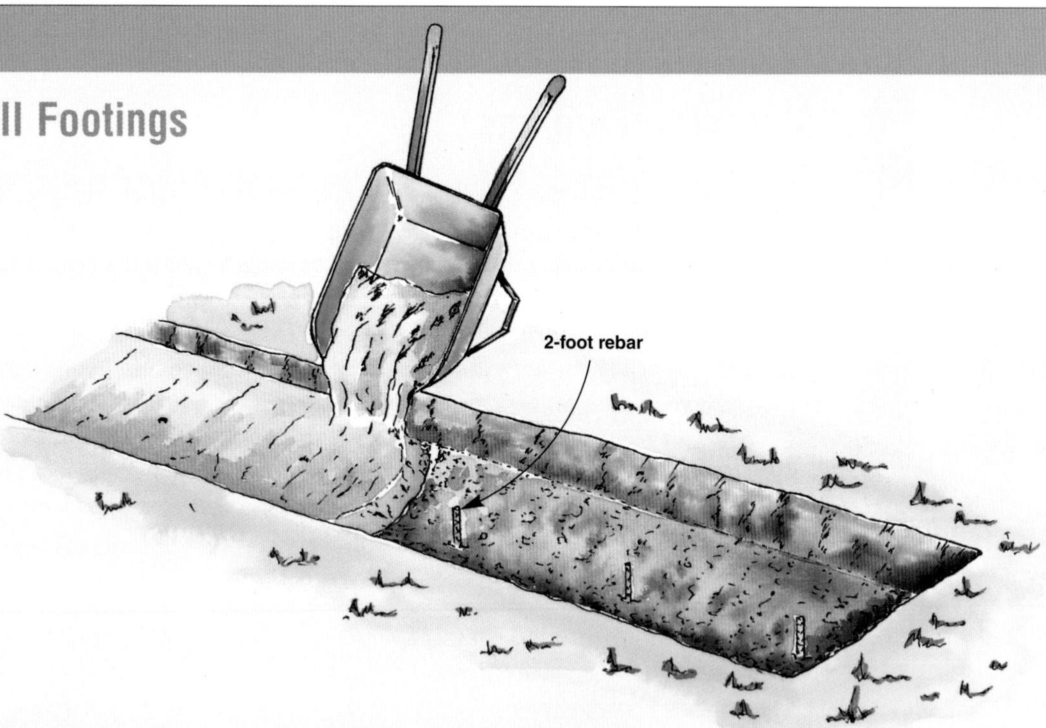

2-foot rebar

FIGURE 2
Pouring the concrete

5 Remove any loose soil from the trench and tamp the bottom. Check the base of the trench with a carpenter's level, or for longer runs, level a mason's line over the length of the trench between the batter boards and measure down from that. In unstable soil (or soil subject to frost heave), lay a 4- to 6-inch subbase of 3/4-inch gravel in the bottom of the trench. Rake it level, tamp the gravel firmly over the length of the trench, and check for level once again.

6 Use a sledgehammer to drive 2-foot lengths of reinforcing bar, "rebar," every 4 feet down the center of the trench. These will serve as the "grade pegs" you will use later to mark and level the top of the concrete, so the aboveground part of the rebar should equal the depth of your concrete footing.

7 Calculate the quantity of concrete you'll need for the job by measuring (in feet) the length, width, and depth of the trench and multiplying the figures to arrive at a cubic-foot measure. A 12-foot by 16-inch by 4-inch trench would be calculated as 12 x 1⅓ x ⅓, or 5¼ cubic feet. For small jobs, 60-pound bags of premixed concrete are most convenient. This 5¼ cubic foot (or 16 square foot, with 4-inch depth) project would require 11 bags of mix; if the depth were 6 inches (making 8 cubic feet), it would need 16 bags. Your builder's supply or home center should have a chart that will allow you to calculate quantities based on your square footage needs. If the job is large enough, you might consider having ready-mix concrete delivered, but be prepared to pay a premium for delivery of small quantities.

8 Before mixing and pouring concrete, get some work gloves and safety glasses (cement is caustic); then enlist the aid of a helper, and clear the work area of any debris that will prevent clear access to any part of the trench. Use a wheelbarrow or mortar box and a mixing hoe to blend water with the concrete mix. Don't work with too much material in one batch, and add water sparingly as you mix—your goal is to make a plastic, nearly fluid mixture, not a soupy or watery one. Starting at one end of the trench, pour the concrete, as shown in figure 2, and move it with a shovel to prevent it from mounding in one spot. Spread it evenly with successive pours, and keep the height below or at the imbedded rebar pins as you move. Work the mix into the corners and eliminate any air pockets with slicing movements of your shovel.

9 Once the trench is filled, use a scrap of 2 x 4 cut to the appropriate length to screed the surface of the footing level with the tops of the rebar grade pegs. Work in a zigzag motion, as shown in figure 3, from one end to the other to knock down high spots and fill in voids at the surface. This action also helps the concrete to set up properly, and provides a slightly rough surface for a good mortar bond later.

10 Leave the stakes and batter boards set up-you'll use them again when you construct a wall on top of the footing. Clean your tools and equipment thoroughly with cold water when you're finished. The concrete will set up in an hour or so, but will not cure to sufficient strength for a few days. To prevent cracking during this period, the concrete must be kept moist. Spray the footing with water a few times each day and keep it covered with plastic. Wait at least a week before beginning any construction work on top of the footing.

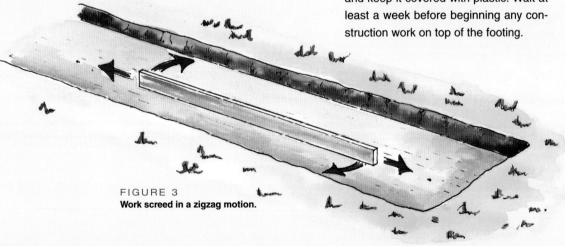

FIGURE 3
Work screed in a zigzag motion.

a low brick wall

Constructing your own brick wall may seem like a formidable task, but once you get the hang of it, building a low brick wall is surprisingly easy. Such walls can serve as interior boundaries in your yard—enclosing a patio, perhaps—or they can separate your front yard from the street. Instructions for building a concrete footing for a low brick wall can be found on page 257. You'll need to allow at least a week between building the footing and laying up the wall so the concrete has time to cure completely.

INSTRUCTIONS

1 Use the stakes and mason's line to mark the outline of the wall, directly over the center of the cured footing. The distance between the two strings (which will match the width of the brick wall) should be equal to the length of one brick. This will equal the width of two bricks plus a ½-inch mortar joint. The lines must be perfectly parallel and about 2 inches above the top of the footing. Lay a "dry run" of two rows of brick on the footing, setting each brick lengthwise against one string and leaving a ½-inch space between each brick, both at the ends and along the sides. Use the carpenter's level to check the tops of the rows, then mark the position of each brick directly onto the foundation. Remove the bricks.

2 Use the hoe to mix your mortar in a wheelbarrow or mortar box, starting with small amounts if you have no experience laying brick. A 60-pound bag of dry, premixed mortar will yield about ½ cubic foot of workable mortar when properly mixed. The mixture should be moist and firm, not soupy. Use the brick trowel to spread an even ⅝-inch layer of mortar within the marked chalk lines on the footing, then furrow the bed with the tip of the trowel.

3 Set the first brick lengthwise on the mortar bed in one corner. Check it for level end to end and front to back. If it's out of level, tap the high corner with the end of the trowel handle. Spread a ⅝-inch-thick layer of mortar onto the end of a second brick. This is called "buttering" the brick. Bevel the edges inward with your trowel so the mortar mounds toward the center. Lay the brick into the mortar bed and at the same time press it against the first brick. The joint should compress and fill to ½ inch. Check and level this brick; then follow this procedure to lay two more bricks, checking for level faithfully and keeping the bricks within the chalk marks on the footing, as shown in figure 1.

TOOLS AND SUPPLIES

4 stakes (1 x 2s would work well)

Mason's line

Tape measure

Line level

Wheelbarrow or mortar box (see step 2)

Hoe

Brick and pointing trowels

Carpenter's level

Joint tool

Pencil (or black pen)

MATERIALS

Bricks (see Tips)

Mortar

2 x 4, 16 inches long

1 x 4, 3 feet long

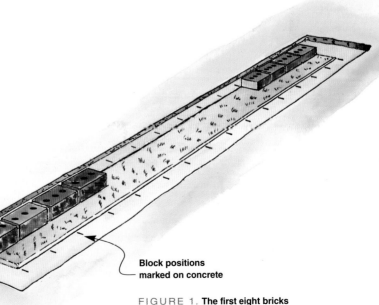

Block positions marked on concrete

FIGURE 1. **The first eight bricks**

Story pole

**Corner blocks
and mason's string**

FIGURE 2
Building up the ends

4 Repeat step 3 on the opposite end of the wall. Attach the corner blocks with the mason's line to the top of both corner bricks, so the line is even with the tops of the bricks. Attach the line level and then adjust any bricks that aren't level. Once both ends of the wall are level, continue laying bricks toward the center of the wall from both ends, checking for level faithfully and keeping the bricks within the chalk marks on the footing. Lay the final brick in this row—called the "closure brick"—by buttering both ends and wiggling it into place. Check for level.

5 Complete the first course by laying a second row of bricks alongside the first. Check for level both along the length and across the two rows; then fill the joint between the rows with mortar. Use a pointing trowel to fill the exposed joints at each end if needed.

6 The rest of the wall is constructed by building up the ends first and then filling in the middle section, as shown in figure 2. Start building one end by spreading a second ⅝-inch layer of mortar on top of one end of the brick course you just completed. Lay the first brick of the second course across the two end bricks of the first course, and level it both ways, making a ½-inch joint. This crosswise brick will serve as a header that will make the second course of bricks overlap the first course by half, keeping the joints staggered so the wall will be stable.

tips

■ You'll probably be working with common brick in a 3½- x 7½- x 2¼-inch size, give or take a fraction. Count on using about 60 bricks for every face square yard of wall, and make sure you purchase brick that's graded for your climate. Make sure you have two solid bricks to put at either end of the capping on the top of the wall.

■ Bricks should be slightly damp when you lay them; otherwise, they'll steal moisture from the mortar joint. Spray them down an hour

or so before using them, so they'll be damp, not dripping wet, when you lay them.

■ Corner blocks and mason's string are used as a guide to keep each course of brick level. To make two corner blocks, first use the handsaw to cut the 16-inch 2 x 4 in half. Then cut a 4-inch x 1¾-inch rectangle out of one corner of each 8-inch block (see illustration). Cut a slot into the middle of the uncut section of each block. Wrap mason's line around this end of each block, securing it in the slot.

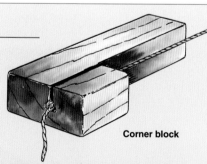

Corner block

■ Use a story pole to check the height of each course as you proceed. Make one by marking a 3-foot-long 1 x 4 with lines that indicate one brick plus a ½-inch mortar joint. Hold the story pole upright against the wall as you work to check the top of each course.

7 Now add the next six bricks of the second course to the wall (two rows of three lengthwise bricks). On top of this, lay the start of the third course of bricks (two rows of three lengthwise bricks without a crosswise header). Then lay the start of the fourth course (one crosswise header and then two rows of two lengthwise bricks). Finish building up the wall end by laying the start of the fifth course (two rows of two lengthwise bricks). As you build, re-member to check for level both along the length and across the width of the wall. Hold the carpenter's level against the end of the wall to check for plumb (as shown in figure 3), and use the story pole to check the height of each course as you build (see figure 2).

8 Repeat steps 6 and 7 to build up the other end of the wall. Once both ends of the wall are raised by five courses, scrape off any excess mortar with the edge of the trowel. A joint tool can be used to clean and smooth the joints.

9 Spread a bed of mortar, and lay the second brick course completely. Check for level individually and along the row as you work.

10 Spread a bed of mortar on top of the second course, and lay the third course. Continue laying courses, constantly checking for level and height with the story pole as you work. Build up end leads as you proceed with each course, remembering that every other course will begin and end with a crosswise brick.

11 Finish the top of the wall by cap-ping it with a row of bricks laid on edge across the wall's width, as shown in figure 3. First lay a mortar bed along the

> **note:**
> Brick can be stacked in a variety of patterns, or "bonds," to build walls. To understand these patterns you need to know that "stretchers" are bricks laid lengthwise along the wall, while "headers" are bricks laid across the width of the wall. The wall in the photo on page 260 is an example of an English bond: it's made of alternating courses of stretchers and headers. The wall described in the instructions (and shown in the illustrations) is made using the simplest of bonds, the running bond. This pattern consists almost entire-ly of stretchers, but a header starts off every other row in order to stagger the vertical joints between the bricks. Before beginning this project, check with officials about local building codes; they may dictate minimum specifi-cations for a brick wall in your area.

top of the exposed course, then butter and lay the individual bricks on edge until the row is closed and complete. Make sure you use solid blocks on the ends and check for level both across and lengthwise.

12 Finish the joints by running the joint tool along vertical joints first, then along the horizontal joints. If there's a place where the joint isn't fully filled out, pack it with mortar using a pointing trowel; then smooth the joint with the tool.

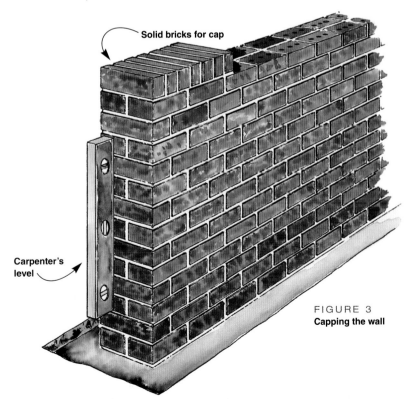

Solid bricks for cap

Carpenter's level

FIGURE 3
Capping the wall

interlocking concrete block retaining wall

Tired of mowing that bank or watching your soil erode? The interlocking concrete block retaining wall systems available these days offer an easy-to-install solution for sloping ground. How the blocks actually connect differs somewhat from system to system, but the basic steps that follow apply to just about any retaining wall up to 4 feet tall. Give yourself plenty of time to complete this project; it's strenuous work that calls for lots of bending and heavy lifting.

TOOLS AND SUPPLIES

Shovel

Hoe

Measuring tape

Mason's line

Line level

Tamper

Carpenter's level

Screed board (a 2 x 4, 28 inches long, would work well)

Broom

Stone hammer

Block chisel

Safety glasses

Torpedo level

Circular saw with masonry blade (optional; see step 6)

Caulking gun

Pencil

INSTRUCTIONS

1 Excavate the slope where the wall will go, using the shovel or hoe. Retain this soil for later use. Measure and mark the lines for a trench—you'll need to leave 12 inches between the back edge of the trench and the soil bank (this is for the crushed gravel that will go between the wall and the bank. Dig the trench 18 to 24 inches wide and about 12 inches deep—or 8 inches deeper than the thickness of the blocks you're using—in order to accommodate a firm gravel base. Skim the bottom of the trench flat and level with a hoe, and check for true by stretching mason's line 6 inches above the ground, end to end, and hanging the line level from it.

2 Fill the trench with 4 to 6 inches of compactible aggregate material. Pack the material with the tamper, and use the carpenter's level to check for level as you work.

3 Add a 1-inch layer of sand on top of this base. Use the screed board to level the sand, checking your work once again with the carpenter's level. This tedious task is worth whatever time it takes-the structural integrity of your wall depends on its base being level and well compacted.

MATERIALS

Compactible aggregate
  material (see tip)
Sand
Crushed gravel
Interlocking concrete blocks
Cap blocks
Masonry adhesive

tip

Compactible aggregate material is made up of various size gravel and sand that compacts into a solid base. Both the composition and the name of this material may differ, depending on where you live. It is not the same as the crushed gravel used to backfill behind the wall.

4 Begin setting the base course of block. Space the blocks slightly apart for drainage, and check each one side to side and front to back as you align them, using a torpedo level. As you work along the wall's length, use the longer carpenter's level to check adjoining blocks (see figure 1). If a block is too low, add sand underneath to raise it; if it's too high, tap it down with a mallet to seat it. If the blocks you're working with have lips, dig out a groove in the sand to accommodate the lips for this first course. In some situations, you may need to remove the lower lip with the stone hammer and the block chisel to allow the blocks to lie flat; be sure to wear protective eyewear when doing so.

5 Fill the space in front, behind, and between the blocks with the crushed gravel. Tamp it down, and sweep the upper surface of the blocks clean in preparation for the next course.

6 Set the second course of block on top of the first, with the center of each block bridging the joint of the blocks below, so all joints are staggered. Make certain the lip of each block hooks over and against the back of the blocks below it as shown in figure 2. If your particular block uses a different setback and locking method, follow the manufacturer's instructions. For exposed, flush-ended walls, you'll have to begin and end each alternating course with a half-block. To split a block, score the top and bottom surface with the edge of the block chisel or the circular saw fitted with a masonry blade. Wet the score line and drive the chisel into the groove until it splits, as shown in figure 3. On walls where the ends will terminate into the slope, prepare a firm bed of foundation material adjacent to the last block, and place a full block over half of the block below so it rests firmly on both the lower block and the foundation material.

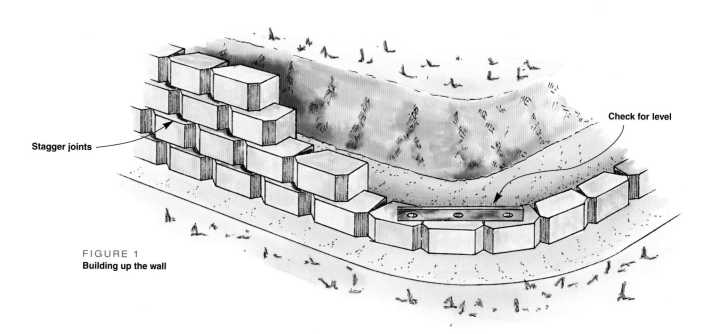

Stagger joints

Check for level

FIGURE 1
Building up the wall

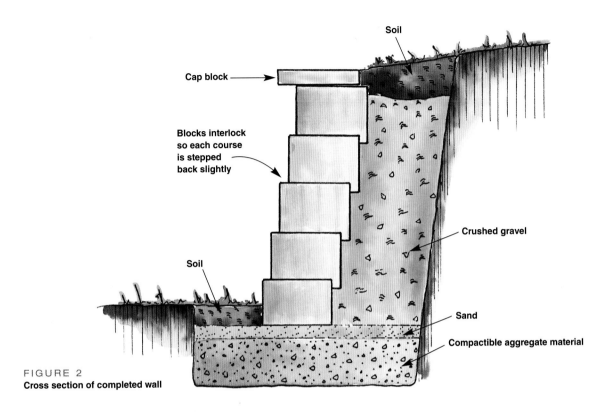

Soil

Cap block

Blocks interlock
so each course
is stepped
back slightly

Crushed gravel

Soil

Sand

Compactible aggregate material

FIGURE 2
Cross section of completed wall

7 Continue laying the third and fourth courses of block, making sure the surface of the previous course is clean before installing the next. Backfill against the wall with several inches of gravel, and use soil from the excavation to fill towards the slope. Tamp all fill material after laying each course. At the final course of block, you can backfill with topsoil.

8 If the top of the wall will be exposed and not covered by plantings, you'll probably want to install cap block. This block is thinner than the structural block and is cemented in place using masonry adhesive and the caulking gun. It can be set flush with the face of the wall or allowed to overhang it. Dry-lay the cap block beforehand and mark its position in pencil. Then sweep the base block clean and cement the caps, using the marks as an alignment guide. Grade additional topsoil as needed to the surface of the cap, sloping it toward the face of the wall slightly so water will run over, and not pool behind, the structure.

FIGURE 3. **Splitting a block**

dry-stacked stone retaining wall

When you need a wall to hold back a bank of soil, consider the simple beauty of a dry-stacked stone wall. Requiring neither mortar nor a concrete footer, a dry-stacked wall 2 feet or less in height can be constructed by just about any do-it-yourselfer. Just remember to pace yourself—this is a wall you'll probably want to build over the course of several weekends; otherwise, you may get some very sore muscles.

INSTRUCTIONS

1 The stones that will make up the top course of your wall are called capstones. These need to be fairly large and flat, so select some of these stones now and set them aside for later.

2 Use your shovel (and the mattock and pick, if necessary) to excavate the slope you will be retaining. The bank should angle back slightly from the bottom to the top (see figure 1, page 270). Use your mattock and pick to remove any rubble (small, irregularly shaped stones) and roots, so the face of the cut is smooth. Reserve the rubble stones and about one-fourth of this soil for later use.

3 Excavate the foundation for your wall by digging a 6-inch deep by 2-foot wide trench at the base of your cut bank. Fill this trench with pea gravel; then add a 2-inch-thick layer of pea gravel (that will rest above ground) on top of that.

4 The first course of the wall is made up of base stones. These should be the largest stones and should have at least one wide, flat surface (wedge the uneven face of any base stone into the pea gravel foundation). Lay out your base stones so that their front ends (at the front of the gravel foundation) are as close together as possible and their back ends are slanting down slightly. The stones at either end of your wall should reach all the way back to the cut bank, since these serve as cornerstones. If a cornerstone is short, find another stone that, when set close behind the first, will reach back to the bank and keep the gravel fill from washing out. The distance between the cut bank and the back of the rest of this first course should average about 1 inch.

5 Add any rubble stones you have available in the space between the base stones and the base. Then lock this first

tips

■ Heavy work gloves and sturdy boots are essential safety gear when working with stone.

■ These instructions are for dry-stacked walls 2 feet or less in height. Dry-stacked walls higher than this require larger stones and a more severe degree of batter (backwards slant); they are best left to experienced stonemasons.

course in place by spreading pea gravel over the rubble and behind the base stones. Use the rebar to set the gravel, especially between the gaps at the back edges of the stones. This step is essential for a strong, stable wall.

6 Brush off any gravel left on top of the base stones. Then lay out the next layer of stones, taking care to place each stone on top of a joint between two of the base stones. Doing so with each layer of the wall will help you avoid "running joints" (vertical gaps running down the wall), which weaken both the strength and the appearance of the wall. Remember, too, when positioning your stones, to maintain the wall's batter of 5 to 10 degrees. Use small rocks as wedges or shims to keep stones level and stable.

7 The stablest walls will have a long "tie stone" running from the front of the wall all the way back to the bank every couple of courses and every 4 or 5 feet of wall length. If you can't find stones long enough to work as tie stones, place two stones close together to serve the same purpose.

8 Build up the wall by continuing to add courses of stone and carefully setting gravel backfill. Remember to constantly check that each course of stone is level from end to end and maintains the batter of 5 to 10 degrees.

9 Lay out the final course of your wall with the capstones you set aside in step 1. Backfill with pea gravel again, but this time use the soil reserved in step 2 to cover the gravel.

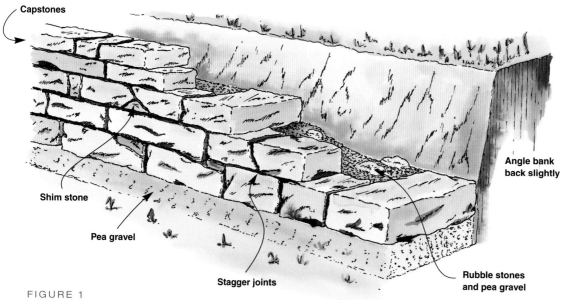

Capstones

Shim stone

Pea gravel

Stagger joints

Angle bank back slightly

Rubble stones and pea gravel

FIGURE 1

landscape
timber
retaining
wall

A landscape-timber retaining wall can hold back sloping ground without a concrete footing or mortared joints. The straightforward construction method and relatively inexpensive materials make this wall a favorite with do-it-yourselfers. Just make sure your bank can be retained by a wall 3 feet or lower in height. Taller walls call for more structural support, and an engineer usually must design walls higher than 4 feet.

TOOLS AND SUPPLIES

Shovel

Measuring tape

Stakes

Mason's line

Tamper

Carpenter's level

Sledgehammer

Drill

5/8-inch spade bit

1/4- and 1-inch spade bits
(optional, see steps 4 and 6)

Chainsaw (optional, see step 3)

Circular saw with a framing
blade (optional, see step 3)

Handsaw (optional, see step 3)

Safety gear (see Tips)

MATERIALS

Compactible aggregate material
(see Tips)

Pressure-treated landscape
timbers (see Tips)

1/2-inch reinforcing bar,
36 inches long

12-inch galvanized spikes

Perforated drainpipe

Crushed gravel

INSTRUCTIONS

1 Excavate and level the portion of the slope where the wall will go. Set this soil aside for use in later steps. If the wall will be more than two or three courses high, you'll need a 12-inch-wide trench to bed the first course of timbers. Lay out the trench with stakes and the mason's line. Dig to a depth of 6 inches in firm soil. (In loose or sandy soil—or soils subject to frost heave—dig a 12-inch-deep trench.) Spread a 6-inch layer of compactible aggregate material in it. Tamp the material flat, and check it with the carpenter's level.

2 Set the first course of timbers and level them with the sledgehammer. Anchor these foundation timbers by first boring 5/8-inch holes through each timber, 16 inches from the ends, and one in the center, as shown in figure 1. Then drive 36-inch lengths of 1/2-inch reinforcing bar, "rebar," through the holes and into the ground until they're flush with the top of the wood. To further stabilize these bottom timbers, pack some of the soil removed from the trench against the front face of the timbers to create a slight slope away from the retaining wall.

3 Lay up the second course so that each timber is set over the joint between two timbers on the course below, as shown in figure 1. This will avoid "running joints" that weaken the wall's structure. Set this and all following courses 3/4 inch back from the one below it, unless you're retaining only 12 inches or less of soil. (This setback allows the wall to lean back into the slope for greater strength.) Cut the timbers to the correct length with a chainsaw if one is available. Otherwise, use a framing blade in a circular saw, and rotate the timber so you can cut in on all four sides to the blade's maximum 2 3/8-inch depth. The cut will then need to be completed with a handsaw.

4 As you set each timber in place, nail it to the course below with 12-inch galvanized spikes, starting at about 8 inches from each end and then at 16-inch intervals in between. If you have trouble driving the spikes with the sledgehammer, predrill the top-course holes with a 1/4-inch spade bit.

5 Starting at the second or third course, you'll need to install anchors or "deadmen" that run perpendicularly to stabilize the wall against the pressure of the soil being retained. (This is especially important for walls taller than 3 feet.) For the low wall in the photograph on page 271, deadmen were set two at a time, spaced 4 feet apart in the front and attached in the back by a 5-foot-long timber. Higher walls will need deadmen installed at every third or fourth course.

6 Once you've set a few courses, you will need to install perforated drainpipe to carry away excess water. Use your level to check the slope—it should be about 1/4-inch for every foot of pipe run, and graded toward an opening you've planned. You can cut an exit hole through the joint of two courses with a chainsaw if you need to exit through an end wall. Lay the pipe about 6 inches behind the wall, and cover it with the crushed gravel as you work upward. Lower walls that will not have to deal with much water can be drained by drilling 1-inch weep holes every 4 feet through the timbers just above the base course, or about 12 inches above the ground.

7 Backfill the area behind the wall and drainpipe with soil removed from the excavation. Compact the earth with a tamper and continue to fill the area above the drainpipe with gravel as you work. When the last two courses are completed, backfill with topsoil, graded to rise just above the top timbers so any runoff will spill over the wall and not pool behind it.

tips

■ Pressure-treated 5 x 6 timbers in 8-foot lengths are a good choice for this project. They're less expensive than larger beams, and if you stack them so they're 6 inches high, calculations will be simple.

■ Because some pressure-treated wood contains the preservative CCA (chromated copper arsenate), wear work gloves when handling the timbers, and add a dust mask and protective eyewear when cutting them.

■ Compactible aggregate material is made up of various-size gravel and sand that compacts into a solid base. Both the composition and the name of this material may differ, depending on where you live. It's not the same as the crushed gravel used to backfill behind the wall.

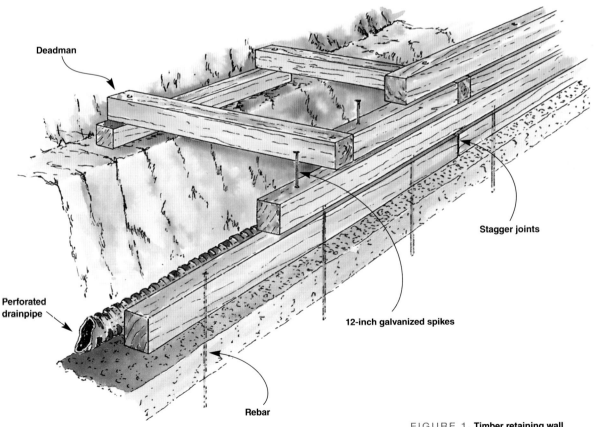

Deadman

Perforated drainpipe

Rebar

12-inch galvanized spikes

Stagger joints

FIGURE 1. **Timber retaining wall**

fences

IF you're the impatient type, a fence may well be the border for you. Walls go up and hedges grow up slower than fences. No matter what your site conditions or the functions desired, chances are good a fence exists that will work for you. And it will do that work while taking up very little of your ground space—a real bonus in small yards.

Fences usually cost less than a wall of the same size. While the average fence requires more maintenance than the typical wall, the amount of upkeep required by a specific fence varies widely, depending on the materials and finish used. All this goes a long way toward explaining why fences are the most popular of garden borders. But the number one reason is probably the fact that there are so many different styles and variations of fencing from which to choose. With the information from the first part of Section Three in mind, let the guide that follows help you narrow your search for the perfect border.

picket

Picket fences are friendly. Typically 3 to 4 feet high, they set a boundary without discouraging neighborly chats, the passing of borrowed cups of sugar, or peeks to check whose tomatoes are ripening first. We tend to think of picket fences as being as American as apple pie, but, in fact, they were used in China as early as the eighth century A.D. and were also common in medieval gardens.

Most picket fences consist of a framework of 4 x 4 posts and 2 x 4 rails with an infill of pickets made from 1 x 3s or 1 x 4s. Preassembled 8-foot sections of fence are available—these usually come with pointed or square picket tops. If you install individual pickets, you can cut the tops to practically any style and even vary the lengths of the pickets so each bay of the completed fence curves.

This style of fence works well if your priorities are establishing a visual boundary, directing human traffic, or creating a backdrop for plants.

Pointed pickets discourage climbing (in either direction), but the fences are usually too short to keep determined intruders out or climbing pets in. In keeping with its friendly attitude, a picket fence offers little in the way of privacy. Relatively inexpensive to build, picket fences are usually painted or stained, so they will require regular maintenance (unless you are cunning enough to convince a friend that the privilege can be his in exchange for a dead rat on a string).

The cheerful picket fence is a staple of backyards everywhere.

board

This fence means business. It's about as close to a wall as a fence can get. At the same time, this no-nonsense boundary offers countless design variations. In fact, few fences have as many design options as the board fence. The size of the infill can vary from fence to fence (or even on the same fence), the boards can abut, have gaps in between, overlap, or—in the case of a shadow fence—be spaced on both sides of a central nailer to provide both privacy and airflow.

Usually, a board fence frame consists of 4 x 4 posts with two or three 2 x 4 horizontal rails attached. The infill is typically vertical boards that can be as narrow as 1 x 3s or as wide as 1 x 12s (boards that are 6 to 8 inches wide are ideal-narrower lumber is not economical, and very wide boards are more apt to warp or crack). This type of fence is fairly difficult (and therefore also fairly expensive) to build.

Consider a board fence if you need privacy, shade, security, or a reduction in noise. (Be careful, though—set in the path of prevailing winds, a solid board fence can cause downdrafts.) The sunny side of a board fence can provide a warm spot to grow tender plants. Plants, especially climbers, will also help soften the sometimes stark appearance of a newly installed board fence. Maintenance needs will vary, depending on whether the fence is painted, stained, or—if made from naturally rot-resistant or pressure-treated wood—left to weather naturally.

What might have been a boring board fence is made elegant by the simple curves at its top.

stakes and palings

Descending from the fortress-like palisades that surrounded early settlements, fences made from stakes and palings still have a somewhat imposing air about them. The rough, unsawn texture of the wood gives these fences a rustic appearance that fits in well with rural settings or informal gardens.

The fences are made by attaching split stakes or saplings with sharp, pointed tops to a framework of 4 x 4 posts and 2 x 4 rails. Construction is relatively simple, but the amount of infill required makes the work time-consuming and the cost high (unless you have a free supply of saplings).

Because of their pointed tops and close-set infill, these fences excel at providing both security and privacy. They're effective at delineating boundaries and tempering the environment (although downdrafts can occur if the infill is spaced too tightly). Left to weather naturally, palings from rot-resistant or pressure-treated wood should require little maintenance. If a stake fence is stained, maintenance needs will increase.

This rustic fence would look out of place in many settings but fits in well with this rural home.

Lattice's open construction makes it perfect for roses and other plants prone to fungal diseases.

lattice

Lattice fencing has been a favorite with gardeners for centuries. Its crisscross design allows for lovely plays of light and seems to beg for the companionship of a climbing rose or clematis. Despite the open, airy effect of lattice, it can—depending on the closeness of the slats—offer a surprising degree of privacy, and it casts an acceptable amount of shade for most gardens. Circular (or other shaped) windows can be cut into lattice fencing to open up attractive views within or beyond the garden. The open nature of lattice helps it to diffuse winds. If the structure is easily climbed, it won't make effective security fencing (although especially thorny roses might help matters here).

You can purchase lattice in prefabricated 4 x 8-foot panels of cedar or treated wood. Most lattice fences consist of a frame of posts and upper and lower rails. The lattice panels are held in place with 1 x 1 strips (nailers) on either side of the posts. The cap rail across the top is typically straight, but fences of this type with scalloped tops are stunning. Lattice fencing is fairly easy and quick to install, so it is relatively inexpensive. The heavier (and more costly) grade of lattice will save you money in the long run. Make sure the staples holding the slats together are galvanized. Maintenance needs will depend on whether the fence is painted or stained or—if built from rot-resistant or pressure-treated wood—left to weather naturally.

This recently installed galvanized steel fence could pass itself off as a fine antique.

ornamental metal

A favorite of the Victorians, ornamental iron fences were so common in Europe, they were melted down and turned into weapons during World War II. Now craftspeople with the ability to hammer heated iron into the twists and arabesques of an ornamental fence are hard to find. Most of us must be content with the prefabricated sections of tubular steel or aluminum available at home centers.

Though metal fences are most commonly found in cityscapes, wrought iron looks spectacular with clematis or roses climbing up and through its intricate rails. The delicate patterns of light and shade cast by such a fence are also a charming addition to most gardens. The more ornamental of these fences have a formal appearance that complements houses

with traditional architecture, while the sleeker, more modern style of metal fence works best with contemporary homes.

To provide security, a metal fence must be tall with narrow spaces between the infill, and preferably spiked tops. These characteristics, combined with a low clearance at the bottom, will also give you a fence that can keep pets and children contained.

Low ornamental metal fences are usually found at the front of the yard, where they serve mainly as psychological barriers-they don't provide much in the way of security or privacy. Maintenance will depend in a large part on the quality of the fence. Check when purchasing one or having one installed for warranties against rust and corrosion.

basket weave

These handsome fences, made from woven slats of thin lumber, should appeal to the crafter who likes to work on a really large scale! (Those less ambitious can purchase prewoven panels to construct the fence.) Weaving the slats is actually easier than you may think, but it does take time. The cost of the materials for the slats or for the prewoven panels is generally moderate.

Effective at providing privacy while allowing air circulation, a basket weave fence is also good for delineating boundaries and tempering the environment. Its effectiveness as a security fence depends on the strength of its wood and the ease with which its framework can be climbed. Such fences look quite striking when stained, but, with all those woven surfaces, that can be a daunting task. If low maintenance is a priority, build yours from rot-resistant or pressure-treated wood and leave it to weather naturally.

This striking basket weave fence makes the grade, while separating a backyard from an alley.

Decorative details can help break the monotony of a panel fence.

panel

The effect of a panel fence is similar to that of an interior house wall. Panel fences are usually constructed with plywood as the infill, but hardboard, plastic, fiberglass, and even glass itself are also options. These tend to be contemporary-looking fences; they don't fit in well with every type of setting. The solid face of this kind of fence will provide a backdrop for plants, but it can feel overwhelming in too small a space.

Panel fences usually go up quickly; their cost will depend on the materials used as infill. Solid ones are excellent at providing privacy and can keep intruders out and pets and children in if their framework is not easily climbed. A panel fence will provide a microclimate for plants, but openings must be designed into the structure to avoid downdrafts in windy sites. The maintenance needs of a panel fence will depend on the material it's built from, but since these fences are usually painted or stained, they need continual upkeep.

post-and-rail and post-and-board

These are rural fences. They're descendants of the rustic stacked-rail worm fences that once zigzagged their way across the American landscape (and which George Washington once declared "expensive and wasteful of lumber"). The pared-down version in use today requires considerably less lumber than most fences and is often used to enclose a large area while still maintaining a view.

These fences can be rustic (as in the case of split-rail fencing) or rather stately (as with the white post-and-board fences surrounding many horse farms). Typically, such fences consist of mortised posts fitted with two to four tenoned rails or dadoed posts with boards. The cost will depend on the type and amount of wood used.

Traditionally used to keep livestock contained, these fences are also effective at delineating boundaries, directing foot traffic, and providing a place for roses to ramble. They don't provide security or privacy, nor do they temper the environment (except for blocking drifting snow). If constructed from rot-resistant or pressure-treated wood and left to weather naturally, these fences will require little in the way of maintenance. Ones that are painted or stained will require regular upkeep.

This three-rail fence establishes a clear border without detracting from the beauty of the landscape.

bamboo

Bamboo is actually a woody grass with hollow, upright stems. According to a Taoist belief, each individual section of the plant's stem represents a step along the path to enlightenment. Traditionally found in the Far East, bamboo fences bring an exotic touch to the garden. They do, however, look out of place in many settings. A bamboo fence that might be stunning in front of a contemporary home on the rugged California coast would look silly in the front yard of a New England Colonial. On the other hand, a bamboo fence is the perfect border for a Japanese-style garden or a backyard koi pond.

Borders made from bamboo can be open or closed, simple or elaborate, depending on their design. Since bamboo usually must be purchased through mail order and shipped, bamboo fences are costly. A less expensive option is to purchase rolls of wire-bound bamboo (which can be found at many home improvement centers) and use them to erect a temporary screen. How long a bamboo fence will last in your area depends on the climate (immature or improperly cured bamboo will decay quickly in a humid environment) and the construction of the fence (treated posts or galvanized steel pipe should be used for the parts of the fence that go into the ground). The warm honey color of bamboo will weather to gray eventually unless you apply an occasional coat of wax or the waterproofing sealers used on decks.

Because bamboo fences come in so many styles, it should be possible (although not always practical) to find one to meet your needs. The most common function of a bamboo fence is as a divider or screen within the garden.

Bamboo's flexibility allows for the sinuous curves and light, airy design of this elegant handcrafted fence.

Chain link
disguised with
a closely planted
hedge helps
keep this pool
safe and secure.

chain link

No one installs a chain-link fence for decorative purposes—this is always a fence with a job to do. You may think of chain link as fit only for jobs such as keeping snarling dogs confined to junkyards, but the right chain link fence in the right place can be both hardworking and, well, if not exactly attractive, at least unobtrusive.

The fence consists of wire mesh attached to straining wires held taut by posts. The wire should be galvanized or coated with colored plastic. Chain-link fences that are coated with black plastic will blend most readily into the landscape. Growing an evergreen hedge against green chain link will also make the fence less obtrusive.

Chain link is one of the less-expensive fencing options and is fairly easy to install once you get the hang of it. Excellent at providing security, chain-link fences do not provide privacy unless they are heavily planted or special inserts are installed. They give climbing plants a leg up but offer little in the way of a microclimate except for blocking drifting snow and serving as a windbreak if densely planted. A well-constructed chain-link fence should need little in the way of maintenance.

wattle

This attractive fence, evocative of the English countryside, derives much of its charm from its rustic simplicity. Consisting of little more than a row of posts driven into the ground and then woven with thin, flexible saplings, this fence has been used since ancient times. The wattle fence is not a long-lasting structure; when used to enclose fields in Europe, it also provided a perch for birds, which then excreted seeds such as bramble and hawthorn. The seeds germinated to become mixed hedges that grew up as the wattle slowly deteriorated. American colonists put wattle fences up as temporary borders until more substantial ones could be erected.

Wattle fencing is usually purchased as individual screens, called hurdles, and will be expensive unless you happen to live close to a hurdle-maker. If you can gather long whips of willow, hazel, bamboo, hickory (or just about any flexible green wood) locally, consider weaving your own hurdles. Much of the character of these handmade fences comes from their imperfections—they're a good choice for those intimidated by power tools or frustrated by the precise leveling and exact measurements most fences call for. Once erected, wattles will require little in the way of maintenance, but they also won't last longer than five to ten years.

Because of this, wattles are most often used as internal boundaries in a garden, providing a screen to shade a patio or to hide the compost pile. They look lovely with flowers such as morning glories or nasturtiums climbing up them, and they are equally at home in the vegetable garden, covered with snow peas or cherry tomatoes.

This low wattle border is being used as a rustic edging beside a walkway.

woven willow

Make a simple but enchanting fence by inserting long willow sticks into the ground at opposite angles and then weaving them together. The willow will often take root and become a leafy living border. Perfect beside a kitchen garden, the fence will not only mark a boundary, but it will also provide a fair amount of privacy (especially when it is in leaf), wind protection, and shade.

Willow whips can be purchased from suppliers, but in many places it's possible to gather your own from riverbanks and roadsides. (Always ask permission before gathering from private property.) Constructing the fence is a simple if fairly time-consuming task (instructions are provided on page 302). If you're interested in growing a woven willow fence, plan ahead—willow is most likely to take root (and is also easiest to weave) if you make the fence in early spring, when the plants are still dormant.

This delightfully planted willow fence provides a charming screen that changes with the seasons.

Setting Fence Posts

Both the appearance and the durability of your fence depend on properly set posts. Time spent to do this task right will be time saved on maintenance and repairs for years to come. Prior to digging, make certain there are no buried utility cables, gas, or water lines in the immediate vicinity of your work. Usually, the local utility companies will check and flag the location of underground services at no charge. You can also hire a company that specializes in locating underground utilities (listed in your phone book's business section under "Utilities Underground Cable, Pipe & Wire Locating Service"). Also, check with your local building department to determine the frost depth in your area and whether frost heave is a concern. In many northern climates, moist, fine-grained soils are subject to winter freezing and thawing cycles, which cause the earth to shift and dislocate even firmly set fence posts. Where frost heave is a problem, the holes must be dug below the frost line and the posts set in a suitable drainage medium.

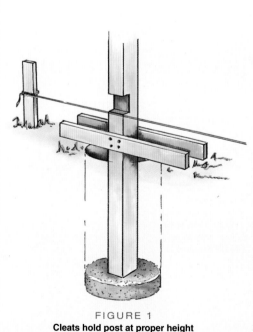

FIGURE 1
Cleats hold post at proper height

INSTRUCTIONS

1 Use a posthole digger to excavate a hole about 4 inches deeper than the depth you plan to set the post. Generally, posts should be set at a minimum of 24 inches, or with at least one-third of their total length in the ground. Gate posts and end and corner posts, which support greater weight, should meet or exceed the one-third rule if possible. Keep the hole width as narrow as possible-about twice the diameter of the post you are planting-unless you intend to use stabilizing cleats or concrete fill (see step 4), in which case you can make the hole three times the thickness of the post.

2 Shovel about 4 inches of ¾-inch gravel into the bottom of the hole and tamp it firmly with a piece of 2 x 4. Reset any layout lines you're using to mark the face of the post instead of its center.

3 If you are setting posts that already have mortises or dadoes cut into them, they'll need to be set to exact height. This is made easier by temporarily attaching cleats (usually lengths of 1 x 4) to the posts to hold the posts in the holes at the proper height (see figure 1). First determine how much of the post you want to have aboveground; then measure down that distance from the top of each post. Use No. 8 x 1½ decking screws to attach cleats to the post at that point.

4 In loose, sandy, or unstable soil, anchors can be used to keep posts firmly in the ground (see figure 2). These are often pressure-treated 1 x 4 strips cut in length to about two and a half times the thickness of the post and nailed to its sides about two-thirds into the depth of the hole. If you're using concrete fill, you can sink six or eight 16-penny galvanized nails into the post at that point (see figure 3).

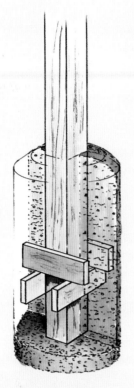

FIGURE 2
Anchors for unstable soil

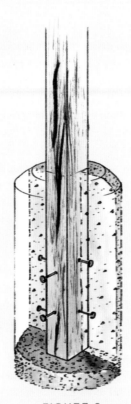

FIGURE 3
Concrete

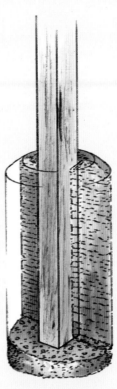

FIGURE 4
Earth and gravel

5 Replace the post in the holes against the layout line, and use a level to determine plumb in both directions. In most soils you can now fill the hole with an earth and gravel mix (see figure 4), tamping with a length of 2 x 4 as you go until you reach the surface. If you plan to use concrete fill, mix all materials dry (even bagged premix) in a wheelbarrow, then add water to make a thick slurry. Shovel the concrete into the hole and tamp it with a 2 x 4 to remove air bubbles. You can either fill the hole completely with concrete, or you can backfill with more gravel to within 4 inches of the surface, tamp, and pour a concrete cap at the top. Trowel the cap downward from the post to shed water.

6 Concrete-bedded posts must be braced for a period of at least 24 hours. Drive a wooden stake about 2 feet from the post on two adjacent sides. Nail a 2 x 4 between each of the stakes and the top of the post, checking for plumb before securing each one. As a general rule, end posts should be set first, then line posts set against the layout lines established between the posts. Fence rails and infill are installed after the posts are set. For mortised or precut fencing, the posts are set as each successive section is completed. Remove the stakes and bracing after the posts are set.

Building Fences on Slopes

Building a fence on sloped ground is a difficult but not insurmountable challenge. Fences can transcend sloped terrain in two ways. Either they can be stepped—each section of fence set at equal intervals to match the rise of the slope, akin to a set of stairs (see figure 2)—or they can be contoured, in which the rails run parallel with the slope, and the fence follows the contour of the ground (see figure 3, page 292).

INSTRUCTIONS

To plot a fence that will be built on a slope, you'll need 100 feet of mason's line, a steel tape measure, a torpedo level and a line level, a plumb bob, masking tape or ribbon, nails, and pieces of cloth. You'll also need a hefty hammer and two wooden stakes (one needs only be 1 foot tall, the other must be tall enough to extend at least 1 foot above the top of the slope when inserted into the ground at the downhill end of the fence line—see figure 1).

To lay out a stepped fence, start at the beginning point uphill, drive the first stake firmly into the ground, and check it for two-way plumb (sideways and forward-and-back) with the torpedo level. This stake does not need to be particularly tall, but it

does have to be stable. Then place the taller stake at the end point downhill and drive it into the ground, plumbed both ways as before.

Tie one end of the mason's line to the first stake and stretch the line to the other stake. Hang the line level on the line at the midpoint, and tie the line to the second stake at the point that it is level.

If the slope is fairly gradual, your line will cover some distance before the downhill stake becomes too short to hold the string at level. On a steep slope, the line may only extend 10 or 12 feet before staking. If your intended fence or wall goes beyond the point of the second stake, you'll need to drive a third stake in line downhill from

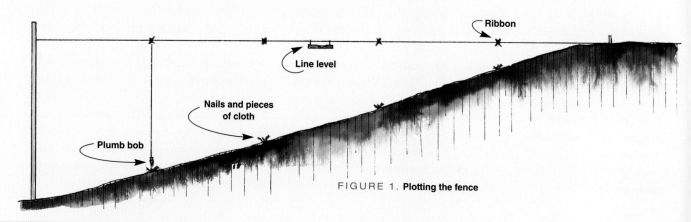

FIGURE 1. **Plotting the fence**

Ribbon

Line level

Nails and pieces of cloth

Plumb bob

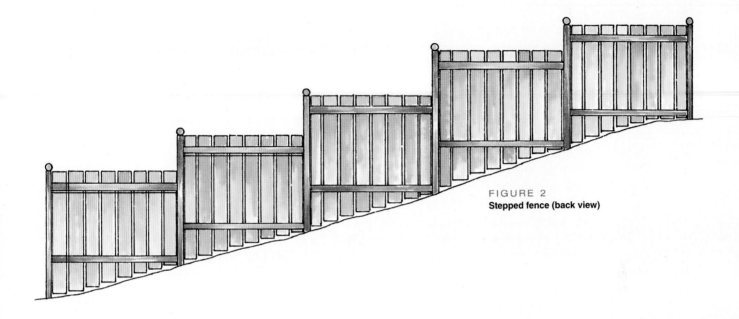

FIGURE 2
Stepped fence (back view)

that, and tie another length of mason's line from the base of the second stake to the top of the third stake so it is level. A fourth or fifth stake might also be required, depending on the topography of your site.

With that done, you can mark the locations for each fence post. Measure along the leveled line(s) and divide the total distance by the length you've planned for each fence section. The sections should be kept at some standard—perhaps 4, 6, or 8 feet— to make best use of precut lumber sizes. So, for example, if your total run is 36 feet and you've planned 6-foot sections, you can accommodate six sections within your fence run. Any remainder can be dropped, or if needed, the line extended to include the additional section. Use tape or ribbon to mark the locations along the level line where each fence post will fall.

These points can then be used as references to transfer the marked locations to the ground. Hang your plumb bob alongside each ribbon without distorting the line, and mark the ground at the pendulum point with nails and pieces of cloth, as shown in figure 1.

To determine the size of each step in the fence, you'll have to figure the overall rise, or height, of the slope. On a single-line layout, this is simply a matter of measuring the distance from the ground to the string at the downhill stake. On multiple-line layouts, that measurement must be taken at each successive downhill stake, and the results added together.

Since the most attractive stepped fences maintain the same step height between sections, you'll want to divide the total rise by the number of sections to arrive at a consistent dimension for each step. So, if the rise is 60 inches and you are planning six equal sections, there will be a 10-inch step between each section of fence. These can be measured from the top of each line post and marked in pencil for later reference when you are setting the posts.

Plotting a contoured fence is even simpler than laying out a stepped structure. Begin by driving a long stake into the starting point at the high end of the slope. Then drive and plumb a second stake into the ground at the end point downhill. Run mason's line between the two stakes, tying it the same distance from the ground at both ends. The line should clear any obstructions or abrupt changes in terrain. If it doesn't, you may have to drive additional stakes between the two points to keep the line clear.

Once the line is strung, begin at the uphill stake and measure down along the line, marking the locations of each fence post with tape to correspond with the length you've chosen for each fence section. Then use a plumb bob, as described before, to transfer those post locations to the ground, where they should be marked with flagged nails.

When it comes time to install the posts for a contoured fence, each one is set to exactly the same height above the ground, so that the fence line follows the terrain's natural contour (see figure 3). This can be accomplished by either backfilling the holes and tamping the posts as needed to achieve the precise height required, or simply setting the posts to "run wild" in length, and trimming their tops accordingly once they're in place. The rail locations are then marked at a consistent height along the posts, measured at an appropriate distance above the ground.

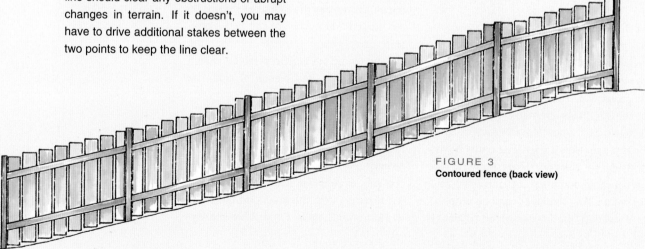

FIGURE 3
Contoured fence (back view)

stick fence

This rustic fence will surround your garden with simple charm, while offering a place for climbers to run riot. Essentially a homespun version of the picket fence, this unpretentious border provides the perfect backdrop for an informal garden. Gathering the fence's infill will require some stick-to-it-tiveness, so tackle this project a little at a time, as befits its laid-back style.

TOOLS AND SUPPLIES

Tape measure

1 x 2 stakes, 12 inches tall

Mason's line

Line level

Plumb bob

Posthole digger

Carpenter's level

Hammer

Loppers

MATERIALS

Green hardwood saplings
(see Tips)

4 x 4 fence posts, 6 or
8 feet tall

2 x 4 rails, 6 or 8 feet long

Sticks (see Tips)

Hammer

Masking tape or ribbon

Strips of cloth

¾-inch gravel

No. 8 x 3-inch weatherized
deck screws

2-inch galvanized finishing
nails

**The following materials are necessary
if setting posts in concrete:**

Concrete

Wheelbarrow

Shovel

Water

16d galvanized nails

Trowel

INSTRUCTIONS

1 Lay out your fence by measuring a distance along your intended line and driving 1 x 2 stakes into the ground to indicate the location of your two end posts. It will simplify matters later if you make this distance a multiple of your rail length, such as 6 or 8 feet. Then drive two more stakes into the ground, each about 2 feet back from an end-post stake. Stretch mason's line between the two outermost stakes with a line level attached at the midpoint. Make sure the line is taut and level.

2 Measure along the string line between the end-post stakes and divide the total distance by the length of your rails. For instance, if your total run is 36 feet and you're using 6-foot rails, you can fit six sections within the run, and you'll need seven postholes. Use masking tape or ribbon to mark the locations along the string line where each post will fall. Then hang a plumb bob alongside each

ribbon and mark that point on the ground with a nail and a strip of cloth. Use the posthole digger to excavate the individual postholes to a depth of 3 feet, centered at the marked points.

3 Set the end posts in place, following the procedure described in Setting Fence Posts, on page 288. Use the carpenter's level to plumb the end posts, then backfill the holes.

4 Reset the mason's line against the end posts once they're fixed in place. Using this string line, set the line posts in place at the proper height, then plumb in both directions and backfill.

5 Using the top of one end post as a reference, measure down to the point where the upper edge of the top rail will go and mark it. Then measure down to the top of the planned lower rail, and make a mark for it. Repeat for all the posts.

---

tips

■ Green hardwood saplings will make the best sticks for this fence.

■ If you don't have a source on your property, clean up (always with permission) behind power companies, road construction crews, or new building projects. Use pruners or loppers to remove any branches from the sticks.

■ Use only pressure-treated lumber or naturally decay-resistant wood (such as cedar, redwood, locust, Osage orange, or cypress) for the posts and rails. Because some pressure-treated wood contains the preservative CCA (chromated copper arsenate), wear work gloves when handling it, and add a dust mask and safety glasses when cutting it.

■ If you're enclosing a garden and want to keep animals out, attach hardware cloth from the lower rail down to the ground before attaching the stick pickets.

6 Measure the center-to-center distance between each post as a double check prior to cutting the rails. Then trim the rails to the proper length. Each rail should butt the one next to it at the midpoint of the post. If that's not the case, minor adjustments can be made by trimming the rails slightly—but remember that they must abut at a post for support. Use the marks made in step 5 to position the rails and then fasten them to the outside of the posts with No. 8 x 3-inch weatherized deck screws.

7 Use 2-inch galvanized finishing nails, driven in at an angle, to attach the sticks to the outside of the rails (positioning the sticks about 4 inches apart will give you a pleasing degree of density). The sticks should touch the ground and extend a bit higher than the desired final fence height.

8 Trim the tops of the sticks with sharp loppers, either straight across or in a pattern of your choice. The bottoms of the fence should be trimmed just above the ground.

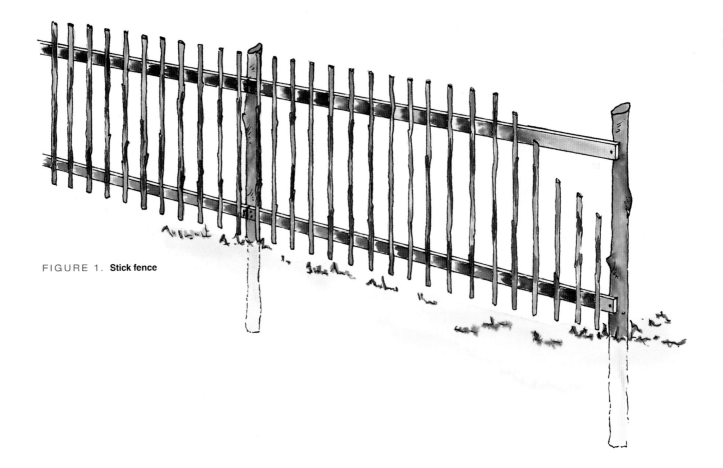

FIGURE 1. **Stick fence**

post-and-rail fence

Here's a fence that will look at home in front of most suburban ranch houses. The style of the fence will vary somewhat depending on whether the rails are split, square, or round. The wood for post-and-rail fences can be found at most large home centers and lumberyards. Because the fence kits are sold with the posts already mortised and tenons precut into the rails, assembly is a snap.

INSTRUCTIONS

1 Lay out your fence by measuring a distance along your intended line and driving 1 x 2 stakes into the ground to indicate the location of your two end posts. Make this distance between the end posts a multiple of your rail length, usually 6 or 8 feet. Then drive two more stakes into the ground, each about 2 feet back from an end-post stake. Stretch mason's line between the two outermost stakes with a line level attached at the midpoint. Make sure the line is taut and level.

2 Measure along the string line between the two end-post stakes and divide the total distance by your rail length. So, if your total run is 36 feet and your rails are 6 feet long, you can fit six sections within the run, and you'll need seven postholes. Use tape or ribbon to mark the locations along the string line where each post will fall. Then hang a plumb bob alongside each ribbon and mark that point on the ground with a nail and a strip of cloth.

TOOLS AND SUPPLIES

Tape measure

Mason's line

Line level

Plumb bob

Posthole digger

Carpenter's level

MATERIALS

Premortised and tenoned posts and rails (rails are usually 6 or 8 feet long)

1 x 2 stakes, 12 inches long

Masking tape or ribbon

Strips of cloth

¾-inch gravel

The following materials are necessary if setting posts in concrete:

Concrete

Wheelbarrow

Shovel

Water

16d galvanized nails

Trowel

3 Follow the steps in Setting Fence Posts, page 288, to set the first post only. Because the posts are already mortised, they must be set to an exact height; the instructions for using cleats to do so can also be found on page 288. Remember, too, that with this type of fence, the posts must be set one at a time, as each section of the fence is assembled.

4 Once the first post has been set, position the second post into its hole. Insert the rails into the first post, then connect the second post to the rails, as shown in figure 1.

5 Use the carpenter's level to make sure the second post is plumb and the rails are level. Then you can set the second post permanently.

6 Repeat steps 4 and 5 until the fence is completed.

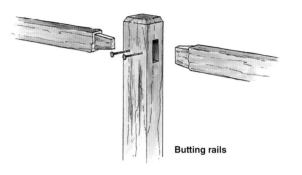

Butting rails

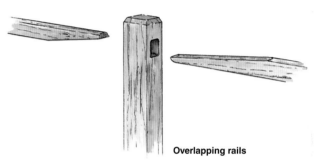

Overlapping rails

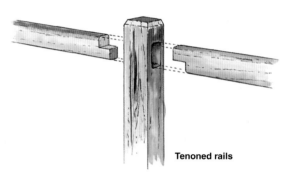

Tenoned rails

FIGURE 2
Rails can join in a variety of ways.

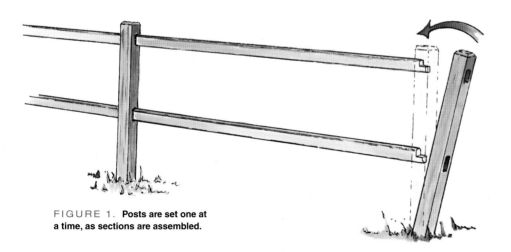

FIGURE 1. **Posts are set one at a time, as sections are assembled.**

tip

Mowing and weeding around the posts of this kind of fence can be difficult. If your fence spans a patch of lawn, lay landscape fabric around the base of newly set posts, or consider planting a low-maintenance groundcover at the base of each post.

picket fence

This is the friendly fence. Build one, and your neighbors are apt to stop and chat when they pass by. Large home centers now offer prefabricated panels of picket fencing that go up quickly, but if you build your picket fence from scratch, you'll have both the satisfaction of knowing it's carefully constructed and the opportunity to individualize your pickets.

NSTRUCTIONS

1 Lay out your fence by measuring a distance along your intended line and driving 1 x 2 stakes into the ground to indicate the location of your two end posts. It will simplify matters later if you make the distance between the end posts a multiple of your rail length, typically 6 or 8 feet. Then drive two more stakes into the ground, each about 2 feet back from an end-post stake. Stretch mason's line between the two outermost stakes, with a line level attached at the midpoint. Make sure the line is taut and level.

2 Measure along the line between the end-post stakes and divide the total distance by the length of each fence section. For example, if your total run is 40 feet and you've planned 8-foot sections, you can fit five sections within the run, and you'll need six postholes. Use masking tape or ribbon to mark the locations along the mason's line where each post will fall. Then hang a plumb bob alongside each ribbon and mark that point on the ground with a nail and a strip of cloth. Use the posthole digger to excavate the individual postholes to a depth of 3 feet, centered at the marked points.

3 Now you can prepare the 4 x 4 fence posts, which can range in length from 72 to 96 inches, depending on your design. Given a level site, it's simpler and more accurate to mark and cut any post-top decorations or notched dadoes into the posts prior to setting them. Using the top of the post as a reference, measure down to the point where the upper edge of the top rail will go (between 4 and 13 inches), mark with the combination square, then mea-

sure to where the bottom of that rail will go, and mark. The distance between the marks should equal the width of the rail boards (3½ inches for 2 x 4s set on edge-typical rail boards). Then, measure down to the top of the planned lower rail (between 30 and 52 inches), and make similar marks for it. Repeat for all the posts.

NOTE: As an alternative, experienced woodworkers can set all the posts and then mark and cut them for horizontal rails after the posts are installed. Depending on the design, and how enduring you wish the fence to be, the rails don't necessarily have to be set in notches; they can be fastened to the surface of the posts with No. 8 x 3-inch weatherized deck screws for a quick and easy installation.

4 Mark and cut any post-top details you have planned. These could include a simple 45° bevel cut, a two- or four-sided 45° point, or an intricate jigsaw-cut finial pattern. A handsaw or circular saw will make a straight and easy cut.

5 Use a marking gauge to measure the depth of the notches-called dadoes-you intend to cut into the posts. These should equal the thickness of the rail boards, or 1½ inches. Once that's completed, set your circular saw to that depth and cut along the shoulder lines of each notch to define the opening. Then continue to make a series of parallel saw cuts through the wood between the shoulder cuts.

6 Using a ¾-inch mortise chisel and a wooden mallet, remove the waste material from the dadoes. Clean and smooth the bottom of each dado with the sharp edge of the chisel.

TOOLS AND SUPPLIES

Tape measure
1 x 2 stakes, 1 foot tall
Mason's line
Line level
Plumb bob
Posthole digger
Pencil
Combination square
Circular saw
Handsaw (optional, see step 4)
Jigsaw (optional, see steps 4 and 10)
Marking gauge
¾-inch mortise chisel
Wooden mallet
Carpenter's level
Cordless drill
Spring clamps
Table saw (optional, see step 11)

MATERIALS

Masking tape or ribbon
Strips of cloth
¾-inch gravel
4 x 4 fence posts, 8 feet tall
2 x 4 rails, 6- or 8 foot long
No. 8 x 3-inch weatherized deck screws
1 x 4 pickets, (cut from 10- or 12-foot lengths of pressure-treated stock)
No 8 x 1¾-inch weatherized deck screws

The following materials are necessary if setting posts in concrete:

Concrete
Wheelbarrow
Shovel
Water
16d galvanized nails
Trowel

tips

■ Use only pressure-treated lumber or naturally decay-resistant wood (such as cedar, redwood, locust, osage orange, or cypress) for your fence. Because some pressure-treated wood contains the preservative CCA (chromated copper arsenate), wear work gloves when handling it, and add a dust mask and safety glasses when cutting it.

■ To determine the exact space between each picket, first decide approximately how much space you want between pickets, based on how dense you wish the fence to look. Add the picket and space width together, and divide the result into the total distance between the post centers. Round this to the nearest whole number. Multiply this number by the picket width to figure out the amount of space the pickets will occupy. Subtract that number from the distance between post centers. This tells you how much space is left for the spaces between the pickets. Divide this by the whole number determined above. (The completed fence will have one more picket than space.) This will give you the width of each space between pickets.

7 Set the end posts in place, following the procedure described in Setting Fence Posts, on page 288. Make sure, if you're bedding the rails in dadoes, that the slots all face the right direction. (Whether the dadoes and rails will be at the front or back of your fence depends on your design.) Set the mason's line to indicate the height of the bottom shoulder of the lower dadoes. Use a carpenter's level to plumb the posts; then backfill the holes.

8 Using the mason's line as a guide, set the line posts in place at the proper height, then plumb in both directions and backfill them.

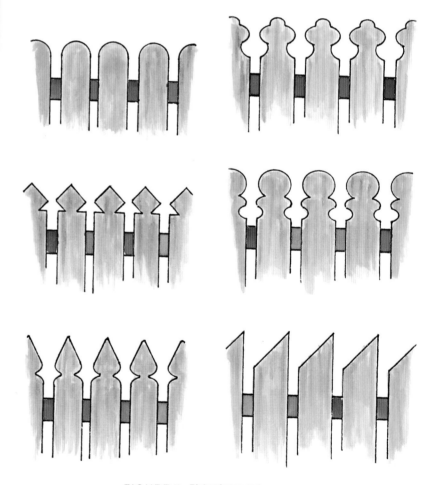

FIGURE 1. **Picket fence styles**

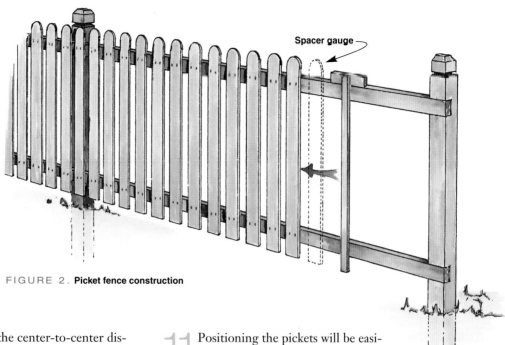

Spacer gauge

FIGURE 2. **Picket fence construction**

9 Measure the center-to-center distance between each post as a double check prior to cutting the rails. Then trim the rails to the proper length. Each rail should butt the one next to it at the midpoint of the post. If that's not the case, minor adjustments can be made by trimming the rails slightly—but remember that they must abut at a post for support, and that changes in the length of the rails will affect the picket spacing. Use No. 8 x 3-inch weatherized deck screws to fasten both the upper and lower sets of rails to the posts.

10 Use a handsaw or circular saw to cut the 1 x 4 pickets from 10- or 12-foot straight lengths of pressure-treated stock. Once the overall lengths are cut, the picket style—ranging from straight-cut oblique or two-sided point to curved-cut round tops or spades (see figure 1)—can be added to the ends by cutting with a jigsaw. When cutting your own pickets, it's easier to clamp two or three together and cut as one than to go individually.

11 Positioning the pickets will be easier with a spacing gauge. To make one, first measure the distance between the top of the top rail and the bottom of the bottom rail. Add this number to the distance you'd like your pickets to extend below the bottom rail. Then add ¾-inches to that number. Now cut a 1 x 4 to that length. Next, use the table saw to rip the board so that its width is equal to the desired space between pickets. Nail a piece of 1 x 4 level with the top of the board (as shown in figure 2).

12 Mark a line on the face of the first post to indicate the bottom of the pickets. Position the first picket on the line; then center and plumb it. Fasten it with No. 8 x 1¾-inch weatherized deck screws. Set the spacer gauge against the edge of the picket with its crosspiece facing outward. Position the second picket to match the height of the first, and fasten it to the upper and lower rails with two screws at each joint. Reverse the gauge, as shown in figure 2, to continue mounting the remaining pickets.

living willow fence

Here's a fence you can build without a hammer or nails. Woven from willow, this border may actually take root, sprout leaves (and pussywillows!), and become a living lattice fence. The best time of year to make this fence is early spring, right before the willow breaks its dormancy.

INSTRUCTIONS

1 Lay out the fence line with two stakes and string or mason's line.

2 Use the spading fork to cultivate a 30-inch-wide trench along the fence line to a depth of about 6 inches. Add compost or composted manure to the trench.

3 Starting on the right end of your fence line, insert the willows whips into the trench so each one is leaning to the left at a 45° angle. The whips should be inserted to a depth of 4 to 6 inches, and spaced about 8 inches apart.

4 Repeat step 3 at the left end of your fence line, only this time each willow whip should angle to the right and be inserted at a midpoint between two of the left-leaning whips planted in step 3. Plant these whips so that they cross just slightly in front of the whips going in the opposite direction.

5 Insert one vertical whip at each end of your fence line.

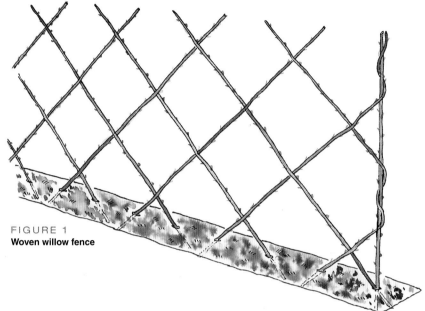

FIGURE 1
Woven willow fence

6 Standing to one side of the fence, begin gently weaving in the simple over and under, diamond pattern shown in figure 1. This will be easiest if you work your way up the fence, weaving one section, rather than one willow whip, at a time. It's important to replace any whips that break or crack; otherwise, that section of fence may die or become diseased. When you get to the end of the fence line, you can trim the ends that extend out past the vertical whips, or you can gently wrap them around the vertical whip and weave them back into the fence's pattern, as shown in figure 1.

7 Tie each intersection loosely with twine.

8 Water your fence daily for the first growing season. Once the fence is established and growing well (toward the end of the first growing season), use loppers to trim the top and shape the fence.

tip

Willow whips (young willow shoots without any branches) can be purchased from suppliers, but in many places it's possible to gather your own willow (you may need to trim branches) from riverbanks and roadsides. Always ask permission before gathering from private property.

TOOLS AND SUPPLIES

Two stakes
String or mason's line
Spading fork
Loppers

MATERIALS

Willow (see Tip)
Twine

GARDEN SEATING

the big book of backyard projects

function
form and
easy
style

Establishing a personal style in your garden means following your own "rules" of creativity, freedom, and ease. When you create a garden for yourself, with seating that appeals to your own needs and feelings, you'll create a place that delights everyone.

FAR RIGHT:
Jimmy Straehla,
Lucky, **1999, 55 x 48 x 28 in. (139.7 x 122 x 71 cm); antique heart pine, lath, granite, copper wire, bottlecaps, old ceiling tin; sawn, nailed, wired.**
PHOTO BY RINNE ALLEN

RIGHT:
Teri Stewart and Serey Andree,
Snake in Fig Tree, **2000, 12 in. x 10 ft. (30.5 cm x 3m); fabric, sequins; sewn, glued, painted.**
PHOTO BY
JANICE EATON KILBY

A garden seat can be, and do, several things. It establishes a point of view from which you can enjoy a natural scene or a picture you've composed with the elements of your garden. If visitors to your garden sit down to rest and take a look at what's in front of them, it's a way of saying, "Look at what I see. Isn't it wonderful?" In addition, outdoor seating gives us a place to enjoy the companionship of friends and family, or to cherish a moment of quiet solitude. Your garden seating is also an object to be enjoyed for its own visual appeal and comfort, and hand-crafting it yourself will give you a feeling of satisfaction very, very different from buying a mass-produced object that's literally one of a million.

form follows function

Before you select seating for your garden or alter what's there, the most important question to ask yourself is, "What do I like to do outside?" Do you dream of a hidden, quiet area where you can go for extended contemplation (sometimes also known as hiding or sleeping)? Then plant some shrubbery and prune it to form a shady hideaway for an armchair or chaise lounge (only one, please, or you'll defeat your purpose). Is there a natural stopping point on a path you walk frequently, or a little nook where you can tuck a bench for a delightful surprise as a stroller rounds a corner? Do you enjoy open-air conversations or eating outdoors? Then carry meals outside for dinner al fresco in chairs with arms wide enough to hold a plate of food and a drink. Do you and your guests always seem to end up outside when you have a party? You can accumulate pillows or lightweight, compact seating that's easy to set up and to store. Do you like to take a book or laptop outside to work? Then find a shady spot to reduce glare. Maybe you just want to escape from "doing" anything constructive. If you have a sturdy tree limb available, a swing is the perfect answer for grown-up play!

location, location, location

The size and location of your garden seating will have to work with the available space, views, exposure (the direction you're facing, as shown on a compass), sun and shade at different times of day, and natural traffic patterns. Think about the seasons you use the garden, the times of day you're most likely to be in it, what you do in it when you get there, and where the most frequently traveled and most isolated spots are.

When do you use your garden the most? Do you like to move garden furnishings around to enjoy different aspects and views as the seasons change? If so, choose seats in portable materials and designs. Are you always shifting your chair to chase available shade at different times of day? You might consider building an easy shade structure in a hot spot, or a portable canopy. Do you usually go out to your garden in the evening, after work? You may want to position a bench to face west, to enjoy the sunset. Asking these questions will help you decide what kind of seating best meets your needs. And remember, comfort counts above all. Lovely as it might be, you won't want to put a backless stone bench in a spot where you'd rather curl up on a chaise lounge with the Sunday paper.

You can also use structures such as arbors, hedges, and planted screens to create privacy and shelter for your seating and to divide up space and define a series of outdoor "rooms." When we're outdoors, we instinctively like to sit with our backs to a wall or a sheltering structure, and to be situated on top of a slight incline that looks out over the surrounding area. A garden seat is a handy device to direct attention to a view and to act as a focal point itself, an object that draws the eye to its placement in the garden. It gets your attention and beckons you closer.

the ground beneath your feet

The first time you have to extract the legs of a garden bench from muddy ground (where they sank when you sat down after a hard rain) you'll understand the benefit of choosing or preparing a site for your garden seat. You want the seat to rest on packed dirt, a layer of loose, nonporous material such as gravel, or a hard surface. It's also better for wood furniture not to be in direct contact with the ground, unless the wood has been chemically treated for that purpose. You might want to highlight your seating by creating a discrete area of gravel, pebbles, bark, or wood chips around and under the seat.

If you're lucky, nature has done the floor decorations for you with native ground-cover, or you can plant a living "floor" underfoot that highlights the seating design. Inquire at a local nursery or garden center to determine the varieties best for your location. If your garden contains a moist, shady area with compacted, poorly drained, high-acid soil, you have a perfect environment to create a wonderful moss "carpet" for your seating. You can also create a moss floor by transplanting palm-size pieces of moss. Prepare the ground by clearing away all existing growth and watering it until it's muddy. Water the moss patch, press it to the ground, water again, then walk on it.

TOP OF PAGE: Cobbles laid in a fan shape in the shady corner of a garden make an informal seating area.

ABOVE: After a home renovation, these gardeners used pieces from an old tile floor to enliven their garden.

LEFT: This bench rests on well-packed dirt.

ABOVE LEFT: Sometimes it's fun to place the legs of a garden seat so your feet actually rest in low-altitude plants and flowers when you're taking your leisure.

ABOVE RIGHT: A pea-gravel patio is the perfect place for these classic modern garden chairs.

RIGHT: All paths lead to this stone patio, a suitable surface for most outdoor furniture.

material possibilities

Most commercially available garden furniture is made of wood, iron, steel, aluminum, plastic, or concrete, and its designs are often inspired by world-famous "classics" (see page 316). Your choices in garden seating expand dramatically, however, when you decide to make your own, and it's a wonderful way to infuse your garden with your own personal style!

First, take a look at what you've got. Do you have a plain concrete bench? Apply a marvelous mosaic design as shown on the Botanical Mosaic Garden Bench on page 367. Is there a tree trunk in the garden, just waiting to be topped with the backrest from an old, legless chair? See the directions for our Beauty and the Beast Chair on page 327, and voila, you're on easy seat!

With the right tools, any material that makes a good surface to sit on, or that can support a surface to sit on, is fair game to become one-of-a-kind garden seating! Choice of materials is determined by your own taste, your analysis of what you want in your garden, portability, the level of maintenance required, durability, and comfort. In each chapter, we'll discuss the unique characteristics and relative merits of lumber, rustic wood, cement, living plants, bamboo, metal, found objects, brick, stone, and fabric.

ABOVE:
The beauty of rustic wood increases with age. If it becomes unstable for seating, let it be a perch for plants or a trellis for vines and roses.

RIGHT:
Durable, long-lasting teak is an excellent investment for furniture exposed to the elements.

ABOVE LEFT:
Katherine Bernstein and Richard Kennedy, cast granite aggregate sculpture, 10 x 11 x 13$\frac{1}{2}$ inches (25.4 x 27.9 x 34.3 cm).

COURTESY OF NORMA CHEREN, ATLANTA, GA. PHOTO BY JANICE EATON KILBY

ABOVE RIGHT:
A picnic table of light weight lumber allows for a movable feast.

LEFT: **Ornate wrought iron is perfect if your look is Victorian.**

ABOVE: **Place a metal and wood park bench like this one at a strategic vantage point in your garden.**

color, scale, and other rules to be broken

ABOVE: **Here, an antique child's rocker is placed next to a large planter to create an interesting contrast of scale.**

TOP OF PAGE: **This funky bench stands out, even with its subtle, weathered color.**

Knowing how the human eye works can be helpful in seating decisions. You can use scale and color to affect the visual perception of an outdoor space. If you have a long, narrow garden with a bowling-alley feel, you can install a bright-colored or oversize seat at the most distant point to draw the eye and visually "shorten" the garden. You can also use scale to play with perspective. By planting tiny, delicate foliage and flowers close to the seat from which you survey your garden, and locating big, coarse-leafed plants at the far end, you'll visually "shrink" the expanse. But don't be afraid to play with scale just for fun, either. Whimsical elements can make your garden a place of charm and true delight.

A rich color can make a commonplace piece of garden furniture look special, and it's a wonderful way to transform flea market finds into gorgeous garden accents.

Purists recommend blues, grays, and blacks to help garden furniture recede into their surroundings, plus the occasional daring red as a focal point. But who said anything about being a purist? Use the colors you like to echo or contrast with nearby flowers or other blocks of color, and don't be afraid to be bold. Worrying about whether you can put magenta next to red is for sissies. When you furnish and decorate your garden, making an unusual or surprising choice is exactly how you define your own style.

In general, bright, hot colors such as orange and red stimulate and excite us, while pastels, blues, and greens feel soothing and calming. White intensifies the color of adjacent objects and flowers, and gray and silver help moderate the transition from one color to the next. But just remember, the most important rule about using color is to choose what pleases you!

LEFT: **Eric O'Leary, Tariki Studio, 1990, stoneware ceramic garden seats, 18 x 16 x 14 inches (45.7 x 40.6 x 35.6 cm).**
COURTESY OF JOHN CRAM, ASHEVILLE, NC.
PHOTO BY EVAN BRACKEN

BOTTOM LEFT: **Who wouldn't want to sit in a giant Adirondack armchair with proportions that make you feel like a kid—or a queen?**

BOTTOM RIGHT: **This rustic bench makes a striking contrast of color and texture against a vivid blue fence.**

classics
of garden
seating BY Enid Munroe

Classics stand the test of time, and garden seating is no exception. Did you know that the bench or chair you already have in your garden may be based on famous designs that are hundreds of years old?

PHOTO 1

Until the 16th century, people used to enjoy gardens as places to walk, but not to sit. The familiar bench supported by carved trestle legs (photo 1) first appeared during the Italian Renaissance. Marble versions were used in the gardens of the villas of the Medicis, the fabulously rich, aristocratic Florentine family. The benches were carefully sited, placed against boundary walls or at the end of a vista. We most often see this bench today made of cast concrete.

Stone turf benches covered with the herb chamomile first appeared in Elizabethan England, the time of England's own renaissance. Constructed of stone and earth, the benches are highly decorative and fragrant, though not very inviting to sit on. Photo 2 shows the chamomile bench at Sissinghurst, the famous Kentish country estate. Made from old bits of masonry, the bench graces the herb garden.

PHOTO 2

Do you have a cast iron garden bench? Wrought iron garden furniture first appeared in the 18th century. Featuring ornate botanical details such as ferns, lilies, and grapevines, they had great ornamental and nostalgic appeal. By the 19th century, newly prosperous entrepreneurs of the Industrial Revolution were buying mass-produced cast-iron versions (see photo 3).

Mass production created other types of metal garden seating. Chairs (photos 4 and 5) were made of wire or metal bent into intricately scrolled designs that gently molded to the body of the sitter. Nineteenth-century European park chairs (photo 6), with their small seats and straight backs, are treasured when they can be found.

PHOTO 6

PHOTO 3

In the 18th and 19th centuries, iron garden furniture makers frequently copied the work of the famous 18th-century English furniture designer, Thomas Chippendale. He incorporated Gothic, French rococo, and Chinese motifs in his work, and reproduction Chinese Chippendale benches of today (photo 7) still feature elaborate geometric designs.

PHOTO 7

PHOTO 4   PHOTO 5

PHOTO 8

Rustic furniture crafted from tree limbs, roots, branches, and twigs emerged as a reaction against formal, French-influenced design at the same time that the famous landscape designer Capability Brown was creating vast natural parks in the English countryside. Rustic design exploits wood's graining, bark, burls, forks, and other oddities. By the mid-1800s, the "new rich" of the Industrial Revolution were also building country retreats furnished in rustic style. Victorians also encouraged ivy and vines to grow around tree stump "stools."

The Victorians loved complicated designs and rich detail. Wickerwork furniture (photo 8) made of rattan, raffia, fruitwood, willow twigs, or other pliable, natural materials lent itself to the decorative taste of the period. In America, the rising middle classes furnished their newly built porches and conservatories with rustic and wicker furniture. Today's vinyl coated, aluminum-framed reproductions (photo 9) simulate the look of wicker while remaining unaffected by the weather.

The wheelbarrow bench (photo 10) was a product of the Arts and Crafts movement of the 1880s, which preached an aesthetic of utility and simplicity (compared to the Victorians, that is). Amusing and practical at the same time, the bench reflected the new idea that garden seating could be moved from one part of the garden to another, rather than remaining a permanently sited fixture.

PHOTO 9

PHOTO 10

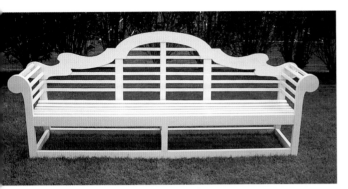

From the beginning of his career in Edwardian England of the early 1900s, Sir Edwin Lutyens designed and created some of England's finest country homes and gardens. He also designed a garden bench that remains a world famous "classic." The Lutyens bench (photo 11) has an elegant scrolled and latticed back that contrasts beautifully with its long, flat seat and wide bottom rails.

Two other classic wooden seats deserve special note. The steamer chair (photo 12) appeared during the great era of ocean liner travel in the early 20th century. It remains a symbol of leisure in the grand style, and reproduction versions still make handy poolside seating. On a humbler note, the beloved Adirondack chair (photo 13) remains a classic and also a mystery, because its true origin is unknown. Adirondacks first appeared in the 1920s, and were originally constructed by nailing together pieces of scrap wood. The chair is frequently confused with the older Westport chair, which is similar and definitely originated in the Adirondack Mountain region of upstate New York.

Seating designers have always taken advantage of new materials to create modern classics. The 1930s bench at La Foce in Tuscany, Italy (photo 14) was designed by Cecil Pinsent to reflect classical influences, but it is made of travertine, a type of cast concrete.

found, recycled, and ready-made objects

IF you're using materials salvaged from dumpsters, demolition sites, tree trimming, junkyards, or your own garage to make your garden seating, good for you! You're doing the planet a favor by not adding to our endless stream of production and consumption. You'll also have all the advantages—and the challenges—presented by the original materials, all mixed together! You'll be inspired to think creatively and to look at the materials you have at hand in a new light.

This happy-go-lucky seat is made from old farm equipment, including a tractor seat, wheel, and horseshoes.

FAR LEFT: **Two logs, a simple plank, and exterior house paint were all it took to create this bench. It stands in front of a section of** *Laughing Trees*, **an outdoor installation by James Malone, Atlanta, GA.** PHOTO BY JANICE EATON KILBY

CENTER: **Jimmy Straehla,** *Transformation*, **2000, 48 x 36 x 28 in. (122 x 91 x 71 cm); antique heart pine, sheet metal, granite, oak tree limbs, copper wire, lath; sawn, screwed.** PHOTO BY RINNE ALLEN

BELOW: **This chair was made from the seat of an old outdoor chair and remnants of antique iron fencing.**

When working with mixed components, you'll need to figure out how to attach similar and dissimilar materials. There's an abundance of metal you can recycle into seating, because metal tends to last longer in a scrap heap. Learn to recognize when it's really unnecessary to weld. Drilling pilot holes and bolting or wiring components together are good ways to connect dissimilar objects, or you may be able to stack piece on top of piece and let the existing weight hold everything in place. If you really must weld because the pieces will be load-bearing, make sure you're not trying to weld aluminum (impossible without special materials) or galvanized tin or steel (doing so produces toxic fumes).

You can apply a coat of sealer, if desired, to arrest the oxidation or weathering of your material. Some craftspeople using salvaged material prefer to leave things "just as they are," while others merrily repaint or refinish.

Tools for working with recycled components are as various as the materials themselves, but never shortchange your safety when working with metal. Always wear safety glasses and gloves.

circle
your
wagons
DESIGNER
Rob Pulleyn

Who said we always have to act like grown-ups, especially when it comes to playing outdoors! Why not start collecting little red wagons for fun, easy seating? Wheel them out for spontaneous festivities, add cushions and throw rugs, and everyone's inner child can come out and play in comfort!

INSTRUCTIONS

1 Arrange the wagons in a circle so your guests can face each other, or in separate conversational groups if you prefer.

2 Fit the cushions into the wagon beds. Cover the cushions with the carpets or rag rugs for extra comfort.

3 To stabilize the wagons and keep them from rolling, tuck the wood shims or blocks between the bottom of the wheels and the ground.

MATERIALS

Variety of four-wheeled metal wagons

Assorted cushions and pillows, approximately the same size as wagon interior

Assorted small carpets and rag rugs

Wood shims or blocks

straw bale
conversation
couch
and chair

DESIGNERS
**Rob Pulleyn
& Lisa Mandle**

These have to be the easiest seats you'll ever make! Straw bales come in sizes that are perfect for making benches and chairs. The length of a bale can fit two people, and the width is just right for a comfortable seat. After a season of enjoyment, the straw makes great mulch for your garden.

INSTRUCTIONS

1 The couch shown uses a total of 19 straw bales, and the chair requires 10. Bales can vary in their dimensions, so be open to altering the plan as necessary. The beauty of this construction technique is that you can always change your mind! Referring to figure 1, arrange six bales side-by-side, butted against each other, to create the seat. Lay the bottom tier of bales, positioning four bales end to end behind the seat. If you wish, you can stabilize the back further by sinking the three pieces of rebar into the ground along the back of the couch, then impaling the back bales on the rebar. Lay four more bales, end to end and centered on top of the four-bale tier, to complete the back. Lay two more bales, one at each end of the couch, to form the armrests. The back ends of the armrest bales should butt against the bales projecting from each end of the bottom back tier.

MATERIALS

29 straw bales, each measuring approximately 18 x 24 x 42 inches

4 pieces of rebar, each 3 feet long (optional)

Assorted pillows, throws, and rugs

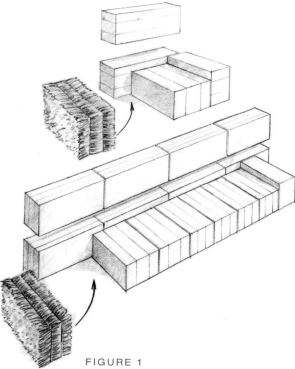

FIGURE 1

2 To construct the chair, stack four bales on top of each other to form the chair's back, then butt the 42-inch edges of four bales against each other to form the seat. If desired, you can stabilize the back bales with a piece of rebar. Position one bale on each side to create the armrests.

3 Decorate the couch and chair with the throws, rugs, and pillows as desired for extra comfort. Covering the seats with a long rug is a particularly good idea, so the straw doesn't tickle bare legs!

beauty and the beast garden chair

DESIGNER
Christopher D. Mello

Do you have a cast-iron chair that's lost its legs, but what's left is still seat-worthy? Try pairing the delicate curlicues of the iron-work with a rough-hewn, sturdy tree trunk. It's easy, and the styles blend together remarkably well.

INSTRUCTIONS

1 If there are any protrusions or bits of metal on the chair bottom where the legs used to be, file them off with the file or knock them off with the grinder.

2 Set the chair on top of the tree trunk, positioning it so the chair is balanced and its front edge overhangs the trunk slightly.

3 The weight of the chair should hold it in place, but if you wish, you can secure it to the trunk. To do so, use the pencil to mark two open places between the ironwork where you can sink the screws into the tree trunk. Drill a ⅛-inch pilot hole at both points, then sink the screws through the washers and into the wood to hold the seat in place.

MATERIALS AND TOOLS

Top half of cast iron garden chair (legs removed)

Metal file or grinder

Tree trunk, 16 to 18 inches high and the same approximate diameter as the chair bottom

Pencil (optional)

Power drill with ⅛-inch drill bit (optional)

Two ¼-inch wood screws, 2 inches long

Two ¼-inch washers (optional)

water-wise living garden bench

DESIGNER
Christopher D. Mello

Three pieces of "found" industrial metal, plus a gorgeous array of easy-care plants, are all it takes to create this sumptuous bench. No cutting or welding is required. The plants are succulents and fragrant herbs of Mediterranean origin that thrive in heat and drought. The metal collects and releases warmth, something these plants love. Visit junkyards to find unique objects that make this bench all your own, and feel free to modify the directions to use a smaller piece of metal.

INSTRUCTIONS

1 Select the site for your bench, and determine where the two ends of the metal seat plate will fall. Position the two metal objects that will serve as the main bench supports approximately 6 to 8 inches inside the ends of the plate, with the pipe positioned under one of the openings in the seat plate. If desired, place additional pipes underneath any other openings in the plate. Push them firmly into the ground, and use the board and level to check that their tops are level, adjusting as necessary.

MATERIALS

- Piece of ½- or ¼-inch metal, approximately 2½ feet wide and 4 to 5 feet long, with random holes piercing the material (the one shown in the photo is called a check plate)
- Hollow metal pipe, 10 to 12 inches in diameter and 16 to 18 inches high (the one in the photo is called a pipe clamp)
- Metal piece or assemblage, 16 to 18 inches high (the one in the photo is a gate valve for a sprinkler system)
- Additional large-diameter pipes (optional)
- Herbs and perennial plants, including: wooly thyme, silver thyme, lemon thyme, common thyme, bronze fennel, lavender, weeping hemlocks, sedums, purple sage, lemon grass, and santolina
- Annuals, including: purple heart, coleus, euphorbia, porcelain berry, catmint, and black sweet potato vine
- Edging stone (optional)
- Old manhole covers or metal plates of similar size (optional)

2 Use the shovel or trowel to fill the pipe supports with the potting soil, and moisten with water.

3 Place the metal seat plate on the supports, making sure the plate's openings are over the pipes filled with soil. Check that the seat is firm and doesn't wobble.

4 Plant some of the herbs in the seat by inserting them through the holes in the plate into the soil below. When you sit on the bench and brush or crush the herbs slightly, they'll release wonderful fragrances.

5 Use the hoe and rake to cultivate the soil around the bench, and plant more herbs, perennials, and annuals in arrangements that please you. The smaller, creeping herbs and succulents work best on the ground and under the seat. Plant the taller plants behind and beside the bench to form a living "frame," staggering them so the shorter plants are positioned in front of the taller plants.

6 Sprinkle mulch at the bases of the plants, covering any bare dirt, and edge the seating area with the edging stones, if desired, planting them on end in the ground. Spray lightly with the garden hose.

7 For a nice final touch, you can sink old manhole covers or metal plates into the ground in front of the bench to serve as footrests.

TOOLS AND SUPPLIES

2 x 4 board

Level

Shovel or garden trowel

Potting soil

Garden hose or watering can

Hoe

Rake

Mulch

flying lawn chair

DESIGNER
Christopher D. Mello

What made you think a lawn chair was only for sitting on a sedate green lawn? With some lengths of chain, you can turn it into a whimsical ornament for a trellis. If you want to sit in your flying lawn chair, do so only if the trellis is constructed to bear the extra weight, the chair's metal is very strong with absolutely no corrosion, and you're confident of the strength of the chain and the welds.

MATERIALS AND TOOLS

Metal lawn chair (legs removed)

Ladder

Tape measure

1/2-inch chain, in a length determined by the height of the supporting trellis

Metal shears

Needle-nose pliers

Welding equipment (optional)

Level

4 double-ended S-hooks, 4 inches

INSTRUCTIONS

1 Measure for the length of the chain attachments. Decide how high you want the chair to hang from the trellis, after making sure the trellis is constructed to bear extra weight. Using the tape measure and allowing for the distance the chair will be elevated off the ground, determine the distance from the trellis crosspiece to the sides of the chair immediately beside the armrests. Use the shears to cut two lengths of chain to match that distance, or use the pliers to unlink them.

2 Now, measure from the trellis crosspiece to the sides of the seat bottom, close to the front and beside each armrest. Cut two equivalent lengths of chain.

3 If you've never welded before, take the chair to a welding shop. Weld the first two chains you cut. Weld one end of one of the chains to the chair seat immediately behind the armrest, leaving the other end free. Repeat with the second chain on the other side of the chair seat. Weld the remaining two chains in place, one end on each side of the front edge of the chair seat.

4 Attach the free end of each welded chain to one of the S-hooks.

5 Hang the S-hooks from the trellis. Use the level to make sure the chair seat is hung evenly, adjusting the chain length if necessary. Squeeze the S-hooks closed with the pliers.

rustic
wood

Before mankind started sawing, planing, or turning wood to create lumber and wooden components, rustic wood was one of our most convenient materials of choice. Rustic construction utilizes found and foraged branches, limbs, and vines in their natural state, with the bark on or off. This type of material therefore has loads of character and individual quirkiness, but it's not appropriate for a seat that requires precision engineering. For example, the form of the oriental bittersweet vine (*Celastrus orbiculatus*) can vary greatly, depending on how it has wound around its host tree.

Rustic materials are abundantly available. With the permission of the property owner, you can cut trees and branches and use them green, or let them dry and then build with them. You can easily collect the leftovers of tree-cutting services or road crews. As a side benefit, you may be performing an environmental service by thinning undergrowth or collecting materials that are considered invasive pests. On the other hand, you can't just drive to a local home improvement center and buy your material in easily quantified, precut dimensions. You have to be prepared to climb, saw, and haul, sometimes from deep in the woods, and the weather can challenge your collecting efforts.

When you collect wood, inspect it carefully for insect holes. If you find any, leave those pieces behind, or you might be importing more damage. You could try heating the wood with a heat lamp to get insects to vacate, but it's preferable to avoid the problem in the first place. Some rustic seating, such as the Wattle Tree Surround on page 334, is built with freshly cut, "green" material to take advantage of its greater pliability. In pieces where pliability is not an issue, you can avoid unanticipated shrinkage or movement by drying cut 1 to 2 inch saplings in a warm, airy place for two to four months before using them.

Rustic construction can be meditative, or relatively fast and free-form, "going with the flow" of the materials and using them as their form dictates. Precision is required only when it comes to making sure the seat is stable and level. There are no real rules to calculating the quantity of materials you'll need, although, depending on its finished size, a seat will require at least four of the largest diameter branches for legs, two for arms, one to three for back supports, four smaller-diameter branches or vines for cross braces, and filler material.

surface decoration and protection

Rustic wood is frequently left unfinished, but you can give it a more finished appearance if you desire. Use sandpaper to remove dirt and burrs and to open up the bark surface slightly. Wearing protective neoprene gloves, brush on a finish coat of one part boiled linseed oil and one part turpentine or mineral spirits, let dry, then apply again. After it's dry, wipe it down with a rag, apply a coat of wax using very fine steel wool, then buff. Bittersweet vine furniture, when treated with a water-repellent wood sealer, can last seven to ten years, or more. However, rustic furniture is so easy to make and casual in nature, durability may not be an issue for you; it's easy to make more when the useful life of a rustic seat has run its course

OPPOSITE PAGE, TOP: **This rustic chair is made from recycled pickets, salvaged cedar, hardwood saplings, and oriental bittersweet. Janice Shields, Cut It Out, Lenox, MA.**

PHOTO BY LINDY SMITH

ABOVE: **Laura Spector, *Rustic Bench with Balinese Temple Umbrella*, 2000, 58 x 48 x 21 in. (147 x 122 x 53 cm); oriental bittersweet, picket fencing, moss; nailed, screwed**

PHOTO BY ENID MUNROE

wattle tree surround

MATERIALS

Seat: Two 4 x 8 sheets, ½-inch exterior plywood

Inner staves: 8 straight hickory or locust saplings, 2- to 2¼-inch diameter x 36 inches

Outer staves: 16 straight hickory or locust saplings, 2- to 2¼-inch diameter x 32 inches

Weavers: 75 willow branches, ¾- to 1-inch diameter x 6 to 7 inches

Seat Supports: 16 willow branches, 1- to 1¼-inches diameter x 5½ feet

Seat trim: 80 willow branches, ¾- to 1-inch diameter x 6 to 7 feet

In the European countryside, you'll often see rustic "wattle" fences woven from stripped limbs and rough branches. This unique tree surround uses the same construction techniques to produce a delightfully rustic surround.

INSTRUCTIONS

Laying out the Stave Circles

1 On a flat surface, butt the long edges of the plywood together. Drive a nail close to the butted edges and 48 inches from either end of the plywood. Use dental floss, tied in a loop around the nail and a pencil, to draw circles with 22-inch and 46-inch radii. Use dental floss because it won't stretch nearly as much as string does. Prop the plywood off the ground, and cut along both lines with a jigsaw. Don't cut up the scraps from outside the circle yet.

2 Clear a ring 4 feet wide around the tree, and lay the seats around the trunk. Lay the outer scraps from the plywood tight around the seat. Make a mark at 8 equal intervals at the inside edge of the seat (about 17¼ inches each). Mark 16 points around the inside edge of the scrap so that they're the same distance

from each other (about 18 inches) and a pair of marks straddles each mark on the inside edge.

Driving and Leveling the Staves

3 Use a hatchet to sharpen one end of all the inner and outer staves. Draw a line 12 inches from the pointed end to indicate ground level.

4 Push an inner stave into the ground at each mark on the plywood and just inside the seat. While standing on the seats so they don't move, use a maul to drive the inner staves 12 inches into the ground.

5 Remove the seat plywood, leaving the outer scraps in place. About 4 inches inside each mark drive an outer stave 12 inches down.

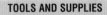

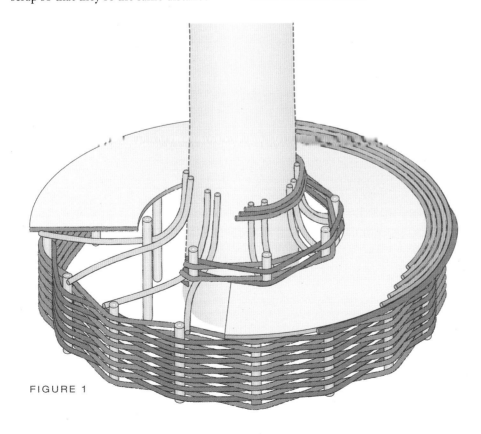

FIGURE 1

TOOLS AND SUPPLIES

Dental floss
Duct tape
2½-inch coated nails
4-inch decking screws
2-inch decking screws
Jigsaw
Hatchet
Sledge
Water level: ½-inch diameter clear
    plastic tube, 12 feet long
    (and funnel to fit)
Bucksaw
Hammer
Lopper
Pruning shears
Cordless drill with #2 Philips driver

NOTE: The dimensions and instructions in this project make a surround for a 2-foot-diameter tree and a 2-foot-wide seat. If you wish to change these measurements, do so when laying out the plywood circle in step 1. Then follow the rest of the steps.

6 Use a water level to mark a trimming line near the top of each stave. You'll need help from a friend for this. Mark one outer stave 17 inches above the ground. Fill a clear plastic tube with water, and tape one end so that it protrudes a few inches above the top of the marked stave, but don't obscure your mark. Spill small amounts of water from the tube until both ends are empty for about 6 inches when they're level with each other. Take the free end of the tube to the next stave, and raise or lower it until your friend tells you that the water in the taped end is even with the mark. Then mark the second stave. Repeat this procedure to mark all the staves. Trim the staves straight across at the level marks.

Weaving the Outer Staves and Adding the Seat

7 Weave willow branches in and out of the outer staves from the ground to 1 inch from their tops. As you start each weaver, put the thicker end on the inside of a stave and nail it in place. Nail the weavers wherever necessary, and leave the narrow free ends inside the staves.

8 The seat supports connect the pairs of outer staves to their inner stave and then travel up the tree trunk (see figure 1, page 335). Mark a line 6 inches down from the top of each inner stave. Identify a pair of outer staves, and screw the fat end of a seat support flush with the top of each stave. Then screw the seat supports to opposite sides of the inner stave just below the mark. Bend the narrow ends so that they run up the trunk. Overbend-

ing the seat supports just past the inner staves will help them stay flatter between the inner and outer circles. Install the rest of the seat supports in the same way.

9 Put the seat on the seat supports, leaving an equal overhang all around the woven circle. Use shorter screws to fasten the seat to the supports several inches from the outer and inner staves. You should be able to draw the supports up against the bottom of the seat.

Trimming the Seat

10 Now cover the seat with a layer of willow branches. Begin by nailing one course of willow trim to the outer edge of the seat. Start with a fat end and, as it gets narrow enough, add the narrow end of another willow branch next to it. Then butt a fat end to the end of the second branch. Continue in this way until you've covered the plywood edge.

11 Cover the top of the seat using the same strategy, starting at its outer edge and working inward.

12 Weave more willow branches from the seat to the tops of the inner staves in the same way as you wove the outer staves.

13 Arrange the ends of the seat supports evenly around the tree trunk, and bind them in place with willow branches nailed around them. Trim their ends even with loppers.

14 Finally, arch willow branches from each inner stave to the second stave along, tucking the ends of the branches into the weaving and securing them with nails.

king of siam
rustic
vine
loveseat

DESIGNER
Laura Spector

You can be emperor or empress of all you survey from this glorious rustic loveseat made of oriental bittersweet vines. The construction technique lends itself very well to improvisation and invention, so relax and have fun while you're making this one-of-a-kind project.

DETAIL: **Braided,
twisted, gnarled,
corkscrewed, or
straight, rustic vines
can give effects rang-
ing from romantic, to
whimsical, to elegant.**

PHOTO BY ENID MUNROE

TOOLS AND SUPPLIES

Chalk

Ruler

Hammer and 3-inch coiled nails,
 or power drill and 3-inch
 coiled screws

C-clamps

Sandpaper

Rags

Paintbrush

Water repellent or wood
 preservative

MATERIALS

4 vines, 2-inch diameter, each
 14 inches long, for the legs

4 vines, 1-inch diameter, each
 18 inches long, for the side
 rungs

2 or 3 decorative vines, 2- to 3-inch
 diameter, each 45 inches long,
 for the front rungs

1 decorative vine, 2- to 3-inch diameter, 45 inches long (or two
 tree saplings, 45 inches long),
 for seat supports

16 picket fencing slats, each
 17 inches long, for the seat

Assorted widths and lengths of
 decorative and straight vines
 to fill in back and arms

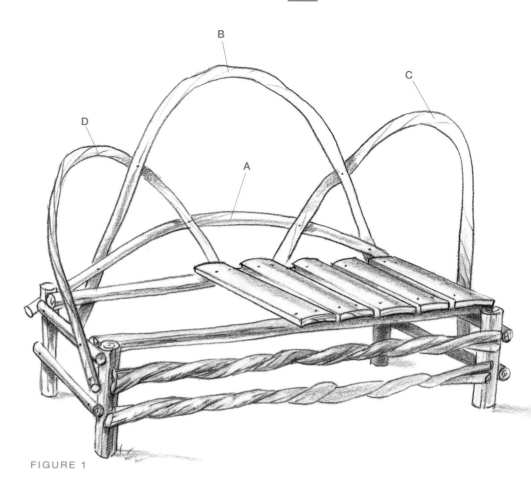

FIGURE 1

INSTRUCTIONS

1 Use the chalk and ruler to draw two parallel lines 10 inches apart on a flat surface, such as a patio. Connect the lines by drawing a perpendicular line 9 inches above the bottom of the two lines.

2 Lay one pair of legs on the parallel lines, and one 18-inch side rung on the perpendicular line. Secure with the hammer and nails or the power drill and screws. Put aside. Construct a second unit of legs and side rung the same way.

3 Now you'll assemble the base while referring to figure 1. Stand the leg units up approximately 42 inches apart. Place a 45-inch decorative vine over the side rung to connect the leg units, and

secure with the nails or screws. Connect the back of the leg units with another 45-inch decorative vine secured over the side rungs with nails or screws. For extra support, add a third decorative vine to the front and secure it just below each side rung and under the first front rung.

4 To assemble the seat, layer the second set of 18-inch side rungs over the front and back rungs; they should measure approximately 12 inches from the ground. Place the seat supports over the two sets of side rungs, and secure with nails or screws. It's preferable to have the front support a bit thicker than the back; this creates an incline from front to back, which makes the seat more comfortable. Screw or nail the picket fencing slats across the seat supports.

5 Install the lower back support (refer to figure 1) by selecting a sturdy vine the approximate length of the base. Bend the vine (A) slightly to create a gentle arch, and nail or screw it to the back seat support.

6 Now you'll install the back and sides by forming three overlapping arches (B, C, and D in figure 1). Select the largest vine, one that's sturdy but flexible, and bend it into a high arch (B). Position the highest point of the arch over the center-point of the bench back, and secure both ends of the arch to the back seat support. Now you'll brace the center arch by creating two smaller, angled arches (C and D). Wrap one end of C behind the right side of the center arch, and one end of D behind the left side of the center arch. Secure the ends. Curve the free ends over and around to the left and right sides of the base and secure with nails or screws.

7 The base structure is now finished, and you can fill in and build up the back and sides by weaving vines over, under, around, and through the three back arches. Work from side to side, and step back occasionally to examine your design choices. Don't forget comfort! Use the C-clamps to hold the vines in place so you can check the design before permanently screwing or nailing them in place.

8 Finish the bench with a light sanding. Wipe down with the rag, then brush on at least two coats of water repellent or wood preservative. Let dry.

If you want to peel the bark from rustic wood, cut the wood just after the tree has put out leaves, and peel it within six weeks for ease of removal.

PHOTO BY RICHARD HASSELBERG

living trees, plants, and bamboo

ABOVE: **For best results, pick a big, hardy tree with long, sturdy limbs for installing a summertime swinging seat.**

ive trees and plants can be part of your outdoor seating projects in several different ways. They can be the integral support for a seat, such as the Lemonade Tree Swing on page 348, or they can form the seat itself, as shown in the Living Tree Armchair on page 345. Plants can add sensory pleasure and decoration, too. It's hard to get much more eco-friendly than this!

working with trees

You must choose the right tree for your project, and learn how to work with it without harming it. If you're attaching a bench or swing, never wrap ropes or chains around a limb; it can girdle it and kill it. Bolts installed in holes drilled through limbs are much better; the tree grows back and strengthens the connection. Extensive cutting or drilling can cause infection and rot in a tree, so cut conservatively. Living seats obviously love and need the sun and rain, but protect young trees from sunburn by hanging row cover fabric or other semi-shade over them during hot, sunny weather.

Assembly is very free form, and your only constraint when training trees to grow in a certain direction is not to bend them so much that they break. The life of the trees is the lifespan of the seat, and you'll have the pleasure of watching it change through the seasons.

Living tree chairs are constructed from tree whips, very young bare-root trees that are 6 to 8 feet tall. You can either grow them yourself, harvest them from the countryside with the landowner's permission, or buy them from a nursery that stocks large, bare-root trees (get advice on climate-appropriate species). Choose flexible trees like willow, alder, or poplar; conifers may be too compact and stiff.

LEFT: **Split bamboo slats were drilled and threaded onto cable to create this elegant swing. It was made by Retana Bros., Agroindeba, San Jose, Costa Rica.**

PHOTO BY SUE AND ADAM TURTLE/TBQ

living decoration

It's fun to grow "living decoration" on your stone, brick, metal, or concrete seating, as long as it's kept moist. When you're building a garden seat, try incorporating components such as cinder block or large, empty pipes that can hold soil, which in turn can sustain living plants. Try filling crevices and joints in stone or brick seating with topsoil enriched with compost, and tuck in moss, baby ferns, creeping herbs, and low-growing flowers such as alyssum, violets, and self-seeding violas to add texture, scent, and color.

You can encourage moss to grow on cool, hard surfaces by painting them with buttermilk. Moss likes to grow in shady places, cracks, and crevices. For a handy moss-starter solution, dissolve one part porcelain clay (found at ceramic supply distributors and craft stores) into three parts water in a jar, shaking it until it's thick and frothy. Combine one part shredded moss and one part liquid fish fertilizer, mix it into the clay/water solution, and apply it to the surface.

bamboo

To Western eyes, bamboo evokes a natural, low-technology lifestyle. It's available in a remarkable variety of diameters and colors, and creates a refined or appealingly primitive effect depending on size and proportion.

Bamboo is also lightweight and relatively inexpensive. For the same reasons that some gardeners dislike bamboo, other people like it: it grows rapidly and prolifically, and unlike redwoods or tropical hardwoods, it's a sustainable resource that makes very good sense from an ecological standpoint.

Bamboo is beautiful without additional surface decoration, but you can use an exterior-grade stain to enhance its texture or to emphasize a particular color. Weathering changes the color of untreated bamboo from green, to tan, to silver grey. In wet climates, moss and lichen may also grow on the surface, giving a mottled, organic effect. If unprotected, outdoor bamboo seating may weaken after several rainy seasons, so check the strength of the seat before you sit! Scrubbing or pressure-washing twice a year with a nonsudsing mildew remover followed by one or two coats of water sealer helps bamboo last up to 10 years. For a longer life, store it in a sheltered place. That's easy, since it's light and easily transported. Add a cushion if you'll be using a bamboo seat for extended sitting.

Your success in building with bamboo will depend on your patience in using the tools and construction techniques for a material that doesn't have any right angles. Bamboo stalks, or culms, are cylindrical, non-uniform, and slightly curved, but it's those very irregularities that make up its visual appeal. So slow down and enjoy the process! When you calculate how much bamboo you'll need for a project, allow for the diameter and length of each pole, just as you do with lumber. Poles can be purchased individually or in bundles of 25 or more from mail-order suppliers. In tropical to temperate climatic zones, you can harvest it locally, sawing it off at the base.

LEFT: **Try incorporating fragrance into your seating design. When you sit down and brush against the scented herbs in the Water-Wise Living Garden Bench, your nose wil enjoy the result!**

tree trunk
plank
bench

If you have two stately trees in your garden, you can actually encourage them, over time, to hold a simple bench in their grasp. Just bear in mind that you want to cause as little injury to the trees as possible. If you're patient, you can use entirely natural processes to fix the bench in place.

MATERIALS AND TOOLS

2 living tree trunks

Handsaw (optional)

Utility knife (optional)

Level

1 hardwood or specialty softwood plank, 2 inches thick, in a length that allows you to fit it very snugly between the two trees*

Stones with tapered edges

4 metal spikes, 4 to 6 inches in length (optional)

Hammer (optional)

*It's essential to use a very hard wood for the plank. Redwood, cedar, or chestnut are suitable.

INSTRUCTIONS

1 When trees suffer a wound or are penetrated by a foreign object, or when they encounter an immovable object as they grow, they respond by growing more material to cover and surround the site. The tree on the left in the photograph has produced a "branch collar" that has grown over the end of the bench. (If you don't wish to cut the tree, skip to step 2 at this point.) Use the handsaw to remove a lower limb from the area where you want to locate the bench. Wedge the bench in place, using the level to make sure it's level. The tree will grow to cover both ends of the bench. Be warned, however, that removing a tree limb or causing a wound always makes a tree vulnerable to infection and rot, and so should be minimized. To facilitate healing, any loose bark around the edges of the wound should be trimmed away with a utility knife to make a clean, regular edge. Trees also heal best if a wound is left undressed and open to the air; don't paint it or put tar on it.

2 A better method, which doesn't injure the tree, is to simply wedge the plank between the trees, then wedge the tapered stones snugly into any gaps. The trees will gradually begin to grow around the ends of the planks, and when they begin to take hold, you can remove the stones.

3 If you wish, before you wedge the plank in place, use the hammer to drive the metal spikes into the trees, two on each end, to serve as supports for the plank. The tree will grow around the spikes.

living
tree
armchair

What could possibly be more ecologically friendly than making your garden furniture from living trees? It's true you won't get instant gratification from this project, but you'll have the satisfaction of watching your handiwork grow. You can also have fun telling your friends, "Excuse me, but I have to go water my chair!"

INSTRUCTIONS

1 Anytime from the fall to the early spring is a good time to plant your chair. To start, use the shovel to dig a hole about 2 feet square and 1 foot deep.

2 Use the tape measure to help you mark four spots inside the hole where you'll position your chair legs. To ensure the finished chair is stable, the legs should be about 1½ feet apart and placed in a square pattern.

3 To create the two front chair legs, plant four of the tree whips where each front leg is located. This will use up eight of the 12 whips. As shown in figure 1, page 346, bind them tightly with the plastic stretch tie tape at the point where they emerge from the ground. Eight inches above the ground, bind them again.

4 Plant two whips at the position for each rear leg. Plant the whips with the largest diameter on the outside perimeter of the chair, and use the smaller-diameter whips on the inside of the chair. The smaller whips will become the chair's arms.

5 To make a frame for the chair, refer to figure 2, page 347, and drive four of the bamboo stakes into the ground. Position them at the outside edges of the legs.

6 To create the front edge of the chair, position one of the bamboo stakes between the front two leg stakes so it functions as a horizontal crosspiece. Cut off a piece of the baling wire with the wire cutters, and use it to wire the crosspiece in place, tightening the wire with the pliers if necessary. The crosspiece should be behind the two front legs of bundled whips.

MATERIALS

12 pliable, live tree whips such as willow or poplar, each 5 to 6 feet tall and ½ inch in diameter

1 stake, 5 feet long

TOOLS AND SUPPLIES

Shovel

Tape measure

Plastic stretch tie tape

7 bamboo stakes, 3 feet long, or scrap wood stakes, 1 inch x ¼ inch, 3 feet long

Baling wire

Wire cutters

Pliers

Hammer

Grafting knife with straight edge blade

Bleach

Water

Pruning shears

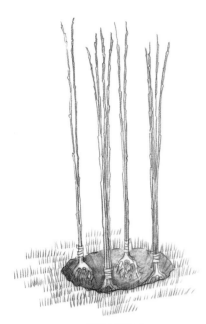

FIGURE 1

7 Bend the whips from the front legs over the crosspiece, arching the whips toward the back legs. Starting with the two inside whips (refer to figure 2), cross them over and under each other to form the chair seat.

8 To make the back edge of the chair, create another crosspiece with a stake, and wire it in place. It's important to note that the whips from the chair seat will be trained underneath the crosspiece (see figure 2). All of the tree whips should now be at the rear of the chair, behind the rear crosspiece.

9 To bend the whips upward, wire a bamboo stake as a crosspiece to the rear leg stakes, about 4 inches above the lower crosspiece. Thread the whips in front of this (upper) rear crosspiece to force the whips upward.

10 You'll now create the chair arms by using the inside whips from the bundles of rear leg tree whips. Bend the inside whips toward the front of the chair, and loop them down to the surface of the chair seat. Where the loop touches the seat, use the plastic tie tape to bind it to the whip that's closest to the outside of the chair seat. For extra support, weave the remainder of the whip into the chair seat. Make sure the ends of these whips end up higher in the chair than the arm loop.

11 Adjust the spacing between the whips to achieve an evenly woven pattern to the chair seat. Where whips cross, securely tie them together with the plastic tie tape.

12 To finish the chair back, use the hammer to pound in the 5-foot stake at the rear of the chair at a point midway between the rear legs. You can weave the whips into a decorative chair back, using the stake for extra support.

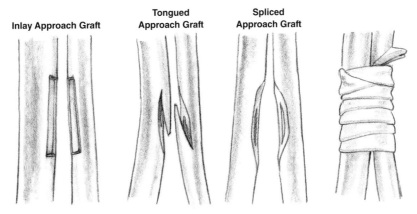

Inlay Approach Graft   Tongued Approach Graft   Spliced Approach Graft

FIGURE 3

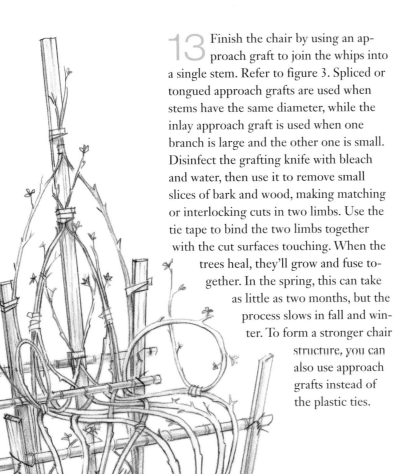

FIGURE 2

13 Finish the chair by using an approach graft to join the whips into a single stem. Refer to figure 3. Spliced or tongued approach grafts are used when stems have the same diameter, while the inlay approach graft is used when one branch is large and the other one is small. Disinfect the grafting knife with bleach and water, then use it to remove small slices of bark and wood, making matching or interlocking cuts in two limbs. Use the tie tape to bind the two limbs together with the cut surfaces touching. When the trees heal, they'll grow and fuse together. In the spring, this can take as little as two months, but the process slows in fall and winter. To form a stronger chair structure, you can also use approach grafts instead of the plastic ties.

14 Graft the tops over a period of time. Start with just two or three whips, and don't graft on any more until the previous graft has "taken," otherwise you may strip bark all the way around the whip, interrupting sap flow, and the portion above the cut will die back. Decide where you want the top graft to be located, and remove a 5 to 10-inch-long strip of bark from each whip. Join and bind the whips with the plastic stretch tie tape. After the graft has grown a ridge of connecting tissue, use the pruning shears to prune away one of the two whips, leaving just enough foliage and buds to ensure one season's growth. After two seasons, prune away the remaining portion of the unwanted whip. Continue to keep an eye on your "lead" whip, pinching back sprouts to help it grow.

15 Keep the chair well watered during its first summer growing season.

When the whips produce side growth, pinch it off. Don't sit in the chair for two or three years until it's grown strong enough to hold your weight.

lemonade tree swing

DESIGNER
Daniel O. Petersen

There's as much art as science to installing a tree swing, and the most important element is picking the right tree to hang it from! Select a substantial hardwood tree if possible. A white oak or live oak is the very best choice. This project also teaches you some important do's and don'ts about installation and safety when working with trees, so you won't harm the tree or hurt yourself in the process. Using both hands for a task while sitting on a limb high above the ground can be risky; always wear a safety belt and use good common sense.

MATERIALS

⅝-inch synthetic three-strand rope*

2 galvanized rope thimbles, ⅝ inch

2 cast galvanized eyebolts, ⅝ x 14 inches

2 flat washers, ⅝ inch

4 galvanized nuts, ⅝ inch

2 locking washers, ⅝ inch

Oak plank, 2 x 10 x 24 inches (can be as long as 42 inches)

*Length depends on tree limb measurement. Avoid manila and cotton ropes, as they tend to decay as they weather.

TOOLS AND SUPPLIES

Ladder

25-foot metal tape measure

Large nut or bolt (optional)

Ball of cotton string (optional)

Vise (optional)

Vise grips

Crescent wrench

Hammer

Grease pencil or permanent marker

2-cycle gas-powered drill, or ½-inch drive electric power drill with a ⅝- or ¹¹/₁₆-inch wood auger bit, 18 inches long

Extension cord for electric drill

Safety belt for attachment to tree

Rope for work line

A friend to help you (essential, not optional)

Roll of electrical tape

Utility knife

Level

INSTRUCTIONS

1 After you've selected a tree for your swing, look for an appropriate limb.

It should branch out perpendicular to the trunk and be a main leader of the tree, 8 to 12 inches in diameter and free of decay and hollow areas.

2 Now you'll measure for the rope that will support the swing. Use the ladder to reach the limb if it's not too high, and measure with the tape measure. Double the measurement to allow for the two ropes dropping down from the host limb. With greater heights, tie the nut or bolt to the end of the cotton string, throw it over the limb, and mark the points where the two ends reach the ground. Add 10 feet more to allow for doubling the rope at the seat attachment.

3 Swing placement is key to the pleasure of the ride! If there's a slope to the ground and a good limb running parallel with the level grade, you can install the swing to face the slope's downhill direction, giving the swinger's feet a back stroke close to the ground, and a front stroke that will take him out and high over the falling slope. Make sure the swing is far enough away from the tree trunk to avoid collision, and clear away any obstacles in the swing arc. Be careful: a very long swing can cover an enormous distance, sending you into unforeseen obstacles.

4 The less time you spend up on the tree limb, the better, so do some preparation on the ground before ascending. First, attach the metal rope thimbles to the eyes of the bolts. Clamp a thimble in the vise, or in the vise grips, and bend the thimble apart with the grips or crescent wrench. Slip the thimble around the eye of the bolt, and bend the thimble back into shape, using the wrench or hammer if necessary. Repeat with the second thimble and bolt.

5 Attach the two ends of the rope to the eyebolt. Have the rope ride in the bed of the thimble so that the metal of the thimble rides against the metal of the eyebolt, instead of rope against the metal.

6 As shown in figure 1, secure the rope to the thimble by braiding it back into itself. Or, you can tie a bowline knot snug to the thimble as shown in figure 2, leaving enough of a tail to tie a figure eight in the end. This will keep the rope from pulling out.

7 Having secured the two ends of the rope to the thimbles on the eyebolts, place the flat washer, the first nut, the locking washer, and the final nut on each of the eyebolts. This is the order they will go on once the bolts are in the tree.

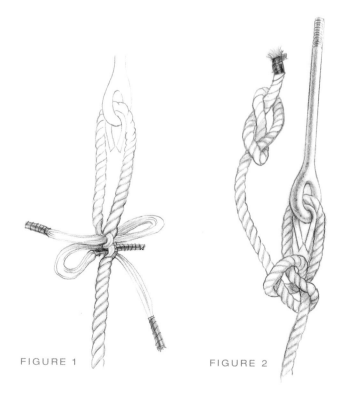

FIGURE 1   FIGURE 2

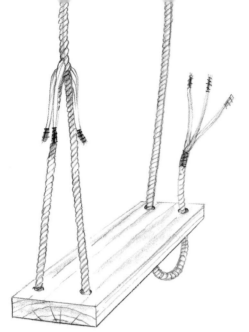

FIGURE 3

8 How you attach the swing to the tree is critical to your safety, the swinger's safety, and the tree's continued good health. When you climb up to work on the limb, it's mandatory that you immediately attach yourself to the limb with the safety belt. Never work alone; always have a friend present. Throw the work line over the limb, and use it to haul tools and materials up and down.

9 Use the tape measure and pencil to indicate the placement of two drill holes in the limb. Set the holes at least as far apart as the length of the swing seat; they can be spaced up to twice that length. (Swings also look better when the space between the ropes at the top narrows to a lesser width at the seat.) Use the power drill with the wood auger bit to drill two plumb holes downward from the top of the limb and through the middle of the limb. Drill the holes through in one smooth continuous motion.

10 Remove the nuts and washers from the eyebolts (to which the ropes are attached). Slip the bolts into the drilled holes from the underside of the limb. Replace the washers and nuts on top, placing the flat washer against the top of the hole, then the first nut, the locking washer, and finally the second nut. Use the crescent wrench to tighten the first nut until the eye end of the bolt on the bottom of the limb and the flat washer on the top side of the limb begin to bite into the limb's bark. Line up the bolt eyes so they face the same direction as the swing arc. After the first nut is tightened, tighten the second nut until the locking washer is flattened between the two nuts. This completes your work in the tree.

11 Now you'll attach the plank seat. The loop of rope hanging from the eyebolts should be dragging the ground. Find the approximate center point of the loop, tape a 3-inch section with the electrical tape, and cut through the rope with the knife in the middle of the taped section. Use the tape measure and pencil to mark a drill hole in each corner, 2 inches in from the sides and corner. Drill the holes.

12 Thread the newly cut rope ends into the holes in each end of the seat: first down through one hole, then back up through the corresponding hole on the same end. Attach the rope end to the rope coming down from the limb, at a point about 18 inches from the seat, using a bowline to create a triangle of rope (see figure 3). Adjust the seat to a comfortable height, and use the level to check that it's evenly hung, then tape and cut off any excess rope. If desired, braid the ends for a finished look.

far east cedar and bamboo bench

DESIGNERS
Carol Stangler and Randall Ray

Craftspeople in the Far East know that elegance is often about restraint, and in their work they will often choose to highlight only one or two perfect details. This luxurious bench is a perfect example, with its simple but beautifully finished cedar construction and mitered bamboo inlay.

MATERIALS

10 culms of black bamboo, each
   4 to 5 feet long

4 x 4 Western red cedar, 8 feet long

4 x 4 Western red cedar, 10 feet long

1 x 2 pressure-treated lumber,
   13 feet total

¾-inch pressure-treated plywood,
   18 x 24 inches

INSTRUCTIONS

1 Wash the bamboo culms and allow them to dry. Paint them with two coats of the clear sealer, following the package directions. Allow to dry.

2 Now you'll make the bench frame. Refer to figures 1 and 2. Measure the two 4 x 4 cedar pieces and cut them to a 45° miter to get two pieces with a 48-inch-long point and two with a 24-inch-long point.

3 Assemble the cut cedar pieces on the work surface, and use the ⅜-inch drill bit to predrill three ¾-inch-deep pilot holes in each corner as shown in figure 3, page 354. Use the ¹⁄₁₆-inch bit to drill an additional 2 inches into the center of each hole.

4 Dust off the shavings. Apply the adhesive to the ends of the cut pieces, assemble, and screw them together with the 2-inch wood screws, countersinking the screws ⅜ inch. Allow the adhesive to dry.

5 From the remaining 4 x 4 pieces, square-cut four legs, each 15¾ inches long. Rabbet the top end of each leg, as shown in figure 4, page 354. Cut and remove the three sections, leaving a tenon that will fit into the corners of the frame.

TOOLS AND SUPPLIES

Clear wood sealer

2 bristle paintbrushes

Tape measure

Miter saw

Power drill with ⅜-inch and ¹⁄₁₆-inch
   bits, a ⅜-inch round-over bit

Paste construction adhesive

30 wood screws, 2 inches long

Fine sandpaper

Chisel (optional)

Circular saw or table saw

Hammer

Pencil

Wood glue

12 tapered wood plugs

Oil-based wood finish in brown/
   black shade

Chalk

Bamboo saw*, or hacksaw with
   a fine-toothed blade for
   cutting metal

Bamboo splitting knife*

Mallet

Miter box

Box of 1⅝-inch ringed panel nails,
   ¹⁄₁₆-inch diameter

*Available from mail order sources for Japanese woodworking tools. A Japanese bamboo saw has a thin blade with 20 to 32 teeth per inch. The bamboo splitting knife is a froe-type knife with a blade approximately ⅛ inch thick, sharpened to a double bevel.

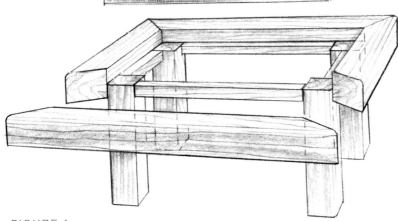

FIGURE 1

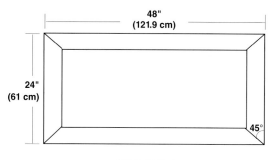

48"
(121.9 cm)

24"
(61 cm)

45°

FIGURE 2

FIGURE 3

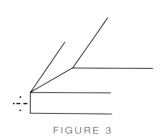

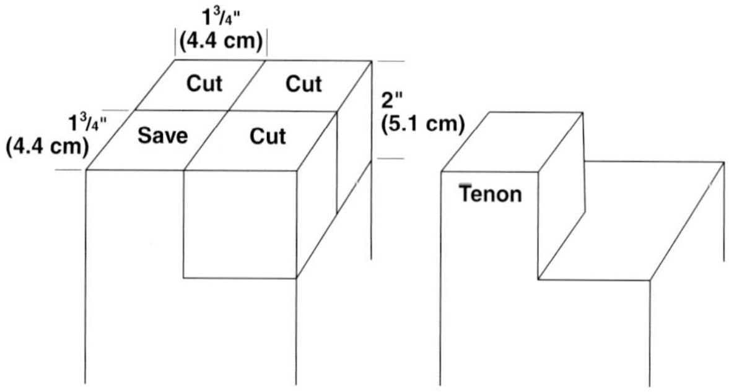

1³/₄"
(4.4 cm)

1³/₄"
(4.4 cm)

Cut   Cut

Save   Cut

2"
(5.1 cm)

Tenon

FIGURE 4

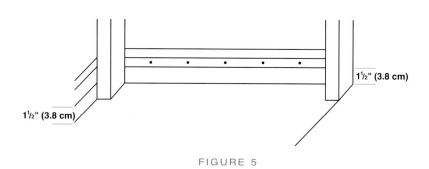

1¹/₂" (3.8 cm)

1¹/₂" (3.8 cm)

FIGURE 5

6 Place the frame face down, apply the adhesive, and set the tenons into the inside corners of the frame. Drill a ¹/₁₆-inch pilot hole 2 inches deep. Screw in the 2-inch screws, and let dry. Sand off any excess adhesive, or use the chisel to remove it.

7 Lay the bench on its side, and pencil a line 1½ inches below the top edge of the frame (see figure 5). From the 1 x 2 boards, cut two pieces 37⅝ inches long, and two pieces 13¾ inches long to serve as cleats.

8 Predrill ¹/₁₆-inch pilot holes every 8 inches along the line you've drawn. Position the cleats you cut in step 6 between the legs, along the 1½-inch depth line. Screw in place with the 3-inch wood screws.

9 Place the bench upside down. Cut three of the 1 x 2 boards to a 14-inch length. Set these stretchers across the width of the bench, between the cleats, as shown in figure 6. Drill two ¹/₁₆-inch pilot holes on an angle, then use the 2-inch wood screws to toenail the ends of the stretchers onto the cleats.

10 Place the bench upright. Measure and cut the ¾-inch plywood to 17 x 41¼ inches. After applying the wood glue to the top edge of the cleats, center the plywood and drop it into the bench. Secure the plywood to the cleats with the 2-inch wood screws, six along each long side, and three along each short side.

11 Use the ⅜-inch round-over bit in the drill to router the outside top edge of the frame and the base of the legs, achieving a pleasing curve. Fill the screw holes with the wood plugs.

12 Clean off any dust or shavings, and use the paintbrush to apply two coats of the clear wood sealer to the cedar, following the package directions. Coat the plywood with the brown/black wood stain. Let dry.

13 As shown in figure 7, use the tape measure and chalk to divide the plywood seat into four equal sections.

14 With the bamboo saw, cut the bamboo into ten 16-inch lengths. Use the knife and mallet to split the bamboo in half lengthwise, creating 20 pieces. Arrange the halves on the seat in a herringbone pattern (see figure 8), adjusting them to get a close fit and an even surface. Cut and split the remaining bamboo, and use it to complete the seat's surface pattern.

15 Refer to figure 9. Use the bamboo saw and miter box to miter-cut the ends of the bamboo pieces into complementary 45° angles, where they meet each other at the chalk lines on the seat. Put a straight angle cut on the ends that butt against the seat frame. Work carefully and precisely to achieve a good fit.

16 Lightly sand the cut ends of the bamboo, and stain the ends with the brown/black stain. Allow to dry, then lay the pieces back into the pattern on the seat. Using the 1/16-inch drill bit, drill a pilot hole through the end of each bamboo piece and 1/8 inch into the plywood base. Secure by hammering the ringed panel nails through the holes. Each nail should slide through the pilot hole. If the hole is too small, the bamboo will split when you try to hammer in the nail. Drill and nail the ends of each bamboo piece in place until the inlay is complete.

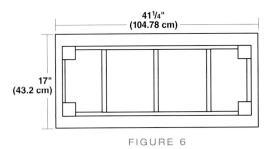

41¼"
(104.78 cm)

17"
(43.2 cm)

FIGURE 6

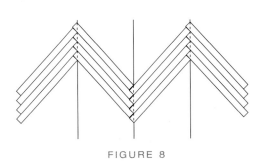

FIGURE 7

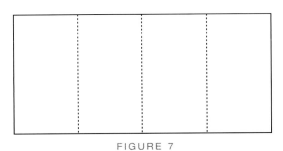

FIGURE 8

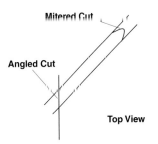

Mitered Cut

Angled Cut

Top View

Side view of mitered split bamboo

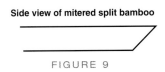

FIGURE 9

brick
and stone

Why not use brick as a decorative insert? See the Recycled Brick and Bedstead Bench on page 360.

brick

You don't have to become a mason to use brick attractively in garden seating. It's possible to make sturdy garden seats that incorporate bricks without the mess of mortar.

Since brick comes in standard dimensions, it's easy to figure out how much you'll need for a project (but check the dimensions with a tape measure). A brick paver usually measures 2 x 3½ x 7¾ inches. To cover a square foot, you'll need about five bricks. So if you want to cover a garden seat that measures 1 x 3 feet, multiply the width by the length, or 1 x 3, to determine the square footage of

3 square feet. You'll therefore need 15 bricks. You can buy new bricks by the piece at home improvement and building supply centers, brick suppliers, and tile companies. For old bricks, look for architectural recycling stores and demolition sites.

Bricks get hot in the sun and acquire moss in damp climates. Old brick may look absolutely delightful in an outdoor seat, but unless you shelter it, winter weather may cause it to crack or crumble. New brick won't have as much character, but it will last longer.

stone

When you use stone to make a garden seat, its origin often determines its decorative effect. The larger the stone, the more it blends into the landscape and looks like it just "grew there." Stone recycled from earlier uses, such as the Recycled Granite Curbing Bench on page 358, has more regular dimensions and a cleaner look.

The advantage of stone is that it lasts almost forever, period. It's impervious to the elements, and if you live in a moist climate, it will probably acquire moss and lichen (if you don't like it, scrub it off with a brush). If you plan to sit long on stone, use a pillow for comfort. Stone's density also means it's very heavy relative to its size, and its main disadvantage is the sheer strength required to lift and move it. Stone work is labor intensive, so lighten the load by collecting a group of friends to help you!

In many areas of the country, you can simply collect stone from the fields. For very large pieces, go to stone yards, or keep an eye on local road-building projects that may involve blasting and removal of large chunks of stone. Offer to remove some of the debris! If you buy materials at a stone yard, they'll usually deliver. If you move a large piece of stone yourself, you'll need a wheelbarrow, a tire iron or piece of rebar (for leverage), and several pairs of helping hands. In desperate cases, you can rent a pallet jack at a local equipment rental business or home improvement center. If you're working with a stone that weighs more than 200 pounds, it's advisable to use the services of a professional backhoe operator to move and position it.

LEFT:
Recycled granite curbing was stacked to create this bench.

recycled
granite curbing
bench

You can rest easy on this bench, because you won't get a ticket for parking on the yellow line! An inventive reuse of old curbing torn up in an urban redevelopment project, this project is simple to construct. For opportunities to salvage wonderful pieces of stone to use in your outdoor seating, check with your local road building authorities, and keep your eyes open at demolition sites and architectural renovations.

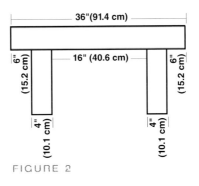

FIGURE 2

INSTRUCTIONS

1 When choosing materials for a stone bench, it's best to select a top piece that has an even, level top and an even bottom to allow it to make good contact with the supporting stones. This is one reason old street curbing can make good seating, as it's fairly uniform.

2 There are three factors to consider when choosing the length of the two bench supports: the height of the bench, the thickness of the seat, and the depth the supports must sink into the ground. The most comfortable sitting height is 16 to 18 inches above the ground. The two pieces that support the bench should sink 4 to 6 inches into the ground. You must take this into account along with the actual thickness of the stone that forms the seat (refer to figure 1). Let's assume you want your bench to be 16 inches tall. Therefore, 16 inches minus the 4-inch thickness of the bench (you've measured it, right?) equals 12 inches, and 12 inches plus 4 to 6 inches (the depth to sink the supports into the ground) equals a supporting stone length of 16 to 18 inches. If you use slim stones for the bench supports, you'll have to sink them even deeper into the ground for strength and stability, and this will affect your calculations accordingly.

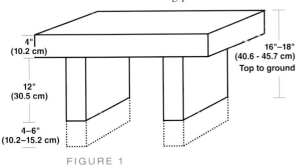

FIGURE 1

3 When choosing supporting stones of the correct length, try to pick some with flat, even tops so the bench will sit solidly on them.

4 Use the tape measure to determine the length of the bench stone. Wearing your work gloves, sink the two supports into the ground so that the bench will overlap them 6 to 8 inches at each end. Refer to figure 2. For example, if you have a 36-inch-long bench and the supports are 4 inches thick, subtract 20 inches. A 6-inch overlap plus 4-inch thickness equals 10 inches. Multiply 10 inches times two and subtract the result from 36 inches. There should, therefore, be a 16-inch space between the supports. But, having said all that, if your bench stone is noticeably thicker at one end, you can balance the asymmetry by increasing the overlap of the thinner end of the bench stone over its support.

5 Use the level to check that the support tops are even (if you have a small level, set it on the 2 x 4 board balanced on the two supports). Adjust the heights if necessary.

6 With your friend's help, carefully set the bench stone in place on the two supports. Check to make sure it's stable and doesn't rock. If it does, slide the stone slightly over the supports to obtain a flatter contact between them.

MATERIALS AND TOOLS

3 pieces of recycled granite curbing, the top piece at least 3 to 5 feet long and the two supporting pieces 16 to 18 inches long*

Tape measure

Heavy work gloves

Shovel

Level

2 x 4 board

A helpful friend

*These dimensions can vary if you adjust your installation procedure accordingly. See step 2.

recycled brick and bedstead bench

DESIGNERS
Johnny and Katina Jones

This bench design combines modern lines with recycled elements that evoke the past: an old iron gate, a bed frame, and bricks that once paved an early city sidewalk. If you haven't welded before, take the project to a metal fabrication shop to be welded.

MATERIALS

9 old bricks

Bed rails

3 scrap metal pieces, the same length as the seat frame

2 pieces of angle iron for the legs, or extra pieces of gate

Old metal gate, 36 to 42 inches wide

Extra decorative metal elements (optional)

TOOLS AND SUPPLIES

Wire brush (optional)

Measuring tape

Safety glasses

Protective gloves

Chalk

Hacksaw

Band saw

Several C-clamps

Welding equipment (optional)

Framing square

Level

Angle grinder

Sanding pad or wire brush (optional)

INSTRUCTIONS

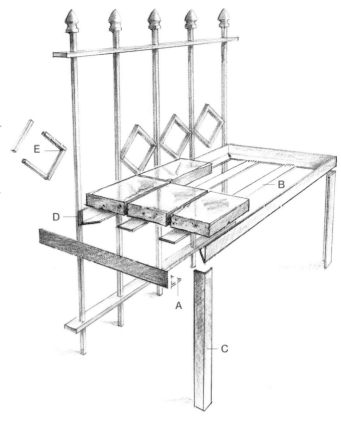

1 Place the nine bricks into three rows of three bricks each.

2 Using the tape measure, check the dimensions of the bricks to determine the seat dimensions.

3 You should always wear protection when working with metal, so put on the safety glasses and gloves. Use the chalk to mark the old bed rails to the dimensions of the bricks, and cut with the hacksaw.

4 With the hacksaw or band saw, miter the corners of the rail pieces to form 90° corners for the frame (A) to hold the bricks.

5 Use the C-clamps to clamp the frame pieces to a heatproof work surface. Turn the lips of the angle iron inward so the frame will provide a "ledge" for the bricks along its perimeter. Make sure they're square. Tack, or spot-weld, the frame, or have a weld shop do it for you. Check the corner angles of the frame with the framing square, and make sure the bricks fit inside. Weld the three pieces of scrap metal (B) to the inside of the frame at 3-inch intervals, where they'll act as an undersupport to keep the bricks in place.

6 To create the two front legs (C), carefully measure the angle iron to the desired height of the bench, and cut it with the hacksaw. Check that the legs are the same height and level, and even them up with the grinder if necessary. The ideal height of any seat is 16 to 19 inches from the ground.

7 Use the angle grinder or sanding pad to clean the tops of the legs. Position the legs flush against the inside front of the seat frame, and weld them in place.

8 Instead of individual legs, you can use extra fencing to serve as legs on the sides of the bench as shown in the photograph. Simply measure pieces of fencing to fit the sides of the seat; in other words, the pieces of fencing should be as long as the seat is deep. Use the hacksaw to cut them to the desired height.

9 Measure the portion of the gate (D) where the seat frame will be attached. The gate serves as the back of the bench.

10 Clamp the frame to the gate, checking to make sure the seat is level.

11 Weld the seat frame to the gate wherever the frame touches the gate, then smooth the welds with the grinder.

12 If desired, weld additional metal decorative elements of your choice (E) to the gate, positioning them inside the spaces between the gate bars.

13 Place the bricks in the seat frame.

cement

cement

First, let's clarify our terminology. Cement and concrete are close to being the same thing but not quite. Portland cement is the lime-based powder you buy at the hardware store. When you combine it with water and sand or gravel, you create a mixture that turns into concrete when it hardens. You can also buy cement mix, which contains Portland cement already pre-mixed with sand in bags.

In the construction technique called ferrocement, you wrap wire mesh around an inner structure (armature) of reinforced metal bar, then pack cement into the form. You can also make ready-made cement seating into something special by applying mosaic; refer to the Botanical Mosaic Garden Bench on page 367.

Cement is messy; wear protective clothing to shield you from the lime's harshness. Site cement projects with care; if you decide to move or replace it, tearing up and removing concrete is quite a chore.

BELOW: **This fantastic cement throne is a mosaic tour de force utilizing mirror shards and other decorative materials.** PHOTO BY CHARLES MANN

LEFT: **With the addition of a couple of pillows, these classical columns are an inventive and attractive use of ready-made concrete forms for seating.**

OPPOSITE PAGE: **Sherri Warner Hunter,** *Garden Throne: A Place to Daydream,* **1999, 65 x 50 x 32 inches (165 x 127 x 81 cm); concrete over polystyrene foam; cut, cemented.** PHOTO BY EVAN BRACKEN

ferrocement

Ferrocement is a very plastic medium, allowing you to create inventive forms for your seating. It's also inexpensive and extremely durable if the concrete is mixed and cured properly. The forms don't have be extremely precise, but take care to build a good armature, wiring or welding it securely so the form won't sag when you apply the cement. Pack the cement firmly into all the spaces, leaving no voids. You must cure the cement by keeping it wet while its molecules form tight bonds with the wire mesh. The longer it's kept in curing mode, the stronger the bond will be. Hardware stores carry all the tools and materials you'll need.

painting and staining concrete

Don't paint cement unless you're prepared to take it down to the bare surface with a wire brush when you have to repaint it every few years; half-measures don't work. You can always choose to leave it natural or to stain it for lasting color.

To paint concrete, first clean the surface with water and a scrub brush. Let it dry, then degrease and etch the surface by scrubbing it with a mixture of muriatic acid and water, following the package directions. The acid is highly caustic, so work in a well-ventilated area and wear safety glasses and heavy-duty protective rubber gloves. Allow to dry, then apply a base coat of waterproof primer with a brush or roller; the base coat is essential to keep the porous concrete from soaking up the paint. Let dry; apply exterior-grade cement paint, then waterproof sealer.

Interior-exterior concrete stains are available at home improvement centers and hardware stores. New concrete must cure for a minimum of 30 days before staining. You'll have to degrease the concrete, strip off any paint or sealer, and chemically etch the concrete with muriatic acid. Let dry, then apply the stain with a synthetic bristle brush or roller, let dry for 24 hours, then reapply in a direction opposite to the first coat.

LEFT: **The fabulous Folk Art Fantasy Bench is a perfect application of the ferrocement construction technique.**

decorating with tiles and mosaic

You can decorate seating with mosaics made from stone, glass, mirrors, broken crockery, ceramic tile, and metals by pressing objects into the final coating of cement before it hardens completely.

You can also add mosaic to a cast concrete bench. A pair of tile nippers cuts thin pieces of ceramic or glass tile. Glass cutters and running pliers are also helpful for cutting mirror and glass. Use cyanoacry-late glue or clear silicone adhesive to adhere the bits to the surface, then apply grout to the crevices using a spatula, trowel, or a tool called a float. Grout comes in various colors, or you can tint it yourself with acrylic paint. After the grout dries for 48 to 72 hours, seal the surface with two coats of clear acrylic sealer. Tools and materials are available at craft stores, hardware stores, and home supply centers.

Warm tones of concrete stain are used very effectively in this outdoor banquette. Steven J. Young, ASLA, SJY Design, Oakland, CA.
PHOTO BY MICHELLE BURKE

botanical
mosaic
garden
bench

DESIGNER
Terry Taylor

When you look at this gorgeous mosaic bench, you can almost imagine yourself in the garden of a Roman villa. Give yourself plenty of leisure time to ponder and assemble the mosaic design, so the artist inside you can come out! You can find all the ceramic pieces you need at thrift stores and yard sales.

INSTRUCTIONS

1 Broken ceramics can be sharp, so always wear your safety glasses when you work. Prepare a supply of shards for the mosaic by using the tile nippers to break the plates in half. Remove the rims from the plates, and trim the rim shards into rectangular pieces 1 to 1½ inches wide. Set the rim shards that contain a portion of the plate's finished edge in one of the meat trays. Break the flat portions of the plates into 1- to 2-inch pieces that are fairly uniform in thickness, and place them in another tray. It's helpful to keep colors separate. Discard the raised "feet" of the plates and any other pieces that are thicker than the rest.

2 Now, trim the plate with the central motif, making it into a circular tile. Use the tile nippers to carefully remove a small portion of the plate rim.

Work toward the raised foot of the plate, removing the rim as you work. Trim the rims as you did in step 1 and set aside. Using the tip of the tile nippers, break away a small part of the raised foot. As you work, you'll be able to place the tip of the nippers on the inside of the foot and trim away the foot, leaving a circular, flat plate bottom.

3 Place the scrap lumber under the bench top to elevate it off the floor or ground, so the top will be easier to move when you're finished.

4 Use the tape measure to check the measurements of the bench top.

5 Photocopy the vine template on page 368 and have the copy enlarged to fit the bench you have purchased. Cut out the pattern with the scissors.

TOOLS AND SUPPLIES

Safety glasses

Tile nippers

Several polystryrene foam meat trays, or similar containers

2 scraps of 2 x 4 lumber, each approximately 3 feet long

Tape measure

Template on page 368

Scissors

Pencil

Fine-tip permanent marker

Thin-set cement mortar

Mixing container for mortar

Water

Notched trowel

Gray sanded grout

Mixing container for grout

Grout spreader or polyethylene foam wrap*

Palette knife

Sponge

Lint-free rags

*These are the foam sheets used to wrap items being shipped.

MATERIALS

15 to 20 ceramic plates and saucers in white, solid greens, and patterned greens, including one plate with a central botanical motif

Concrete garden bench with removable top

6 Center the flat, circular tile that you created in step 2 on the bench top. Use the pencil to sketch a larger circle around the tile as a border area. Place the vine pattern on the bench, and trace around the pattern with a pencil. Flip the pattern over to the other side of the circular tile and trace it again. If you're satisfied with the placement of the central motif and vine pattern, trace over the pencil lines with the permanent marker.

7 In the mixing container, mix a small amount of the thin-set mortar with water according to the manufacturer's instructions.

8 Use the small, notched trowel to spread the mortar on the circular area you sketched on the bench top for your central motif. Position the circular plate bottom in the mortar, and use the plate rims to accent the border area. Use the tip of the trowel to remove any excess mortar that may have squeezed up between the tiles.

9 Working in one small area at a time, spread the mortar around the top edge of the bench. Use the finished plate rims you made in step 1 to create a finished edge of mosaic on the bench top.

10 Start filling in the vine pattern with the solid-colored shards. Spread a small amount of mortar in an area, and use small shards to fill in the vine and leaf shapes, trimming pieces with the tile nipper as needed. Be sure to keep the design lively by varying your placement of colors. Don't try to make the vine pattern absolutely symmetrical and evenly colored; small variations and irregularities add to the charm of the piece.

11 As you work, fill in the small areas between the leaves and vine with white shards. If you have excess mortar in these spaces, fill them in with white shards before the mortar dries.

12 Spread the mortar on the uncovered areas of the bench, and continue filling in with shards. Placing white close to the vine pattern will give the color extra sparkle, but you don't have to make the background completely white. It will be more interesting if you sparingly add bits of green and patterned shards.

13 Allow the mosaic to dry overnight before grouting.

14 Mix the gray sanded grout in the container according to the manufacturer's instructions.

15 Use the grout spreader or the polyethylene foam wrap to spread the grout over the surface of the mosaic. Use pressure to force the grout into all the spaces between the shards. After allowing the grout to set up for about 15 minutes, begin removing the excess grout with the polyethylene foam wrap or rags. Follow the manufacturer's recommendations on the grout packaging for removing any grout "haze" that develops.

16 Allow the mosaic to cure according to the grout's package directions before placing the bench in your garden.

17 Freezing water can cause mosaic to crack, so you'll want to protect your bench from moisture during the winter. Cover it with plastic sheeting, or store it in a sheltered location.

folk art
fantasy
bench
DESIGNER
Robert Cheatham

With shapes and swirls inspired by Art Nouveau, this garden bench sits squarely in the folk art tradition of making fantastic outdoor constructions with cement, chicken wire, and paint. You'll have fun deciding exactly where you want the vinelike tendrils to grow in your own bench.

INSTRUCTIONS

1 First you'll make the bench "feet." Use the metal shears or wire cutters to cut out four pieces of chicken wire. Cut the pieces big enough so that when a piece is wrapped around the end of a 4-foot rebar and the rebar is inserted into a glass vessel, 3 or 4 inches of the chicken wire will stick out of the vessel. Wrap a piece of chicken wire around one end of each piece of 4-foot rebar.

TOOLS AND SUPPLIES

Metal shears

Wire cutters

Hacksaw

Table vise for making bends in rebar (you can also use a trailer hitch with the ball removed, or a fork in a nearby tree)

Needle-nose pliers

10-gallon plastic bucket

Shovel

Hammer

Heavy-duty protective rubber gloves*

Cement trowel

Garden hose with spray attachment, or plastic mister bottle

Rags or burlap (optional)

*Rubberized fabric gloves are available in hardware stores. They offer the best protection against the sharp ends of the wire mesh.

MATERIALS

50-foot roll of chicken wire, 2 feet wide with 1-inch mesh size

10 pieces of ⅜-inch steel rebar, each 4 feet long

4 glass or porcelain forms, such as screw-on glass light covers, lamp bodies, or other hollow vessel shapes

Two 60-pound bags of sand mix cement

Water

5 pieces of ⅜-inch steel rebar, each 18 inches long

Roll of rebar tie wire

1 can each outdoor-grade epoxy spray paints in red, blue, and green

2 Refer to figure 1. Using the bucket and shovel, mix water with the cement to pouring consistency according to package directions, making only enough to fill all four vessels. Before it has time to set, pour the cement into each vessel, lightly tapping the sides of the glass to settle any air pockets. Set the vessels in an upright position with the pieces of rebar pointing up, and allow them to dry for three days. With the hammer, rap the glass of the vessels hard enough to break away and remove the glass or porcelain shells.

3 Now you'll start to form the bench frame with two of the "feet." Insert the rebar protruding from a "foot" into the vise, roughly 18 inches from the bottom of the foot. Make a bend. Repeat with the second foot. The bends will not be exact 90° angles but will have more of a curve to them (see figure 2). Position the two front feet in front of the back two feet. Point the bent front pieces back toward the two upright pieces of rebar protruding from the back feet. Allow a 16- to 18-inch span to help form the seat, then make a second bend in both pieces of "front feet" rebar so the rods point upward. They will help form the back of the bench.

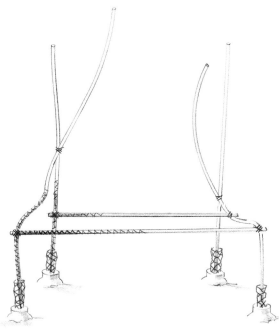

FIGURE 2

4 Refer to figure 2. Place a 4-foot piece of rebar horizontally across the two front pieces of rebar, an inch or two below the point where the two front pieces start to curve backward. Cut pieces of the tie wire with the wire cutters, and wire the bar firmly in place on both ends. Do the same with another 4-foot crosspiece in the back.

5 Using the remaining 4-foot sections of rebar, fill in the framework of the seat and back with vinelike "tendrils" of rebar as shown in figure 3, bending and curving them. Connect them with the tie wire to the front and back pieces of horizontal rebar. To temporarily prevent the upper ends of the "tendrils" from falling over, lightly wire them in place.

6 Wire the 18-inch sections of rebar in between the bent, 4-foot sections to fill in the seating area.

FIGURE 1

7 Use the shears to cut the chicken wire into narrow 10- to 12-inch lengths, and start tightly wrapping the cut mesh around the rebar form. Put on the protective gloves to protect against the sharp ends of the mesh. As you wrap, the mesh should closely follow the desired contours, and in structural and weight-bearing areas like legs and joints, attach at least six layers of mesh for strength. Use the needle-nose pliers or short bits of the tie wire to pull the mesh close in to the rebar. You can also use the shears to cut and fold the chicken wire.

8 When you've wrapped the form with the chicken wire to the desired shape and thickness, apply the cement. A mix of cement the consistency of toothpaste is needed so it will adhere to the wire. Wearing the protective gloves, apply the cement with the trowel and your hands, making sure to press the cement all the way into and around the rebar so there are no gaps or air pockets (see figure 4). Work as fast as you can so you can apply all the cement in one session. After about an hour, the cement will be set up enough so you can smooth the surface.

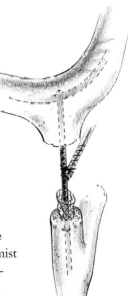

FIGURE 4

9 Using the spray attachment on the garden hose or the mister bottle, mist the cement until it's sopping wet. It's extremely important to keep the bench in the curing stage by hosing it down or misting it every four hours. Keep the bench wet for at least 24 hours and for up to four days. To maintain wetness overnight, saturate the rags or burlap with water and lay them over the bench. Continue to mist the piece periodically. The longer you can keep the bench in curing mode, the stronger the bond will be between the steel and cement.

10 After the bench has cured for 24 hours, mix and apply another coat of cement, if desired, to smooth out the surface and fill any voids where the cement has dropped out. Let it set up, then mist it and resume the curing process.

11 After the cement has cured and fully dried, spray-paint the bench with outdoor-quality epoxy spray paint. To achieve the look shown in the photograph, apply red to the feet, blue to the legs and the perimeter of the seat, and green to the seat, arms, and back "vines." At the margin of each color, use a delicate touch with the spray paint, blending each tone into the next one without harsh borders.

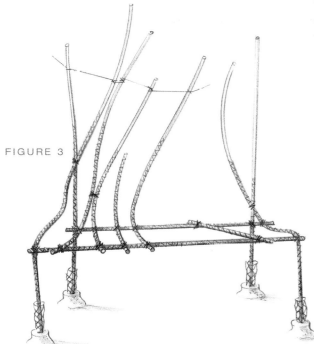

FIGURE 3

wood

ABOVE AND RIGHT: A minimal surface finish complements the gentle arc of the back and simple slat design of this bench.

building with wood

Lumber is one of our most popular and versatile materials for creating garden seating. With the proper tools, you can cut and shape wood into just about any form you can conceive. You can stain or paint it any color you like, opening up the range of decorative possibilities dramatically. As a material, wood is very strong relative to its weight, and it just plain feels good when you sit on it.

The main disadvantage of wooden outdoor seating is the lengths to which you have to go to protect it against the effects of being outdoors in the first place! You can buy expensive, extremely durable hardwoods, such as plantation-grown teak, to make your project, or use less expensive pressure-treated (PT) softwood lumber, which has been treated with chemicals to make it last up to 10 times longer than untreated lumber. Some PT lumber is also treated so it can tolerate direct ground contact. When you cut PT, wear gloves and a respirator to avoid the chemicals, and seal it with a finishing coat. A third option is to use specialty softwoods, such as cypress, cedar, or redwood, which are naturally weather-resistant. Some consumers avoid redwood, not wishing to contribute to forestry pressures on diminishing native American redwood forests.

sealing, staining, and painting wood

Sun and water can cause wood to turn gray, crack, or rot. A protective layer of paint, stain, clear finish, or water sealer extends wood's longevity dramatically, and a yearly application of water-repellent sealer with a UV filter helps hardwood or specialty softwood outdoor furniture last for decades. If you're scrupulous about maintaining the sealed or painted finish, softwood will last almost as long. Before applying finish, sand the wood to a smooth finish, then remove any dust with a tack cloth. Brush the finish on the clean, dry surface, adding extra coats as recommended.

If you want to show off the grain of hardwood or a specialty softwood and protect it from cracking, apply a coat of penetrating finish water sealer. It doesn't color the wood, though the wood may darken slightly. To further protect decay-resistant redwood and cedar furniture, apply a water repellent with UV protectors and a mildew inhibitor; reapply annually.

Wood stains come in many colors, finishes, and degrees of opacity. For outdoor seating, choose a penetrating stain that also contains a water sealer. A penetrating oil stain soaks in, dyeing wood while allowing the grain to show; it penetrates softwood poorly, however. A pigmented oil stain is handy for changing or matching wood colors, but it can obscure the grain. Water stain is clear and dyes the wood permanently, but it's slow-drying and hard to apply. Re-stain wood every three to five years.

Paint covers up flaws and allows you to be creative with color. Use only exterior-grade paint. Oil-based enamel dries slowly, but it's durable, washable, and provides slightly better coverage than latex enamel. Latex is easy to thin and clean up with water. Apply a primer first to seal the wood and help the paint "grab" the surface. Let dry, then brush on the paint.

why bother?

the beauty of the old,
the unfinished,
and the weathered

In some cases you may not want to finish or refinish a piece of outdoor furniture. Hardwoods such as teak, or specialty softwoods such as cedar, will eventually weather to a lovely silvery gray, and this might be all the finish you want for your outdoor seat. You'll have to make the decision whether to allow the weathering and aging process to proceed, or if you want to retard it with sealer, stain, or paint so the material will last longer.

ABOVE: **Weather and time reveal the colors these French garden chairs have been painted over the years.**

TOP RIGHT: **If you choose, you can allow your outdoor furniture to collect moss and lichen so you can enjoy its varied colors and textures.** PHOTO BY RICHARD HASSELBERG

RIGHT: **Plant your seat! If you have a seat that's so decrepit it's no longer useful as a seat, try giving it new life as a plant stand or a decorative item in its own right.**

If you're lucky enough to inherit or acquire an old wood (or wicker, or metal) outdoor seat, stop for a moment to appreciate its appeal. The nicks, chips, cracks, marks of wear, and layered surfaces of paint are visual testimony to the passage of time, to the history of the particular piece of furniture, and to the lives of the people who loved and used it before you. The Japanese have a special word, *sabi*, for the patina of age. It's history and poetry combined in an object, to be cherished and not necessarily refinished.

You can "distress" wooden furniture to make it look as if it's been around a long time. Use sloppy, mottled applications of paint in muted tones, and sand selected edges and points to simulate wear. You can also literally batter the furniture with chains (ouch!), brush a contrasting paint or stain over the surface, and quickly wipe most of it off with a rag to leave an "aged" residue in the crevices and depressions. Finally, if a seat has truly outworn its usefulness as a seat, it can make a lovely plant stand in the garden.

The weathered and oxidized surfaces of old garden furniture can be beautiful just as they are.

easy living
trestle
swing

Swings suspended from freestanding trestles were very popular with the Victorian gentry, and they're popular again today because of their versatility. This project doesn't require a porch or tree for hanging, only a flat area to stand on. The gently curved seat and back are very comfortable, and its size makes it a cozy swing for two.

INSTRUCTIONS

Building the Seat

1 Use the grid pattern shown in figure 1 to enlarge full-size templates for the curved back supports (A) and seat supports (B). Draw the templates on stiff cardboard or thin plywood, and cut them out with scissors or with a jigsaw depending on the material. Use the templates to trace the three back supports (A) and the three seat supports (B) onto your stock. Then saw out the curved pieces with a jigsaw.

2 Cut the half-lap joints on the back supports (A) and seat supports (B), as shown in figure 2, page 378. Each piece has a tongue that's half the thickness of the wood. Lay out the joints and cut them with a handsaw or on the table saw. Test-fit the pieces, adjusting the depth of cut if necessary.

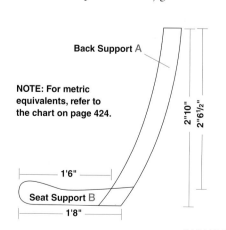

Back Support A

NOTE: For metric equivalents, refer to the chart on page 424.

2"10"
2"6½"

1'6"

Seat Support B

1'8"

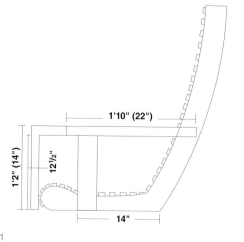

1'10" (22")

1'2" (14")

12½"

14"

FIGURE 1

TOOLS

Tape measure

Scissors

Small compass

Rafter angle square
    (speed square)

Handsaw

Jigsaw

Circular saw with rip guide

Table saw (optional)

Power drill with #8 pilot drill bit
    and #8 countersink

¼-inch drill bit; ¾-inch
    and ⅞-inch spade bits

C-clamps

Bar-style clamps in assorted
    lengths from 30 to 36 inches

Scrap wood blocks

Palm or random-orbit sander

MATERIALS

88 linear feet 1 x 2 cedar

4 linear feet 1 x 4 cedar

6 linear feet 2 x 4 cedar

6 linear feet 2 x 6 cedar

12 linear feet 2 x 8 cedar

42 linear feet 6 x 6 cedar

HARDWARE AND SUPPLIES

Thin plywood or stiff cardboard
    to make templates

100 #8 x 1½-inch wood screws

12 #8 x 2½-inch wood screws

28 #8 x 3-inch wood screws

2 screw eyes, ⅜ x 1½-inches

2 screw eyes, ⅜ x 2½-inches

2 screw eyes, ½ x 3-inches

4 lag bolts, ½ x 5-inches

8 lag bolts, ½ x 8-inches

4 S-hooks, 1½ inches

2 lengths of ⅛-inch chain,
    each 6 feet long

150-grit sandpaper

Rags

Exterior wood stain

Paintbrush

A helpful friend

3 Fit one half-lap joint together, making sure the shoulders are tight, then clamp the back and seat supports to the work surface. Countersink and drill five pilot holes for #8 x 1½-inch screws through the back support (A) and into the seat support (B), spacing the holes evenly across the lap joint. Secure the joint with five screws, and set the seat assembly aside.

4 Assemble two more seat assemblies from the two remaining back supports (A) and seat supports (B), following step 3.

5 Cut the four seat rails (C) to length.

6 Now secure the seat rails (C) to the seat assemblies. Working with the first assembly, align two seat rails (C) with the bottom edge of the seat support (B), one at the rear and one at the front as shown in figure 2. Clamp the rails to the supports, and countersink and drill two pilot holes for #8 x 3-inch screws through the seat support and into the end of each rail. Space the holes approximately ¾ inch from the top and bottom edges of the rails. Secure the rails to the supports with two screws at each joint.

7 Repeat step 6 to attach the remaining two seat rails to another seat assembly.

You should now have two seat assemblies, with two seat rails attached to each, and one seat assembly with no rails.

8 With your friend's help, stand the two seat assemblies that have rails upright on the work surface, pointing the rails toward each other. Position the remaining seat assembly between the rails, and lightly clamp all three assemblies together. Adjust the rails on the middle seat assembly as needed, and tighten the clamps. Countersink and drill two pilot holes for 3-inch screws through each side of the middle seat assembly and into the ends of each rail. You'll need to toe-nail the holes by drilling at an angle since the rails are directly opposite each other. Secure the rails by driving screws through the seat assembly and into the ends of the rails.

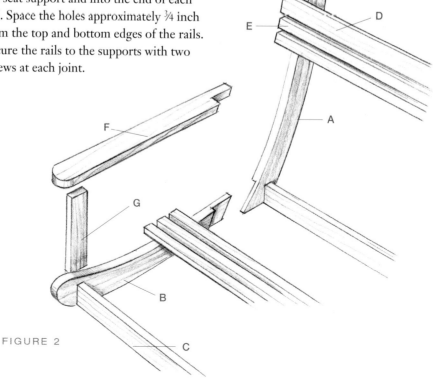

FIGURE 2

Adding the Seat Slats

9 Cut all the seat slats (E), including the top slat (D), to length. Before you assemble the slats, smooth and round over any sharp edges with 150-grit sandpaper and a pad sander.

10 Place the top slat (D) in line with the tops of the back supports (A) and even with their outside faces, and clamp it in place. Countersink and drill two pilot holes through each end and in the middle of the slat for 1½-inch screws, centering the holes over the back supports. Then secure the top slat (D) to the back supports, using a total of six screws.

11 Now you can add the seat slats (E), starting below the top slat (D). To create even gaps between all the slats, position three ¾-inch-thick scrap spacer blocks between the top slat and the first seat slat, placing a spacer over each seat assembly. Align the seat slat so its ends are even with the back supports (A) and with the top slat (D) above. Clamp the slat in place, or have your friend hold it steady while you countersink and drill one pilot hole for a 1½-inch screw through the slat and into each seat support. Screw the seat slat (E) to the back supports, using a total of three screws.

12 Repeat step 11 to attach all of the seat slats (E) to the back and seat supports (A and B) of the swing.

Making and Attaching the Arms

13 Cut out the two arms (F) and the two arm supports (G). Lay out the 1¾-inch radius on the ends of the arms with a compass, then cut the curves by sawing to the lines with a jigsaw.

14 Square a line across the bottom face of one arm (F), 2 inches back from its curved front edge. Clamp one arm support (G) to the arm so that its face is flush with the inner edge of the arm and one edge of the support is on the line you just marked. Countersink and drill two pilot holes for 3-inch screws through the arm and into the arm support, and screw the support to the arm.

15 Repeat step 14 to attach the other arm to its support.

CUTTING LIST

CODE	DESCRIPTION	QTY.	MATERIAL	DIMENSIONS
A	Back supports	3	2 x 8	1½" x 7¼" x 40" shape as per template
B	Seat supports	3	2 x 6	1½" x 5½" x 24" shape as per template
C	Seat rails	4	2 x 4	1½" x 3½" x 21¾"
D	Top slat	1	1 x 4	¾" x 3½" x 50"
E	Seat slats	22	1 x 2	¾" x 3½" x 50"
F	Arms	2	2 x 4	1½" x 3½" x 22"
G	Arm supports	9	2 x 4	1½" x 3½" x 12½"
H	Trestle legs	4	6 x 6	5½" x 5½" x 84" from long point to long point of miters
I	Side rails	2	6 x 6	5½" x 5½" x 36" from long point to long point of miters
J	Corner braces	2	6 x 6	5½" x 5½" x 11" from long point to long point of miters
K	Top beam	1	6 x 6	5½" x 5½" x 72"

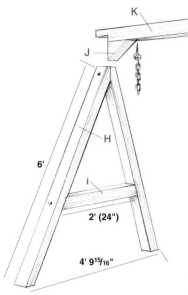

K

J

H

6'

I

2' (24")

4' 9¹⁵⁄₁₆"

FIGURE 3

16 Position one arm assembly against one end of the swing. Check that the back of the arm is flush with the back edge of the back support (A), and that the bottom of the arm support (G) is flush with the bottom of the seat support (B). Clamp the assembly in place, and countersink and drill two pilot holes from the inside face of the back support (A) and into the arm (F). Center the holes in the arm, and secure it to the back support with two 2½-inch screws. Similarly, attach the arm support (G) at the front of the assembly by countersinking and drilling four pilot holes from the inside face of the seat support (B) and into the arm support. Secure the support with four 2½-inch screws.

17 Repeat step 16 to attach the remaining arm assembly to the opposite side of the swing.

18 With the swing constructed, you can install the hanging hardware. Drill two ¾-inch holes through each arm (F) with a spade bit for the hanging chain to pass through. Locate the first hole 3 inches in from the back of each arm and centered on its width. Drill the second hole toward the front of the arm, centered widthwise and directly adjacent to the arm support.

19 Install one ⅜ x 1½-inch screw eye into each outer back support (A), and one ⅜ x 2½-inch screw eye through each arm support (G) and into each outer seat support (B). Drill a ¼-inch pilot hole for each screw, locating the holes 2 inches from the bottom of the arm supports and back supports and centered on their width.

Building the Trestle

20 With the swing complete, you're ready to tackle the trestle. Cut out the four trestle legs (H), the two side rails (I), and the two corner braces (J). Using the rafter angle square and circular saw, mark and cut the legs (H) with a 70° miter on the top ends, and a 20° miter on the bottom ends. Make sure the miters oppose each other so that the long points of the miters are on the same face of the beam. Mark and cut 20° opposing miters on each end of the side rails (I). Clamp the brace stock (J) to a work surface, then mark and cut 20° opposing miters on each end. The top face of each brace should come to a point. Set the corner braces (J) aside for now.

21 Position two trestle legs (H) on the floor with their top miters touching. Then place one side rail (I) between the legs roughly halfway down their length, or until the miters of the rail fit snug between the legs. Check that the rail is level and square with the legs by measuring up from the bottom of each leg. Clamp the miter joint at the top of the legs and clamp the rail between the legs.

22 Drill one ⅜-inch pilot hole through each leg (H) and into the ends of the side rail (I), and one hole through one leg at the top miter joint and into the opposite leg. Drill the holes in the legs and rails about 8 inches deep. Drill the holes in the miter joints at the top of the legs 5 inches deep. When drilling for the side rail, angle the bit to the leg so the holes are parallel to the rail. Center the holes on the width of the leg and rail, and center the holes over the joint at the top of the legs. Join the mitered legs (H) with a 5-inch lag bolt, and secure the side rail (I) to the legs with two 8-inch lag bolts. Remove the clamps.

23 Repeat step 21 to assemble the remaining two legs (H) and rail (I) into a second A-frame unit.

24 Cut the top beam (K) to length. On both ends of the beam, mark a line across the bottom face 5½ inches in from the end, and mark another line across the end itself 2¾ inches from the top face. Cut to your marked lines with a handsaw or circular saw to form a rabbet 2¾ inches deep x 5½ inches long at each end of the beam.

25 Going back to the A-frame assemblies, measure about 7 inches down from the top of each miter joint, and square a line around the legs. The line should be 5½ inches wide, or the width of the top beam (K), on the inside and outside faces of the A-frame. Cut to your layout lines with a circular saw and remove the waste to create a flat area at the top of the A-frames for the top beam (K).

26 Enlisting your friend's help once again, stand the two A-frames upright at their intended resting spot, and place the top beam (K) across the frames. Make sure the shoulders of the rabbets you cut in the beam are snug to the inside faces of the frames. At each end of the beam, drill a ⅜-inch pilot hole through the top of the beam and into the leg assembly, centered on the miter joint. Secure the beam to the top of the trestle with a 5-inch bolt at each end.

27 Stiffen the trestle to prevent racking by adding the two corner braces (J). Position each brace inside the frame between the top beam (K) and the miter joint at the top of the A-frame, and clamp it in place. Drill a ⅜-inch pilot hole through each end of the brace and into the beam and frame, angling the bit as you drill. Drill the holes about 8 inches deep, then secure each brace to the beam and frame with two 8-inch lag bolts.

28 Now install the hanging hardware on the trestle. On the bottom face of the top beam (K), measure 12 inches in from both ends, and drill a ⅜-inch pilot hole centered on the beam's width. Install a 3-inch screw eye into each hole at each end of the beam.

29 Using two lengths of chain and four S-hooks, hang the swing from the trestle. Use the S-hooks to attach the chain to the screw eyes in both the trestle and the swing. Be sure to pass the chain through the holes in the arms (F) of the swing before attaching it to the screw eyes. Adjust the length of the chain to provide a comfortable sitting and swinging height. Sixteen to 18 inches from the seat to the ground is optimum.

30 Finish the trestle swing by sanding all the parts smooth and rounding over any sharp edges. Then wipe off any dust with a dampened rag, and paint the swing with an exterior wood stain in the color of your choice.

eat and run
convertible
and picnic table
bench

IF you enjoy sitting in a favorite outdoor spot for contemplation, and you love spur-of-the-moment picnics, here's just the project to combine the two activities. You can transform this comfortable bench into a picnic table and seat then back again in less than a minute.

DESIGNER
Alan Michael Hester

INSTRUCTIONS

Making the Base Assembly

1 Dimension the pieces as specified on the cutting list, using the chop saw or the radial-arm saw. Cut complementary 10° miters on both ends of the front and back legs (A and B) and on both ends of the crosspieces (C). The miters give the front and back legs a slight angle for stability and also allow the seat and tabletop to lie flat when you assemble the project.

2 Notch the back legs (B) to receive the back support (D), as shown in figure 1, page 385. Lay out the 3½ x 1½-inch-notch, 5 inches from the short point of the miter at the top of each back leg (B). Use a square to mark the notch, then cut to your layout lines with a jigsaw or on the band saw.

3 Before assembling the base, drill the back legs (B) for the bolts that will connect them to the top supports (F). Locate the hole in each back leg as shown in figure 1, centering the hole widthwise and 3¾ inches from the top of the leg. Drill a ⁵⁄₁₆-inch hole though each leg.

4 Now you'll assemble the legs to the crosspieces (C). Because you're working with mitered pieces, be careful when assembling the legs. The right and left leg assemblies don't "match." They're mirror images of each other.

For the first assembly, lay a back leg (B) and front leg (A) in front of you. Lay the front leg on top of the back leg, with their bottom ends flush, and mark a line onto the back leg by tracing the miter at the top of

TOOLS

Chop saw or radial-arm saw

Jigsaw or band saw

C-clamps

Power drill with ⁵⁄₁₆-inch and ³⁄₈-inch drill bits, and Phillips #2 driver bit

#8 countersink and #8 pilot bit

Socket wrench with ⁷⁄₁₆-inch and ½-inch sockets, or adjustable wrench

Tape measure

Small square

MATERIALS

17 linear feet 2 x 4 western red cedar

30 linear feet 2 x 6 western red cedar

3 linear feet 2 x 8 western red cedar

HARDWARE AND SUPPLIES

24 deck screws, #8 x 2½ inches

8 carriage bolts, ⁵⁄₁₆ x 3½ inches with nuts and washers

2 hex bolts, ⁵⁄₁₆ x 3½ inches with nuts and washers

2 eyebolts, ³⁄₈ x 4 inches

CUTTING LIST

CODE	DESCRIPTION	QTY.	MATERIAL	DIMENSIONS
A	Front legs	2	2 x 4	1½" x 3½" x 17" from long point to short point of 10° miter
B	Back legs	2	2 x 4	1½" x 3½" x 29" from long point to short point of 10° miter
C	Crosspieces	2	2 x 4	1½" x 3½" x 25" from long point to short point of 10° miter
D	Back support	1	2 x 4	1½" x 3½" x 53"
E	Seat slats	2	2 x 6	1½" x 5½" x 72"
F	Top support	2	2 x 8	1½" x 7¼" x 16"
G	Tabletop/ back slats	3	2 x 6	1½" x 5½" x 72"
H	Stop blocks	2	2 x 4 scrap	1½" x 3½" x 3" from long point of 10° miter

the front leg. Then lay a crosspiece (C) on top of the legs, with its top edge flush to the top of the front leg and even with the line you marked on the back leg. The 10° miter at the rear of the crosspiece should align with the rear edge of the back leg, while the short point of the miter at the front of the crosspiece is flush with the outer edge of the front leg. Clamp the assembly.

5 Mark the crosspiece for the carriage bolt holes. With the assembly still clamped, drill a pair of ⁵⁄₁₆-inch holes at each joint, drilling through the crosspiece and leg. Insert a carriage bolt into each hole, and tighten the nut on the inside of the leg with a wrench.

6 Repeat steps 4 and 5 to construct the second leg assembly, making sure you have the mitered pieces in the correct relationship to each other.

7 Now join the two leg assemblies to the back support (D). Fit the back support into the notches in the two leg assemblies, ensuring that the ends of the support are flush with the outer edges of the assemblies. Countersink and drill pilot holes for two #8 x 2½ inch screws through each end of the back piece (D) and into the leg assembly, centering the holes on the thickness of the legs. Use the drill and the Phillips driver bit to sink the screws flush with the face of the support.

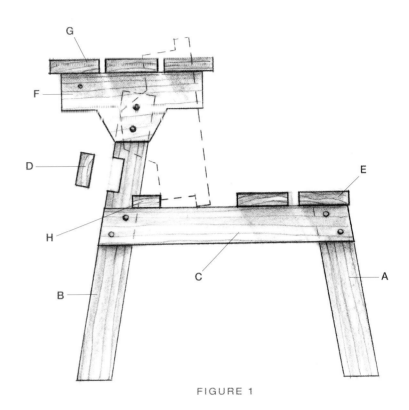

FIGURE 1

Building the Seat and Top Supports

8 You're ready to attach the two seat slats (E) to the base assembly. Position the outer edge of the front seat slat (E) on top of the crosspieces and flush with the long point of the miter on the front legs (A). Position the second seat slat (E) next to the first slat, keeping a 1-inch gap between the two slats. Make sure the slats are centered lengthwise on the base assembly, with an 8-inch overhang on the ends. Drill and countersink as before, driving two screws per joint through the slats and into the crosspieces below.

9 Now you'll make the top supports (F). Lay out the cut lines on each support blank. On each end of the blank, square a line 3½ inches below the top edge, and make a mark 4 inches in on the line. Then find the center lengthwise of the blank, and mark 2 inches on either side of center at the blank's bottom edge. Connect these points to the 4-inch marks above using a ruler. Once you've laid out the blanks, use a jigsaw or the band saw to cut the supports to final shape.

10 Drill a 5/16-inch hole through each top support (F). Center the hole lengthwise on the support, and 2 inches up from the bottom edge.

Attaching the Tabletop/Back

11 Now you'll create the top assembly. Attach the three tabletop/back slats (G) to the top supports (F) as shown in figure 1. Working with the slats upside down on the bench, position the two outer slats so they overhang the supports by 1 inch and leave ¾-inch gaps between individual boards. Check that the overhang on both ends of the slats is 8 inches so that the tabletop slats (G) will line up with the seat pieces (E). Clamp the slats to the supports. Then flip the assembly right-side up and countersink and drill pilot holes for #8 x 2½-inch screws as you did on the seat slats. Secure the tabletop slats to the top supports using two screws per joint.

12 Slip the top assembly over the base assembly. Match up the holes in the back legs with the holes you drilled in the top supports, and insert a 5/16-inch hex bolt and washer through each hole. Tighten the nuts on the bolts with a wrench, but

don't overtighten. You'll want a little "play" so the bolts can pivot when you raise the tabletop or lower it into its bench seating position.

13 Pivot the tabletop into its horizontal position, and clamp the top supports to the back legs to steady the tabletop. If necessary, use a level to check the top for level. Then drill a ⅜-inch hole through each top support and leg assembly. You can judge the hole location by eye, drilling it approximately 2 inches above the pivot bolt. Insert the ⅜ x 4-inch eyebolts through the holes to hold the table firm.

14 Remove the eyebolts and pivot the tabletop down to its alternate position as the bench back. To register the back at a comfortable angle for sitting, add the stop blocks (H) on the crosspieces behind the back. Holding the back in position, clamp the stop blocks so they butt against the back, then pivot the back up and secure it with the eyebolts so it's out of the way. Now screw each block, using two screws per block, to its corresponding crosspiece, countersinking and drilling pilot holes at a slight angle through the block.

15 Finally, you'll need to lock the bench back. First, pivot the tabletop into the bench back position. Working from the inside of each back leg, use a ⅜-inch bit to drill through the back of each existing hole in the legs and through the top support to create a new, matching hole in the top support. When you have the tabletop set up in its alternate bench back position, put the eyebolts through the legs and top supports to secure the back. This also gives you a handy place to keep the bolt when it's not in use!

extra-comfy
loveseat

DESIGNER
George Harrison

When you sit in your new loveseat, you'll understand why we think this may be one of the most comfortable garden seats ever crafted. Its lines are inspired by classic Adirondack design, but the difference in comfort is remarkable! The secret is in the templates you'll make and use to cut the contoured pieces of your loveseat.

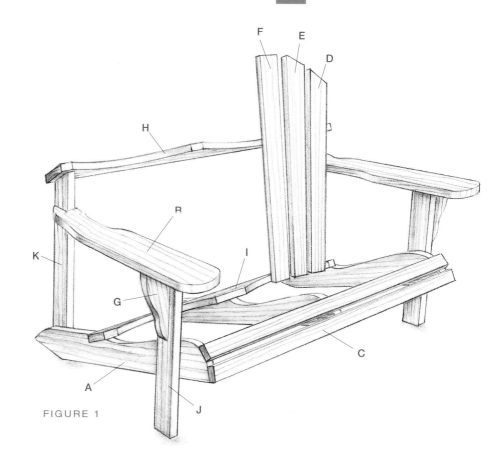

FIGURE 1

TOOLS

Band saw or jigsaw

Power drill with #8 pilot drill bit, #8 countersink, and ⅛-inch drill bit

Table saw or circular saw with rip guide

Router with ¼-inch roundover bit

C-clamps

Rasp

Measuring tape

Small square

Bevel gauge

Awl

Scrap wood blocks

150-grit sandpaper

MATERIALS

48 linear feet of 1-inch-thick x 5½-inch-wide cypress or pressure-treated lumber

HARDWARE AND SUPPLIES

½ sheet (4 x 4 feet) of thin scrap plywood, or stiff cardboard

1 pound #8 x 2-inch deck screws

Water sealer or paint (optional)

Paintbrush (optional)

INSTRUCTIONS

Cutting Out the Chair Parts

1 All of the chair pieces are made using templates, except for the seat slats (C), which you can cut to size on the table saw or with a circular saw. The angles and subtle curves are the key to the loveseat's comfort. If you take your time making the templates, they'll faithfully duplicate the contoured shapes of the chair parts. Enlarge the templates shown on pages 391 and 392 on grid paper, and trace the shapes onto stiff cardboard or thin plywood. Make sure to mark the pilot holes where indicated.

Cut the templates by carefully sawing to your lines with a jigsaw or on the band saw, then fair and smooth the curves with a rasp and 150-grit sandpaper. Drill ⅛-inch holes through the templates at each pilot hole location.

2 Once you've made the templates, lay them on your stock and trace around them. Use an awl to transfer the pilot hole locations onto the stock. Cut out each piece with the jigsaw or on the band saw, cutting up to your traced lines.

3 Countersink and drill all the pilot holes through the chair pieces, except for the back slats (D, E, and F). On these slats, countersink and drill pilot holes only through the lower holes; you'll drill the upper holes later. Be sure to countersink and drill three pilot holes in each seat slat (C), one centered on the slat's length and two holes ½ inch in from each end.

4 To ease the sharp edges of the chair, use the router with the ¼-inch roundover bit. Rout all the edges, or arris, except for those areas where joints will meet. Leave these areas sharp and crisp.

Assembling the Chair Frame

A note about the joinery before you begin assembly: All the joints in this chair are screwed together. You can install the screws much more easily and prevent splitting by boring ⅛-inch pilot holes for the screws in the stock. Once you've aligned the two parts that form a joint, use the ⅛-inch bit to drill through your previously countersunk pilot holes in the first part and into the second, mating piece.

5 On each seat support (A), make a mark 5¾ inches in from the front at the bottom face of the leg. Make another mark at the back of the leg, 2 inches in from the back, as shown. You'll use these marks to align the front and back legs (J and K).

6 Using the straight front edge of your workbench or a straight board as a gauge, position one front leg (J) over one seat support (A), aligning the bottom of the leg and the flat area on the seat sup-

port with the straight edge. Position the front leg with the mark you made on the seat support in step 1. Set a bevel gauge to 60°, and use the gauge to position the leg at the correct angle relative to the seat support. Clamp in place. Screw the front leg to the seat support with two #8 x 2-inch deck screws. Repeat the process with the second front leg and another seat support, this time arranging the pieces as a mirror image of the first assembly. These assemblies will be used on the right and left sides of the loveseat.

7 Join the right and left sides with the lower back support (I), screwing the support into the notches at the tops of the seat supports (A).

CUTTING LIST

CODE	DESCRIPTION	QTY.	MATERIAL AND DIMENSIONS
A	Seat supports	3	1" x 5½" x 37", shape as per template
B	Arms	2	1" x 5½" x 31", shape as per template
C	Seat slats	9	1" x 1½" x 42"
D	Back slats	4	1" x 5½" x 30", shape as per template
E	Back slats	4	1" x 5½" x 31½", shape as per template
F	Back slats	4	1" x 5½" x 31½", shape as per template
G	Arm brackets	2	1" x 5½" x 7⅛", shape as per template
H	Upper back support	1	1" x 5½" x 41½", shape as per template
I	Lower back support	1	1" x 5½" x 42", shape as per template
J	Front legs	2	1" x 5½" x 20⅝", shape as per template
K	Back legs	2	1" x 5½" x 26", shape as per template

Attaching the Arms

10 Before you attach the arms (B), secure the arm brackets (G) to the front legs (J) to support them. Clamp the brackets flush with the tops of the legs, then screw through the legs and into the brackets, using two screws per bracket.

8 Add the remaining seat support (A) by slipping it under the lower back support, then screwing through the back support and into the seat support. If the middle seat support needs stabilizing, add one seat slat (C) at the front of the chair frame, locating it on top of the three seat supports and flush with their bottom front ends.

9 With the chair assembly on a flat surface, such as a benchtop or the floor, use a square to position the back legs (K) square to each seat support (A). Align the legs to the marks you made in step 1. Clamp the legs, then screw them to the supports.

11 Position the arms (B) on top of the brackets (G), making sure the notch in the back of each arm fits snugly against the back leg (K). Trim the notch if necessary. At the front of the chair, screw each arm (B) into the top of its corresponding arm bracket (G) and front leg (J). Then level each arm by measuring the distance of the arm to the floor at the front of the chair, and use that measurement to adjust the back of the arm relative to the back leg (K). Once the arms are level, screw through the back legs and into the arms to secure them.

Extra-Comfy Loveseat Templates

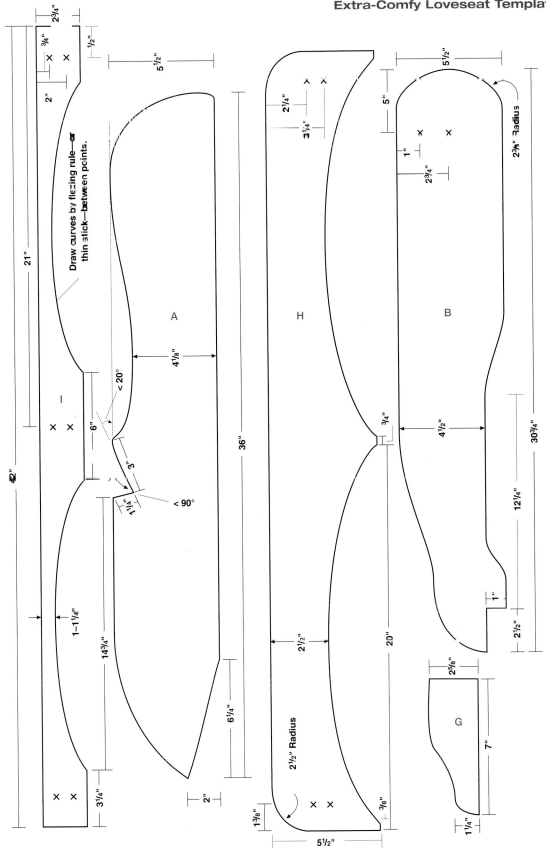

NOTE: For metric equivalents, refer to chart on page 424. Templates are not to scale.

Extra-Comfy Loveseat Templates

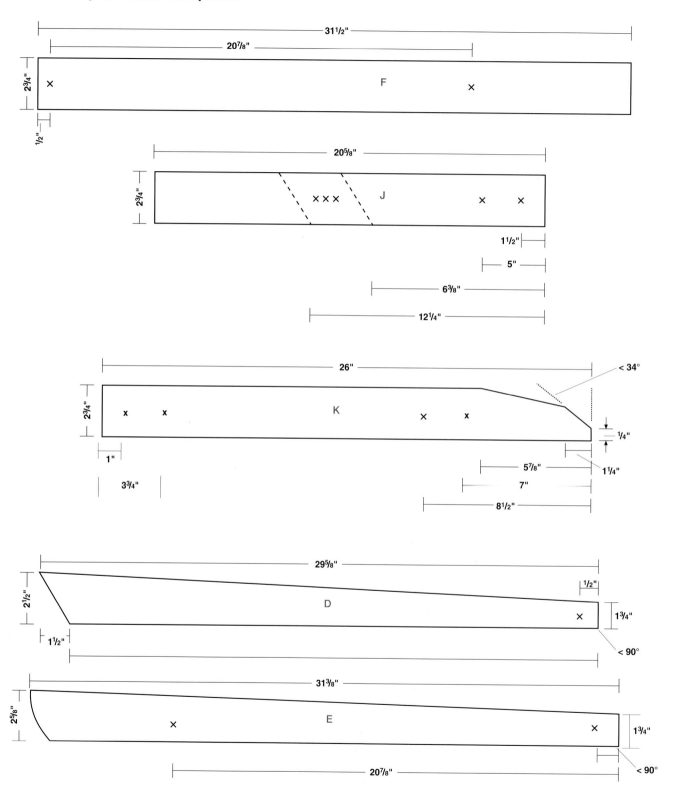

NOTE: **For metric equivalents, refer to chart on page 424. Templates are not to scale.**

low country
joggle
bench

Some folks in the American South say the first bench of this type was built by a man in the 1800s for his elderly mother, who had arthritis and needed a little "bounce" to stand up from a seated position! Simple to build and fun to use, the long seat flexes when you sit on it. You can gently bounce up and down, or rock back and forth on the curved feet.

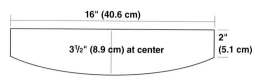

16" (40.6 cm)

3½" (8.9 cm) at center

2" (5.1 cm)

FIGURE 1

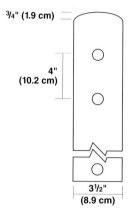

¾" (1.9 cm)

4" (10.2 cm)

3½" (8.9 cm)

FIGURE 2

INSTRUCTIONS

Note: You can make the bench shorter if desired by decreasing the length of the seat (F). The longer the bench is, the more it will tend to "joggle" or bounce in use.

Making the Leg Assemblies

1 Cut out the four feet (A), four legs (B), and eight braces (C).

2 Set the base of the circular saw to a 45° angle and use it to miter both ends of each brace (C).

3 Referring to the dimensions in figures 1 and 2, lay out the curves at the bottom of the feet (A) and the gentle arches at the top of the legs (B). Use the scrap stick to generate the curves, or use the length of string with the pencil tied at one end to draw the radius. Saw to the layout lines with the jigsaw; cut from both sides of the stock if necessary. Use the spokeshave or 150-grit sandpaper to smooth and fair the curves; smooth, bump-free curves on the feet will give a smoother rocking motion.

4 Lay out the three dowel hole locations in each leg (B) as shown in figure 2. Drill the holes with a 1¼-inch spade bit, using the scrap block beneath the work to prevent tearout. Place a small square on the work as a guide to help you drill the holes square to the surface.

TOOLS

Circular saw

Jigsaw

Small square

Tape measure

Spokeshave or block plane

Power drill with Phillips #2 driver bit; #8 countersink and pilot bit; ⅜-inch, ¼-inch, ³⁄₁₆-inch drill bits; 1¼-inch, 1-inch, ¾-inch spade bits

Bar-style clamps, 30 inches

Hammer

Paintbrush

MATERIALS

1	1 x 2 fir, 8 feet long
1	5/4 x 12 fir, 10 feet long
2	4 x 4 fir, 8 feet long
2	1¼ inch dowel (fir/pine), 6 feet long
1	¼ inch dowel (fir/pine), 2 feet long

HARDWARE AND SUPPLIES

Scrap stick, ⅛-inch thick x 2 feet long, or nylon string (optional)

Pencil

150-grit sandpaper

Scrap wood block

Masking tape

12 lag screws, ⅜ x 7 inches with washers

16 deck screws, #8 x 1½ inches

4 deck screws, #8 x 2½ inches

Exterior-grade stain, oil-based enamel paint, or latex enamel paint

5 Make a centermark lengthwise on one side of one foot (A), and a corresponding centermark widthwise on the bottom side of one leg (B). Align the centermarks so the foot is centered on the leg, and clamp the foot and leg together.

6 Drill two ¾-inch counterbored holes in the bottom of the foot (A) in line with the leg (B). Drill the holes about ⅜ inch deep, or deep enough to allow the head of a lag screw and a washer to recess into the foot. Then drill a ⅜-inch clearance hole into each counterbored hole, drilling through the foot (A) and ⅛ inch into the leg (B). Wrap a flag of masking tape around the bit to indicate the correct drilling depth.

7 Remove the clamp and the foot, and drill two ³⁄₁₆-inch pilot holes into the end of the leg (B), using the shallow ⅜-inch holes to locate the bit. Drill the holes about 3 inches deep.

8 Attach the foot (A) to the leg (B) with two ⅜ x 7-inch lag screws and washers. Be sure that the heads of the lag screws don't protrude past the bottom face of the foot.

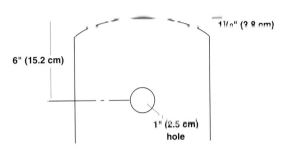

6" (15.2 cm)   1¹⁄₈" (2.8 cm)

1" (2.5 cm) hole

FIGURE 3

9 Position the two braces (C) on the leg assembly, with their corresponding miters snug against the foot (A) and the leg (B). Use the countersink and pilot bit to drill holes for screws. Secure each brace to the foot and the leg by driving a 1½-inch screw through each mitered end.

10 Repeat steps 5 through 9 to construct three more leg assemblies.

CUTTING LIST			
CODE	DESCRIPTION	QTY.	DIMENSIONS
A	Feet	4	3½" x 3½" x 16"
B	Legs	4	3½" x 3½" x 19"
C	Braces	8	¾" x 1½" x 8" from long point to long point of 45° miters
D	Dowels	6	1¼" x 21"
E	Dowel pins	12	¼" x 2"
F	Seat	1	1⅛" x 11¼" x 10'
G	Seat pin	2	1¼" x 6"

Assembling the Bench

11 Cut the six dowels (D) and the 12 pins (E) to length.

12 On each dowel (D), measure in ⅞ inch from each end, and drill ¼ inch holes through the dowel. Keep the holes parallel with each dowel by clamping the stock on top of a scrap board, then eyeball a square placed near the dowel as you drill through the dowel and into the scrap.

13 Stand two leg assemblies upright and approximately 12 inches apart, and insert a dowel (D) through each of the three holes in the legs (B). Let the dowels protrude about 1 inch beyond each leg. Now tap a pin (E) through each of the holes in the dowels with the hammer to lock the dowels in place. Align the dowels so the pins are level or parallel with the

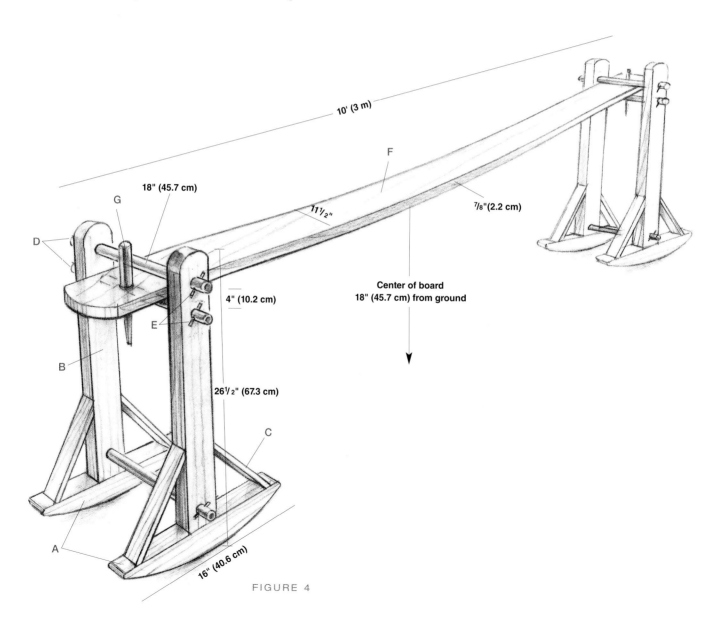

10' (3 m)

F

18" (45.7 cm)

G

11½"

⅞"(2.2 cm)

D

4" (10.2 cm)

E

Center of board
18" (45.7 cm) from ground

B

26½" (67.3 cm)

C

A

16" (40.6 cm)

FIGURE 4

floor. To further strengthen the bottom dowel, drive a 2½-inch screw through each leg and into the dowel, toe-nailing at an angle through the leg and into the dowel. Repeat the assembly procedure with the remaining leg assemblies, dowels, pins and screws to make the second seat support.

14 Lay out and saw the curved ends on the seat (F) as shown in figure 3. Refer to figure 3 to locate the hole in each end of the bench, then use the 1-inch spade bit to drill the holes while using a backing block of scrap to prevent tearout.

15 Cut the two seat pins (G) to length. Use the block plane or spokeshave to taper the pins from 1¼ inch diameter at one end to ¾ inch at the opposite end. Use your fingers and eye to judge that the pins are round, then remove any tool marks and smooth them with 150-grit sandpaper.

16 As shown in figure 4, place the two bench supports about 9 feet apart on the floor. Slide one end of the seat (F) between the top two dowels (D) of one support, until the hole in the seat is just past the dowels. Tap a seat pin (G) firmly into the hole in the seat. The dowel should extend roughly 2½ inches above the top of the seat.

17 Slide the free end of the seat (F) between the dowels (D) on the second support. Secure the seat in the same manner as before, driving the remaining seat pin (G) into the hole in the seat. With the seat in place, test its bounciness!

18 It's easier to apply a finish to the bench if you separate the assemblies. Remove the two seat pins to free the seat and the seat supports, and sand off any sharp edges or roughness. Wipe clean, and brush on the paint or stain. Let dry.

metal

You don't have to be a working black-smith with a forge to make metal garden furniture. With the right tools, you can easily work with recycled metal scrap, off-the-shelf materials, or prefabricated metal components such as the scrollwork that you'll trim and weld to make the Elegant Iron Chaise Lounge on page 407.

Simply put, metal is either ferrous (it has iron in it), or nonferrous (it doesn't have iron in it). Steel is iron with extra carbon added. If sun heats it up, hose it down and cover it with a seat cushion. Metal is impervious to weather if you prime and paint it; touch up any corrosion annually with a rust-preventative paint, and scrub off moss with soap and water. You can also have metal powder-coated, an industrial process that bakes on the paint for a very durable finish. Check the phone book for suppliers.

Precision is very important in metal projects. Unlike wood, metal can't easily be shaved down that extra quarter of an inch, so remember to measure twice before you cut! On the other hand, if you cut too much off a piece of iron or steel, you can just reweld the pieces together, remove any excess welding material with a grinder, and cut again.

Just like lumber, iron and steel are sold in assorted stock lengths and sizes, although the shapes are more varied: ½-inch round rod, ½-inch square rod, ¼-inch flat bar, and 1-inch round tubing, for example. You buy metal by the linear foot, or by the piece if it's a prefabricated component. You can purchase iron and steel stock from local industrial suppliers and metal distributors. Prefabricated parts can be ordered by mail from ornamental iron suppliers. Many welding shops will gladly supply both stock and components.

You can do a great deal of metalwork with a vise and a hacksaw, but you can also simply take the parts for your project to a weld shop or metal fabricator for extensive cutting or welding.

OPPOSITE PAGE TOP: **Forged steel bench painted with interior latex paint so it would rust and acquire an "aged" patina. Hays Cash Design, 1999.**
PHOTO BY REED PHOTOGRAPHY

LOWER LEFT: **Nancy Owens, *Fire Escape Bench*, dimensions various; steel; cut, welded, painted.**
NANCY OWENS, LANDSCAPE ARCHITECT, NEW YORK, NY

painting and sealing metal

Metal is a beautiful material in itself. You may simply want to knock off the larger pieces of rust with a wire brush, then put a coat of sealer on to arrest the oxidation process.

Before painting metal, it's important to prepare the surface. Remove every bit of rust with a wire brush and sanding blocks, then clean the surface with soap and water. If the surface has a lacquered finish (if you can remove flakes with the straight edge of a razor blade, it's there), sand off the lacquer with fine steel wool dipped in denatured alcohol. Clean again with soap and water, then scouring powder, and finish by wiping it down with denatured alcohol or another solvent. The repeated sanding and scouring may seem like overkill, but these processes create tooth on the surface that will grab and hold the paint better.

Paint the dry metal with rust-inhibiting metal primer, and let it dry. Brush on exterior-grade paint. The primer and paint must be chemically compatible, either oil-based or acrylic (water) based. Acrylic is easier to clean up, but oil-based paint provides better, more durable protection. After the final coat of paint dries, brush or spray on a couple of coats of clear sealer for more protection against the elements.

You can use artist's brushes to paint freehand designs on the surface, or use stencils. Buy a stencil brush and ready-made stencils at craft stores, or make the stencils yourself. Try tracing leaves from plants in your garden onto a piece of thin cardboard, acetate, or blank stencil material, then cut away the inside with a craft knife. Lay the stencil on the metal surface and spray, sponge, or brush on paint. You can also use leaves or other objects as "reverse stencils," laying them on the surface and spraying around the perimeter, leaving a pretty ghost image. Let dry, and finish with clear sealer.

Cynthia Wynn, *Harriet Zoom*, 1996, 36 x 26 x 29 in. (91 x 66 x 73.6 cm), **painted metal scrap; cut, welded.** PHOTO BY CHUCK PEARSON

floral
plaid
lawn
chair

DESIGNER
Jean Tomaso Moore

Down-home garden seating meets fine decorating in this wonderful chair! Easily applied acrylic paint, tape, and foam stamps reproduce a classic leaf-and-plaid pattern. With this project, you can renovate even the shabbiest metal lawn chair.

TOOLS AND SUPPLIES

Wire brush

Sandpaper

Rag

Ruler or tape measure

Pencil

Carpenter's square

Foam brushes in assorted sizes

Foam stamps in maple leaf and fern designs

MATERIALS

Metal lawn chair

Rust-resistant acrylic spray primer

Acrylic spray paint in light yellow, olive green, and khaki

Acrylic craft paint in several shades of green, including teal and forest

1 roll each of painter's tape in 1- and 2-inch widths

Clear acrylic spray sealer

INSTRUCTIONS

1 Prepare the surface of the chair by using the wire brush to remove all rust and loose paint. Sand down the chair to create as smooth a finish as possible, then dampen the rag and wipe away surface debris.

2 Following the directions on the can, spray on several coats of the primer and allow to dry.

3 Select one of the lighter shades from your color palette of acrylic spray paints, and spray on two coats to serve as the base color. (Yellow was used for the base coat of the chair pictured.) Let dry overnight.

4 With the ruler or tape measure, find the center point on the back of the chair. Use the carpenter's square to draw a vertical pencil line along the center of the entire chair, including the seat, back, and backside.

5 Apply the 2-inch painter's tape along the center of the pencil line, running a line of tape over the seat, the back, over the back, and down the backside of the chair. Press the tape firmly in place, being especially careful with the edges.

6 With the ruler, measure points approximately 2 inches on both sides of the tape. Following the points, use the carpenter's square and pencil to draw parallel lines on the chair. Apply the 2-inch tape along the center of the newly drawn lines.

7 Decide how you'll space the first set of horizontal lines. Their spacing doesn't have to be uniform, but use the ruler to keep the lines straight and square. Mark the lines in pencil, and put the 1-inch tape on top to form the horizontal pattern. Press the tape down firmly, ensuring the edges are secure.

8 Spray the chair with the khaki spray paint or another color of similar tone. Leave the tape in place and allow to dry.

9 With the original taping still on the chair (and masking the lightest color), tape the chair again both horizontally and vertically with 1-inch tape. Apply the tape in an alternative pattern. Place two to three strips of tape in each direction to create the initial plaid.

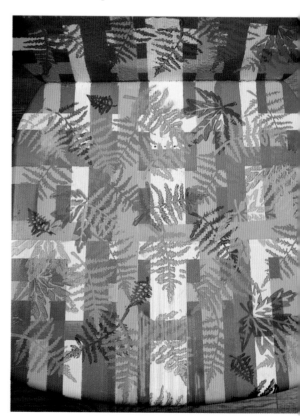

10 With the tape firmly in place, spray the chair with the third and darkest color, olive. While the paint is still wet, peel off the layers of tape one piece at a time to reveal the masked colors underneath. On this chair, the original taping masked the yellow, the second masked the khaki, and the top layer was the olive green.

11 To add additional colors to the plaid, apply more tape in vertical and horizontal patterns, and use the foam brushes to apply other shades of acrylic craft paints. Peel the tape off when the paint is still wet, but allow each color to dry before adding additional tapings.

12 When you're satisfied with your plaid design, use a small paint-brush to touch up any messy edges.

13 Use one of the foam brushes to apply the acrylic craft paints to the foam leaf and fern stamps. Layer leaf prints onto the chair in various shades of green and blue-green. Press the stamp firmly against the chair, and pull it cleanly away to prevent smearing.

14 When you've applied all the stamped images you desire and the paint has dried, spray on several coats of the clear acrylic spray to seal and protect the chair.

elegant iron chaise lounge

DESIGNERS
Doug Hays and Penny Cash

You don't have to be a master blacksmith to create this gorgeous lounge chair! Its fabulous flourishes and curlicues are actually ready-made scrollwork used for gates and railings, and you can buy them from ornamental iron suppliers. The other metal stock you need is easily found from the same sources, or through steel distributors. If you've never welded before, take the parts to a local welding shop.

INSTRUCTIONS

1 Lay out the pieces on the table or floor. Set aside the two "S" scrolls, which you'll cut apart later. Roughly arrange the scrolls as shown in figure 1, page 408. Prefabricated scrollwork often has slightly inconsistent dimensions, and you may have to bend it a little to make it fit.

2 Take the two "S" scrolls you put aside earlier, and fit them in the laid-out pieces. Use the marker to indicate where they need to be cut (see figure 2, page 408). Secure a scroll in the vise, cut it with the hacksaw, and add the piece to the layout. Repeat with the second scroll.

3 As shown in figure 1, the two pieces of ½-inch round stock that run the length of the lounge on both sides will form the support for the slats. In turn, the arrangement of the scrollwork determines the contour of the slat support. You'll make two bends in each support by hand, with the support anchored in the vise. You may also choose to have a local weld shop make the bends for you.

When you plan where you'll make the bends, the backrest should be at least 30 inches high to allow you to lean your head back and take a nap! A comfortable angle for reclining is 22 to 30°. Allow 19 to 21 inches of the seat to support your rear and thighs, and 26 inches for your lower legs. With these "comfort parameters" in mind, use the chalk to draw a line on your work surface along the top of the scrollwork. The line should touch most of the ironwork. Measure the length of the line by running the piece of string along it, then measure the string.

4 Secure a piece of the ½-inch round stock in the vise, and use the abrasive blade on the miter saw or the chop saw to cut it to the length of the string plus at least 12 more inches. Measure and mark where the first bend will be. When bending metal bar, it's best to bend in increments instead of one big effort, which is harder and may torque the metal. Clamp the round stock into the vise again, give it a slight bend, and check it against the scrollwork layout to make sure it's achiev-

TOOLS AND SUPPLIES

Large worktable or clear floor
area, 5 x 10 feet

Fine-tip permanent marker

Vise

Hacksaw

Piece of chalk

Piece of string, 8 feet long

Tape measure

Miter saw with abrasive blade,
or chop saw

Welding equipment (optional)

Paintbrush

Primer for steel, spray-on
or in a can

Exterior-grade paint for steel,
spray-on or in a can

MATERIALS

14 feet of ½-inch round,
hot-rolled, mild steel

31 feet of 2½ x ¼-inch flat,
hot-rolled, mild steel

6 pieces of metal scrollwork
with a curlicue on each
end, each piece 28³⁄₈ inches
long and 9⁷⁄₈ inches wide*

4 pieces of metal scrollwork
with a curlicue on each end
and in the middle section,
each piece 28³⁄₈ inches long
and 9⁷⁄₈ inches wide*

2 finials,* 3⁷⁄₈ inches tall

*You can mail-order scrollwork
and finials from metal fabricators and suppliers to architectural firms, or order
them through a local welding shop.

ing the necessary shape. If so, bend it a little bit more until it forms the desired angle. Make the second bend but don't trim the piece yet. Repeat with the second piece of ½-inch round stock. Lay out both pieces against the scrollwork, and mark where they need to be trimmed. Trim them with the power tool, or put them aside for the weld shop to cut.

5 Now you'll cut the slats from the 2½-inch x ¼-inch flat stock. The slats are 19 inches long and are spaced about 1 inch apart. In the photo, the last two slats following the scrollwork are 2 inches wide. Don't waste your time try-ing to cut the slats without power tools. Use the miter saw with the abrasive blade, or the chop saw, to cut them, or take the stock to a metal fabricator to be cut.

6 At this point, if you haven't welded before, take the parts to a local weld-ing shop. With the scrollwork still lying flat on the work surface or floor, tack-weld

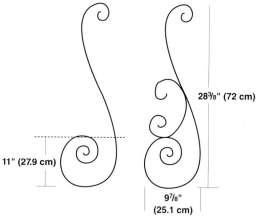

11" (27.9 cm)

28³⁄₈" (72 cm)

9⁷⁄₈"
(25.1 cm)

FIGURE 2

it together to form the two sides of the lounge. While everything is still flat, weld the side supports onto the scrollwork. Stand each side upright and temporarily brace them. Now you'll weld on the slats. Make sure the two sides are square, plumb, level, and the right distance apart, using a slat as a spacer. Weld the pieces together with permanent welds, starting at the bot-tom and working your way up.

7 Weld the two finials to the upper ends of the seat supports.

8 Paint the metal with the primer, pay-ing close attention to the nooks and crannies. Allow to dry, then paint with the exterior-grade metal paint.

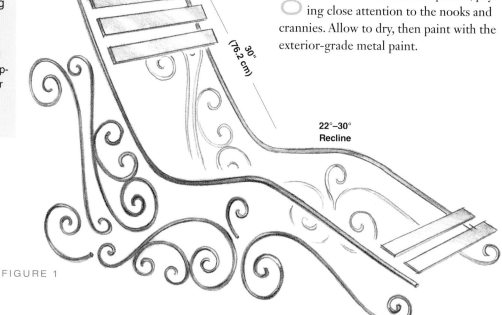

30"
(76.2 cm)

22°–30°
Recline

FIGURE 1

sparky, the three- legged chair

DESIGNER
Cynthia Wynn

This contemporary chair combines copper wire, rebar, and recycled roofing tin in an inventive design that doesn't require welding. Curled feet and elegant curves add graceful and whimsical elements, topped by spark plugs used as decorative accents!

TOOLS AND SUPPLIES

Safety glasses

Protective gloves

Tape measure

Fine-tip permanent marker

Bench vise

A helpful friend

Bolt cutters

Sharp utility knife

Small, handheld propane torch

Lighter or striker

Hammer

Chipping hammer

Cable cutters

Needle-nose pliers

Needle-nose vise grips

Regular vise grips

Large jaw vise grips

2 C-clamps, 3- to 6-inch size,
    depending on the width of
    your workbench

Piece of flat bar, 24 inches long

1-inch pipe, 3 feet long

Pipe bender

Hand punch or awl

Poster board

Scissors

Fast-drying spray paint

Tin snips, or a high-speed drill
    with a hummer wheel

Sandpaper or synthetic scouring pad

Rag

Solvent

Semigloss wood lacquer

Paintbrush

MATERIALS

6 lengths of #3 rebar, 10 feet each

Salvaged roofing tin, enough to make
    one 3 x 3 x 1½-foot triangle
    and one 1 x 1 x 1-foot triangle

48 feet large-gauge copper wire*

50 feet of 16-gauge copper wire

25 feet of 20-gauge copper wire

4 spark plugs

*Copper wire salvaged from 220 electrical
cable works perfectly.

INSTRUCTIONS

1 You should always wear safety glasses and protective gloves when working with metal or wire, so put them on. First, you'll create the decorative curls for the back and feet of the chair. The two back legs will have curls 5 inches in diameter, and the four legs will have curls 2½ inches in diameter. Cold-bending rebar into small shapes is challenging, and you'll find it helpful to have a friend to assist you with this step. Use the tape measure and marker to mark all six lengths of rebar at a point 4 feet, 5 inches from one end.

2 One at a time, clamp each length of rebar in the bench vise with the short end pointing down and the mark at the top of the vise jaws. Grip the long end of the bar close to the vise jaws and pull down, bending the bar into an approximate 45° angle as shown in figure 1.

3 Remove the bar from the vise, and reclamp its long end into the vise with the bottom of the V-shape pointing up. Pull the short end of the bar up until you have a curl like the one in figure 2.

4 Use the bolt cutters to trim the short end off the curl, cutting at a point about 3⁄4 inch before the crossover point.

5 Repeat the process of clamping and curling on the opposing end of the bar to make the second, duplicate curl for the back. As you bend the second curl, it's important to bend up on the opposite side of the long end of the bar, so that when the curl is trimmed and laid side by side with the other bar for the back, the curls match but the bars go out in opposite directions, as shown in figure 3.

6 Repeat steps 2 through 5 to make all four legs.

7 Have your friend help you with this stage. One by one, clamp the curl of each leg in the bench vise and simultaneously pull out and down, tightening the curl into a 2½-inch circle. At least two of the leg curls are mirror opposites, like the back curls.

8 Use the bolt cutters to trim off the short ends of the foot curls about 3⁄4 inch from the crossover points.

9 Salvage the wire from the 220 cable by using the cable cutters to cut the cable into twenty-four 2-foot sections. Slice the casing open with the knife to free the individual wires, then strip them of their insulation by slicing lengthwise with the knife.

10 Hammer both ends of the 24 pieces of wire to flatten them.

11 Large-gauge wire is stiff and difficult to bend, but you can anneal the wires, softening them by heating each one until it's red hot. Light the propane torch with the lighter, and use it to heat each wire. Allow the wires to cool. If the wire becomes work-hardened again as you work with it, anneal it again so it's malleable.

Making the Chair Frame Back

12 Now you'll make the back of the chair frame. Use the pipe bender to curve the two pieces of rebar intended for the back, starting at the curl and ending halfway down. Bend the two bars to match each other as shown in figure 4.

13 Use the annealed copper wire to lash together the two rebar curls. Put the flattened end of the wire between the curls, and clamp the curls together with the bench vise. Hammer the flat end of the wire that's sticking out so it wraps around the rebar.

14 Begin wrapping the wire around both pieces of the rebar, keeping tension on the wire with your hands or by clamping the needle-nose vise grips to the wire's end when possible. To ensure a tight lashing, pinch and twist the wire with the needle-nose pliers, and after each wrap, tap the wire into the space between the rebar with the chipping hammer.

FIGURE 1

FIGURE 2

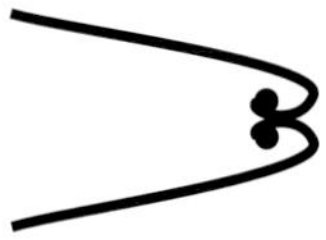

FIGURE 3

FIGURE 4

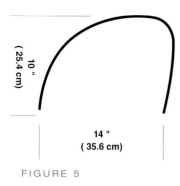

10 "
(25.4 cm)

14 "
(35.6 cm)

FIGURE 5

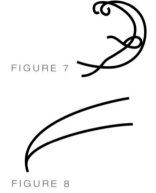

FIGURE 6

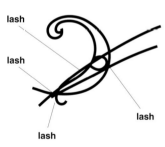

FIGURE 7

FIGURE 8

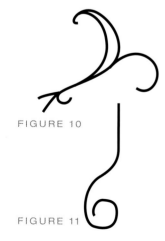

lash

lash

lash

lash

FIGURE 9

FIGURE 10

FIGURE 11

Making the Back Brace

15 Make the brace for the back of the chair by taking one of the short pieces of rebar (left over from the bar you trimmed after making the curl), clamping it in the table vise, and bending a U-shaped cross support. Bend the U so it's slightly uneven to give the chair a more jaunty air. The U-shaped bracket will be 14 inches across; where its bend stops, there will be two 10-inch lengths. See figure 5.

16 Trim off the excess rebar with the bolt cutters, leaving straight, 10-inch lengths at the ends of the U.

17 Using the flat bar and two C-clamps, clamp the V to the worktable, leaving the 10-inch lengths sticking out. Slip a 3-foot section of the 1-inch pipe over a 10-inch section of the rebar to provide extra leverage, and bend the section up into a right angle. The brace should now look like figure 6.

18 Spread apart the two free ends of the lashed-together back section so that the U-shaped brace fits between them at the end of the curved portion of the back. The 10-inch sections of the brace should stick straight out behind the chair back. Clamp the back and the brace together, and lash them together tightly with the annealed wire. Use the lashing technique described in step 14 at this point, and at all other points where required.

19 Use the pipe bender to bend together the remaining portions of the back toward each other. Cross them at a point about 10 inches from their ends, and lash together securely with the annealed copper wire.

20 Now you'll bend the bottom half of the chair back so it matches the top half. Use the C-clamps to clamp the entire piece face down on the worktable, placing the bar directly under the U-shaped brace. The 10-inch pieces will be sticking up. Grasp the crossed section and push up. Move the bar down 4 inches and push up again, repeating the process until you've achieved the desired curve. See figure 7.

Making and Attaching the Legs

21 To create the chair's back leg, repeat steps 12 and 13. Then, starting from the curl, bend a curve halfway up each bar as shown in figure 8. Lash the two curls together to form one back foot.

22 With the curls pointing down, attach the back foot piece to the chair back. The foot should be positioned under the crossed portion of the chair back. The curled portion of the back foot piece will be positioned outside the crossed ends of the chair back, and the two "arms" of the foot piece will pass under the two curved corners of the U-shaped brace at the inside of the chair back. Lash the back foot section to the chair back in four places as shown in figure 9: two by the crossed portion of the chair back and two to the right angles of the U-shaped brace.

23 You'll use the two straight pieces of the back foot section to create the front leg supports. Clamp as necessary and bend each piece down, curving them to point backward toward the back foot (see figure 10).

24 You'll use the two remaining pieces of curled rebar to construct the front legs. Take a bar and put its curl in the vise. Bend back against the curl to accent the fiddlehead shape of the front feet. Refer to figure 11. Repeat with the second bar.

25 Use the tape measure and marker to indicate a point 18 inches from the bottom of the curl. Clamp the bar in the vise with the curl pointing down, and bend a right angle at that point. Measure and mark a point 16 inches from the front of the right angle. Reclamp, and bend another angle that's not quite as sharp. With the bolt cutters, cut the remaining rebar off 12 inches from the middle of the second angle. Bend the 12 inch portion back to match the curve of the chair back.

26 As shown in figure 12, bend the ends of the front leg support so they fit into the heel of the front leg piece. With the bolt cutters, trim off about 7½ inches.

27 Lash the front legs to the chair at four points on each leg: two at the back of the chair, one at the seat, and one at the heel of the front foot. Cross the 12-inch portions of the front legs behind the back of the chair, splaying out the front legs to make the chair more stable. Check the stability of the chair as you lash on the front legs, adjusting as necessary.

28 The U-shaped brace for the front is the last piece you'll bend. Repeat steps 15 through 17, achieving the profile shown in figures. 13 and 6. This U-brace will measure 16 inches across and 10 inches long. Bend it a little unevenly to give the chair design character!

29 Fit the front brace between the two front legs, and lash it in two places on each side. You've now completed the chair frame.

Making and Attaching the Seat

30 Use the poster board and marker to make patterns of the inside areas of the chair seat and back, and cut out the patterns with the scissors. Lay the patterns on the salvaged roofing tin, and use fast-drying spray paint around the pattern edges to mark the area you'll cut.

31 Cut out the tin with the snips, or secure the tin with the clamps and cut it with the hummer wheel on the drill. Be careful, the edges are sharp! Check the fit of the tin to the chair frame and trim any excess.

32 Use the sandpaper or synthetic scouring pad to smooth the edges of the tin and remove any burrs.

33 Use the hand punch or the awl and hammer to make holes every 3 inches around the edge of the tin, ⅜ inch from the edge.

34 Wire the tin to the frame with the 16-gauge copper wire. Use the wire snips to cut two pieces of wire per hole. Thread the wire through the tin and around the rebar frame, twisting the ends of the wire together with the needle-nose vise grips to ensure a tight connection. Hide the twisted ends under or behind the chair.

35 For a fun finishing touch, use the 20-gauge copper wire to wire the spark plugs to the raw ends of rebar that stick out in the chair back. First, lash the wire around the rebar and the plugs, then tighten them by lashing between the rebar and plugs.

36 Wipe the chair with the rag and solvent to remove any dirt or grease. Let dry, and finish it by applying the semigloss wood lacquer with the brush.

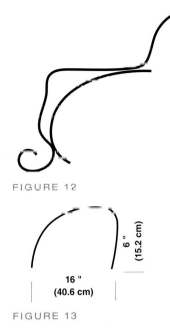

FIGURE 12

FIGURE 13

shade and accessories

ABOVE: **On a hot summer day, the most logical place for a garden seat is under a giant shade tree. If you don't have years to wait for that tree to grow, however, you have other options.**

S hade is probably the single most important factor affecting the comfort of your garden seating. And in today's stressed world, we also retreat to our gardens to enjoy delicious peace and privacy.

You probably already know the spots in your yard that tend to get the most sun or stay the coolest throughout the year. In brief, northern and eastern exposures are cool, south is always warm, and west can be unbearable after a hot summer afternoon. If you want a west-facing seat so you can enjoy the sunset, plan to block at least some of the harsh midafternoon sun by installing a canopy or an umbrella. You may want to create a sheltered, sunny spot where you can sit and enjoy the fragrances of your flower garden; if so, planting or building a windbreak is easy!

Thick hedges and shrubs are ideal for creating sheltered alcoves in the garden; plant one main hedge, then other hedges perpendicular to it. If you're short on time, choose low-maintenance varieties that require only light pruning to keep their shape. Evergreens are a practical year-round solution because they don't lose their leaves. There are also some deciduous shrubs that will continue to give shelter in the winter

RIGHT. Instead of building an arbor, you can use shears to gradually carve out a niche in a hedge that's big enough for a seat.

BELOW: A wisteria arbor arches across this pebble patio to create a shady outdoor room.

because their branches grow so thickly. These include viburnum (*Viburnum*), forsythia (*Oleaceae*), and winter honeysuckle (*Lonicera fragrantissima*).

Fragrant, sheltering vines and garden seating just seem to go together, don't they? Climbing hydrangea (*Hydrangea petiolaris*), honeysuckle (*Lonicera*), climbing roses (*Rosa*), Carolina jessamine (*Gelsimium sempervirens*), clematis (*Clematis*), and jasmine (*Jasminum*) create wonderful shade and shelter when they grow on a supporting trellis or arbor. Check the vine's growth habits; wisteria (*Wisteria*), and trumpet vine (*Campsis radicans*) are vigorous growers that need strong supports.

Building an arbor or pergola can be a daunting proposition with all those columns and cross beams. Why not copy the earliest arbors by interlacing the tops of trees or shrubs over your seating area? You can also construct the Morning Glory Garden Bench on page 416, using arched wire fencing to create the world's simplest built-in trellis. Plant it with quick-climbing, flowering annuals such as morning glories (*Ipomoea*), moonflowers (*Ipomoea alba*), or hyacinth bean (*Dolichos lablab*), or float a piece of fabric over the top to create instant shade.

Ready-made objects can provide easy shade solutions. You can always bolt an umbrella to the back of a chair. If you have a shabby sun umbrella or a rain umbrella that has seen better days, why not remove the fabric and turn it into a mini-trellis, growing quick vines up the handle and along the "fingers" of the skeleton? Is there an old gate quietly rusting in your storage shed? Install it in the ground next to a seat that could use some shelter, and plant it with quick-growing vines for an almost instant windscreen.

ABOVE LEFT:
Crossvine (*Bignonia capreolata*) is a semi-evergreen, flowering vine that keeps its leaves throughout the year. Give it a sturdy support to grow on.

ABOVE RIGHT:
The flowering shrub Rose of Sharon (*Hibiscus syriacus*) grows to 12 feet (3.6 m) tall, and is easily trained to form an arbor.

simple
rustic arbor

DESIGNER
J. Dabney Peeples

The rhododendron branches used to construct this arbor create an inviting arched shape, though you can use many different woods for varying effects. The runners of a Russian olive (*Elaeagnus*) shrub were pruned and trained to grow up and over the arbor structure, covering it beautifully with silvery gray leaves. As a bonus, Russian olive has delicious berries and gives off a wonderful fragrance.

TOOLS AND SUPPLIES

Pruning saw

Measuring tape

Fine-tip permanent marker

Assorted cement coated nails,
  2 to 3 inches long

Hammer

Wire

Shovel

Plant ties

Pruners

MATERIALS

4 rhododendron branch
  uprights, each 7½ to 8 feet
  tall and 2½ inches in diameter

4 branches to serve as rafters,
  each 3 feet long

14 to 18 crosspieces,
  each 2 feet long

Assorted smaller branches for filler

4 pieces of rebar, each 2 feet long

Shrub or vine of your choice
  (*Elaeagnus* is shown in
  the photo)

INSTRUCTIONS

1 Use the pruning saw to cut the branches to the lengths specified. To create the arched shape of the arbor, the uprights themselves should gently arch. When the uprights are joined, they'll create a walk-through 3 to 4 feet wide.

2 To make the sides of the arbor, lay out two of the uprights on the work surface, making sure the arched bends are oriented toward the same direction. Use the measuring tape and marker to mark 16-inch-wide intervals on the uprights. Using nails of a length that will penetrate both pieces without going all the way through, nail the 2-foot crosspieces to the two uprights, making a ladderlike form. If the nail does pierce both branches, bend it over with the hammer, and rust will eventually help disguise it. Complete the other side of the arbor with the remaining two uprights and crosspieces.

3 Place the two finished upright sections on their sides, so the tops touch and the sides are parallel. Nail the rafters about 1 foot below the top of the uprights, then nail two crosspieces to each rafter to connect them even more securely to the upright.

4 Stand the arbor on its feet, and nail the smaller, filler branches to the sides and top. If you place the smaller branches creatively, you can make it look as though the arbor grew where it stands.

5 Place the arbor in your garden. To secure it, drive the rebar into the ground at the points where the uprights touch the ground, leaving about 1 foot of the rebar above ground. Use the wire to attach the uprights to the rebar.

6 Dig a hole three times as wide as the root ball of the shrub or vine, at the base of the arbor on the outside. Plant the shrub or vine, and water and feed it as recommended. As it grows, attach it to the arbor with the plant ties, and prune new growth to encourage it to grow up and over the arbor.

morning glory
garden bench
with
wire fence trellis

DESIGNER
Jane Wilson

This is one of the easiest bench-and-trellis combinations we've ever seen! Wire fencing is a snap to use to form the arch, and you can plant it with morning glories or other quick-growing vines, or throw fabric over it for instant shade. You can also modify the design to make a longer bench for a comfy spot to stretch out and take a nap. Just increase the length of the bench slats. Directions are also given for making an easy covered cushion for your bench.

MATERIALS

for the trellis bench:
Roll of galvanized, vinyl-coated, 24-inch-wide wire fencing with 2 x 3-inch mesh openings

5 pieces 2 x 2 x 8 pressure-treated (PT) wood approved for ground contact, or hardwood

5 pieces 1 x 2 x 8 PT or hardwood

1 piece 2 x 4 x 8 PT or hardwood

2 pieces 1 x 6 x 8 PT or hardwood

for the bench cushion:
One piece of 54-inch-wide cotton polyester duck fabric, 53 inches long, in a forest green color

Foam cushion form, 24 x 48 x 2 inches thick

TOOLS AND SUPPLIES

for the trellis bench:

Protective gloves

Wire cutters

Ruler or tape measure

Fine-tip permanent marker

Power drill with ⅛- and ¼-inch
    Phillips head bits

C-clamps, 5-inch

Triangle or carpenter's square

Hammer

A willing friend

Crescent wrench

Miter box (optional)

Handsaw (optional)

for the bench cushion:

Tape measure

Scissors

Straight pins

Thread to match fabric

Sewing machine

Electric iron

Can of spray-on water repellent
    for fabric

Hardware

44 #8 Phillips head wood screws,
    1½ inches long

4 bolts, ¼-inch diameter
    and 4 inches long, with
    4 matching nuts

4 8d nails, 3 inches long

12 6d nails, 2 inches long

INSTRUCTIONS

Making the Trellis Bench

1 Wearing the protective gloves, use the wire cutters to cut a 16-foot length of the wire fencing from the roll.

2 Refer to figure 1. Sandwich each cut end of the wire fencing between a pair of the 5-foot 2 x 2 arch uprights (A) and a pair of the 5-foot 1 x 2 upright supports (B), with their sides flush on the outer edges. All the 1 x 2 supports (B) should be on top, on one side of the fencing, and the 2 x 2 uprights (A) on the bottom, with the fencing in between. Use the ruler and marker to indicate pilot holes 2 inches in from the ends of each support (B), and drill the pilot holes with the ⅛-inch bit, taking care to avoid the wire. Sink the wood screws through the pilot holes to secure each "sandwich."

3 While the assembly is still flat on the ground with the 1 x 2 upright supports (B) on top, you'll attach the inner and outer arch crosspieces (E and F). On the top side of the assembly, position a 1 x 2 outer arch crosspiece (F) flush against the inner ends of the two arch supports (B). Slip a 2 x 2 inner arch crosspiece (E) underneath, centering it under the 1 x 2 (F) with the wire fencing

in between. Clamp together with the C-clamps, and secure with a wood screw at each end. Remove the clamps. Repeat on the other side of the assembly, against the other two arch supports.

4 Use the ruler to measure 7 inches in from the arch supports on each side. At each 7-inch point, repeat the "sandwich" assembly of 1 x 2 (B) fencing, and 2 x 2 (A). Measure in another 7 inches from each assembly, and install two more "sandwiches." You should now have six of these assemblies installed along the fencing. When you stand the arch up, the 2 x 2 uprights (A) will be on the inside of the standing arch, where you'll attach cross braces (C), which in turn will support the bench slats (D).

5 Flip the trellis assembly over so the 2 x 2 uprights (A) and 2 x 2 inner arch crosspieces (E) are on top. Use the ruler and marker to measure and mark 16 inches in from the end of each upright (A). Place a 2 x 4 cross brace (C) at the marks on a pair of the 2 x 2 uprights (A), positioning the cross braces on the outside of the marks. Use the triangle or square to make sure the cross brace is square to the uprights, so the bench will be level when it's installed. Clamp together with the C-clamps.

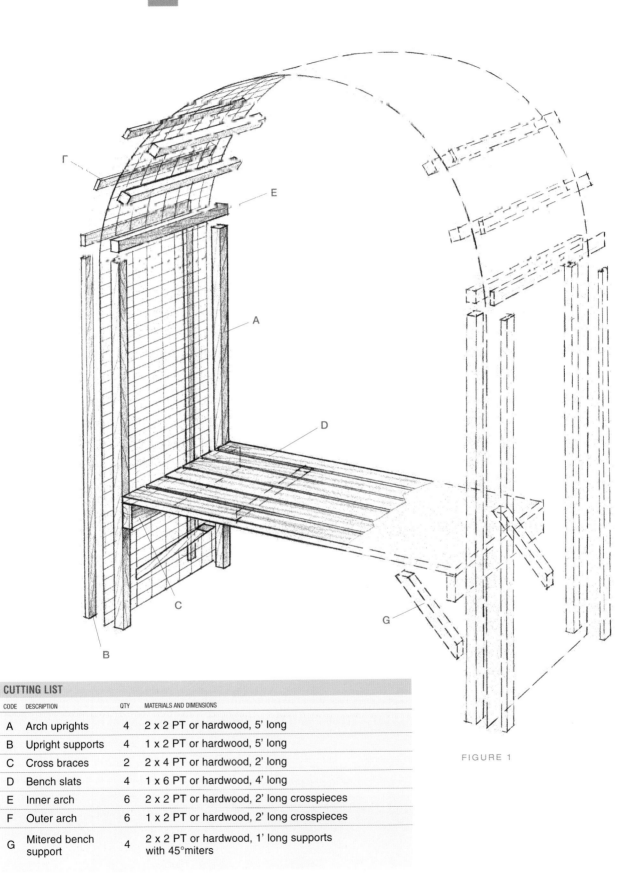

Γ

E

A

D

C

B

G

FIGURE 1

CUTTING LIST

CODE	DESCRIPTION	QTY	MATERIALS AND DIMENSIONS
A	Arch uprights	4	2 x 2 PT or hardwood, 5' long
B	Upright supports	4	1 x 2 PT or hardwood, 5' long
C	Cross braces	2	2 x 4 PT or hardwood, 2' long
D	Bench slats	4	1 x 6 PT or hardwood, 4' long
E	Inner arch	6	2 x 2 PT or hardwood, 2' long crosspieces
F	Outer arch	6	1 x 2 PT or hardwood, 2' long crosspieces
G	Mitered bench support	4	2 x 2 PT or hardwood, 1' long supports with 45°miters

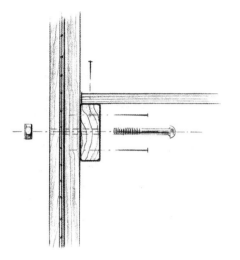

FIGURE 2

6 Refer to figure 2. Now you'll install a 4-inch bolt at each end of both crosspieces (C) to strengthen the joins. About 1 inch below the edge of the crosspiece (C), drill a ¼-inch hole through all three pieces (A, B, and C). Slide in the bolt so that its nut end will be inside the arch, and tighten the nut with the wrench. To further stabilize the connection, hammer in a 3-inch 8d nail about 1½ inches below the bolt, so the nail passes through the crossbrace (C) and into the upright (A). Remove the clamps. Repeat to install the other three bolts.

7 With the help of a friend, form an arch from the wire and wood assembly, with the inner arch crosspieces (E) inside the arch. Pull the bottom of the arch together until a bench slat (D) can rest on the cross-pieces (C), spanning the inside of the arch at both ends. The outside edges of the two outer bench slats (D) should be flush with the edges of the crosspieces (C). Screw the slats to the crosspieces, using two screws at each end. Place the two remaining slats (D) inside on the crosspieces, spacing all the slats approximately ³⁄₁₆ inch apart. Secure with screws.

8 Now you'll cut the mitered bench supports (G) from the remaining 2 x 2. As shown in figure 3, use the miter box and handsaw to cut a 45° angle on one end, then make four more opposing 45° cuts 12 inches apart to create four supports mitered at both ends.

9 Lay the arch on its side, and fit a support (G) up in each corner below the bench. Nail in place with the 2-inch 6d nails, using two nails on each end of each support. Stand the bench up, making sure it's level. Plant morning glories for daytime color and moonflowers for evening scent, and enjoy!

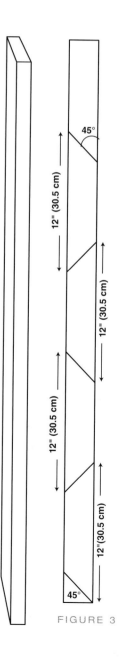

FIGURE 3

Making the Bench Cushion

1 The finished bench cushion will be 2 inches thick and measure 24 x 48 inches. Use the tape measure and scissors to measure and cut a piece of fabric measuring 51 inches across and 53 inches long. This includes extra material for ½-inch seam allowances and the thickness of the finished cushion.

2 Fold the fabric over, right side in. Use the straight pins to fasten the longest edge together.

3 Refer to figure 4. Thread the sewing machine and sew a ½-inch seam (A) along the longest edge, leaving a 10-inch opening in the middle. Remove the pins, and lightly press the seam open with the iron. Now center the seam (A) in the "tube" of material, and sew ½-inch seams along the short edges (B) to close up both ends (see figure 5). Press the seams open with the iron.

4 Now you'll create the four corners of the seat cushion using a simple mitering technique. With the cover still wrong side out and the longest seam centered, twist the fabric diagonally at one corner, so the raw edge of one of the short seams is centered in the corner, as shown in figure 6. Pin together, and use the tape measure to measure in from the corner, along the centered seam, the same distance as the thickness of the cushion insert. Sew a seam at that point, inside the corner, from one side of the corner to the other. Remove the pins. Repeat with the other corner and the other short seam. Use the scissors to trim excess material from the corners.

5 Turn the cover right side out. Make sure the raw edges of the opening in the long seam are tucked inside, and sew a ¼-inch seam on either side of the opening to hold the raw edges inside.

6 Slip the foam cushion form into the cover through the opening.

7 Spray the cushion with the water repellent according to package directions, and allow to dry. Install on the bench seat.

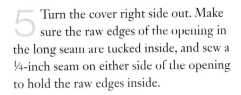

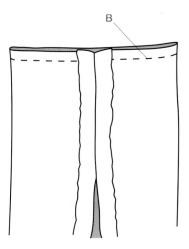

FIGURE 5

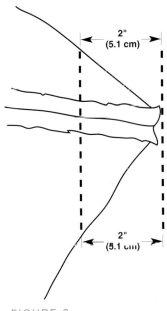

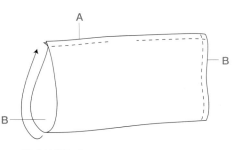

FIGURE 4

FIGURE 6

metrics conversion charts

length

INCHES	MILLIMETERS (MM) CENTIMETERS (CM)	INCHES	MILLIMETERS (MM) CENTIMETERS (CM)	INCHES	MILLIMETERS (MM) CENTIMETERS (CM)
1/8	3 mm	7 1/2	19 cm	21	53.3
3/16	5 mm	8	20.3 cm	21 1/2	54.6
1/4	6 mm	8 1/2	21.6 cm	22	55 cm
5/10	8 mm	9	22.9 cm	22 1/2	57.2 cm
3/8	9.5 mm	9 1/2	24.1 cm	23	58.4 cm
7/16	1.1 cm	10	25.4 cm	23 1/2	59.7 cm
1/2	1.3 cm	10 1/2	26.7 cm	24	61 cm
9/16	1.4 cm	11	27.9 cm	24 1/2	62.2 cm
5/8	1.6 cm	11 1/2	29.2 cm	25	63.5 cm
11/16	1.7 cm	12	30.5 cm	25 1/2	64.8 cm
3/4	1.9 cm	12 1/2	31.8 cm	26	66 cm
13/16	2.1 cm	13	33 cm	26 1/2	67.3 cm
7/8	2.2 cm	13 1/2	34.3 cm	27	68.6 cm
15/16	2.4 cm	14	35.6 cm	27 1/2	69.9 cm
1	2.5 cm	14 1/2	36.8 cm	28	71.1 cm
1 1/2	3.8 cm	15	38.1 cm	28 1/2	72.4 cm
2	5 cm	15 1/2	39.4 cm	29	73.7 cm
2 1/2	6.4 cm	16	40.6 cm	29 1/2	74.9 cm
3	7.6 cm	16 1/2	41.9 cm	30	76.2 cm
3 1/2	8.9 cm	17	43.2 cm	30 1/2	77.5 cm
4	10.2 cm	17 1/2	44.5 cm	31	78.7 cm
4 1/2	11.4 cm	18	45.7 cm	31 1/2	80 cm
5	12.7 cm	18 1/2	47 cm	32	81.3 cm
5 1/2	14 cm	19	48.3 cm	32 1/2	82.6 cm
6	15.2 cm	19 1/2	49.5 cm	33	83.8 cm
6 1/2	16.5 cm	20	50.8 cm	33 1/2	85 cm
7	17.8 cm	20 1/2	52 cm	34	86.4 cm
				34 1/2	87.6 cm
				35	88.9 cm
				35 1/2	90.2 cm
				36	91.4 cm

length (formula)

U.S.	MULTIPLY BY	METRIC EQUIVALENT
Foot	0.3048	Meter
Yard	0.9144	Meter

area

U.S.	MULTIPLY BY	METRIC EQUIVALENT
Square inch	645.16	Square millimeter
Square foot	0.09290304	Square meter
Square yard	0.8361274	Square meter
Acre	0.40469	Hectare

mass

U.S.	MULTIPLY BY	METRIC EQUIVALENT
Ounce	0.02834952	Kilogram
Pound	0.45359237	Kilogram
Ton	0.9071847	Tonne

volume

U.S.	MULTIPLY BY	METRIC EQUIVALENT
Fluid ounce	29.57353	Milliliter
Gallon	3.785412	Liter
Cubic inch	16.387064	Cubic millimeter
Cubic foot	0.02831685	Cubic meter
Cubic yard	0.7645549	Cubic meter

temperature

FORMULA

Degrees Fahrenheit
Minus 32
Times 5
Divided by 9
Equals degrees celsius

GARDEN FLOORS section
acknowledgments and photo credits

Special thanks to:

J. Dabney Peeples, Arthur Campbell, Graham A. Kimak, and many of the fine clients of J. Dabney Peeples Design Associates, Inc., Easley, SC. All spent a great deal of time taking us through their gardens, our notepads and cameras in tow.

John Thelen of Landmark Landscapes, Swannanoa, NC, who contributed expertise, tools, and a whole lot of physical labor to create the section's how-to photographs. Thanks also to his clients, Stuart and Jean McLennan, also of Swannanoa, who allowed us to dig up their yard.

Veronika Alice Gunter, assistant editor, whose extraordinary organizational abilities are surpassed only by her patience and diplomacy. This section would not have been possible without her.

And thanks especially Mary Weber, the section's consultant. Her expert technical knowledge, keen eye for detail, enthusiastic interest in the subject, and unfailing good humor (often in the face of avalanches of deadlines) made her an exceptional partner in this project.

Much thanks to the landscape architects and others who submitted photography for this section:

Arbor Engineering, Greenville, SC; Tom Keith, architect: pages 19 (middle), 96–97 (top)

Bomanite, Madera, CA; Dino Tom, photographer: pages 24–25, 116–117, 118–119, 120, 121, 122, 125

Brick Industry Association, Reston, VA: pages 21, 27, 64

Broussard Associates Landscape Architects, Clovis, CA; Terry Broussard, ASLA, architect; Larry Falke, photographer: pages 86–87, 120 (bottom)

J. Dabney Peeples Design Associates, Inc., Easley, SC; Graham A. Kimak, photographer: pages 103 and 136 (bottom left and right)

Daniel's Landscaping, Campbellsport, WI; Daniel Stukenberg, architect/photographer: pages 72–73

Hanover Architectural Products, Hanover, PA: pages 112–113, 115, 116 (top), 117

Kellogg Landscape Architecture Construction, Inc., Bastrop, TX; Sandra Chipley Kellogg, architect and photographer: page 90 (bottom)

Graham A. Kimak, Greenville, SC; landscape designer/photographer: page 137 (top)

Landplan Studio, Fair Lawn, NJ; Dennis Muhr, architect/photographer: page 105

Missouri Botanical Gardens, St. Louis, MO, Jack Jennings, photographer: pages 24–25 (bottom), 79 (upper left)

Signe Nielsen Landscape Architect, P.C., New York, NY; Signe Nielsen, architect/photographer: pages 26 (top of column), 69, 78, 79 (bottom row), 89, 98 (bottom), 102, 108 (top), 109 (top and bottom), 129, 131, 132 (top right and bottom), 134 (left)

Dana Schock and Associates, Sudbury, MA; Dana Schock, ASLA, architect/photographer: cover, pages 15 (top), 23 (bottom left), 58

SJYDesign, Oakland, CA; Steven J. Young, architect; Michelle Burke, photographer: pages 16 and 74

Ken Smith, New York, NY, architect: page 138 (right top and bottom)

Mary Smith Associates, P.C., Quincy, MA; Mary Smith architect/photographer: page 85 (top)

Tile Heritage Foundation, Healdsburg, CA; Joseph Taylor, photographer: page 68

Additional photography credits:

Chandoha Photography, Annandale, NJ: page 81

Derek Fell's Horticultural Picture Library, Gardenville, PA: pages 92 (top), 132 (top left), 135 (bottom), 137 (bottom)

Thom Gaines, Asheville, NC: pages 22, 26 (bottom of column), 29 (bottom of column), 108 (middle and bottom), 109 (middle)

Dana Irwin, Asheville, NC: page 139 (bottom)

Dency Kane, New York, NY: pages 99 and 101

Janice Eaton Kilby, Asheville, NC: page 139 (top)

Charles Mann Photography, Santa Fe, NM: pages 15 (bottom), 57, 70, 71, 84, 91, 111 (top), 120 (top)

Jerry Pavia Photography, Bonners Ferry, ID: pages 18 (top), 19, 24–25 (top), 26–27, 28, 29 (top), 30–31 (top), 55, 64, 66–67, 75, 94, 95 (bottom), 96–97, 106–107

James Haig Streeter, San Francisco, CA: pages 65 and 82

GARDEN FLOORS, CONT.

We also want to acknowledge several artisans whose work is showcased in this section:

Circle of Stone, Haywood County, NC; David Reed, stonemason: page 95

Gardensphere, Sugar Grove, NC; Robbie Oates, stonemason: pages 38 (bottom), and 92 (bottom)

Michael Huba, Albany, NY; artist/photographer: page 110

Landscape Gardeners, Biltmore Forest, NC; Art Garst, landscape designer: page 20–21

Finally, special thanks to those who allowed us to photograph their gardens:

Roger Bakeman, Atlanta, GA: page 111 (bottom)

Trena and Ed Parker, Biltmore Forest, NC: page 59

ASHEVILLE, NC:

John Cram: page 63

Elizabeth Eve: page 60–61

Dr. Peter and Jasmin Gentling: page 38 (top)

Andrew Glasgow: pages 114, 114–115

Mary Johnson: pages 18 (bottom), 84–85

William and Barbara Lewin: page 22

Christopher Mello: page 135 (top)

Heather Spencer and Charles Murray: pages 16–17 (bottom)

GREENVILLE AND EASLEY, SC:

Jack and Joyce Clarkson, Easley, SC: pages 100, 104

Michael and Kathy Evans, Greenville, SC: pages 27 (top) and 116 (bottom)

Janice and Bill Hagler, Greenville, SC: page 90 (top)

Porter and Ann Roe Rose, Greenville, SC: pages 76–77, 88

PATHS AND WALKWAYS section acknowledgments and photo credits

Many thanks to the following people and firms from around the world who contributed photographs:

Photographs Submitted by Landscape Architects, Path Builders, Path Owners, and Photographers:

Pages 216 (bottom) and 220: James M. Chadwick, Los Gatos, CA; James M. Chadwick, architect; Melgar Photographers, Santa Clara, CA, photographer

Page 146–147: John Cram, Asheville, NC

Page 226 (bottom): City of Austin, TX; Carol M. Foy, architect/photographer

Page 233 (top): Michael/Todd, Inc., Naples, FL; Jeff Petry, ASLA, architect; William C. Minarich, photographer

Pages 226 (top), 233: Michael/Todd, Inc., Naples, FL; Jeff Petry, ASLA, architect/photographer

Page 224: Dana Schock and Associates, Sudbury, MA; Dana Schock, ASLA, architect/photographer

Pages 157, 205, 209 (bottom), 221 (bottom): Hord Coplan Macht, LLC, Baltimore, MD; Carol Macht, ASLA, architect; Bob Creamer, photographer

Pages 161, 196, 193, 200, 202 (top), 209 (top), 221 (top): JOS Landscape Architect, Newtown, PA; Jayne O'Neal Spector, architect/photographer

Page 145: Ehrich & Ehrich Landscape Architects, Cranbury, NJ; Dennis Muhr, architect/photographer

Page 224 (bottom): Ehrich & Ehrich Landscape Architects, Cranbury, NJ; Dennis Muhr and Gary Hansen, architects; Dennis Muhr, photographer

Page 208: Simmons & Associates, Inc., Indianapolis, IN; J. Craig Hitner, architect; photography by Chilluffo Photography

Pages 144, 204, and 211: Magrane Associates Landscape Design, San Francisco, CA; Penney Magrane, architect; Mark McLane, photographer

Page 203 (top): Barba & Groh Landscaping, Inc., San Juan, Puerto Rico; Gustavo Barba, architect; photography by Gustavo Barba and A. Thomas Groh

Pages 184, 186 (top), 192, 210, 215 (top), 217, 220 (top), 227: J. Dabney Peeples Design Associates, Inc., Easley, SC.; Graham A. Kinak, photographer

Page 186 (top): Graham A. Kinak, Easley, SC, landscape designer/photographer

Page 223: J. Dabney Peeples Design Associates, Inc., Easley, SC; Jack Thacker/Traditional Concepts, Inc., Greenville, SC, residential designer; Tony Pridgeon, Pridgeon Masonry, Spartanburg, SC, brick mason; Graham A. Kinak, photographer

Pages 163, 225 (bottom), 231, 232: Michigan 4-H Children's Garden, Michigan State University; East Lansing, MI; photography by Norman Lownds, assistant professor and curator

Page 185: Alfred B. Maclay Gardens, Tallahassee, FL

Pages 186, 195: Randy Burroughs, photographer

Special thanks to those who allowed us to photograph their paths and their supplies:

Jesse Israel and Sons Garden Center, Asheville, NC

J. Dabney Peeples Design Studio Display Gardens, Easley, SC
(The talented team here was immensely helpful in many ways.)

J R Stone Sales Inc., Asheville, NC

The Home Depot, Asheville, NC

Turf Mountain Sod Inc., Hendersonville, NC

UNCA Botanical Gardens, Asheville, NC

Helga and Jack Beam residence, Asheville, NC

Brown residence, Greenville, SC

Clarkson residence, Greenville, SC

Gannon residence, Greenville, SC

Graham A. Kinak residence, Greenville, SC

David and Deborah Lichtenfelt residence, Greenville, SC

Little residence, Greenville, SC

Mary McKinney residence, Greenville, SC

Morton residence, Greenville, SC

Glenn and Jan Spears residence, Greenville, SC

Wallenborn residence, Asheville, NC

Williams residence, Greenville, SC

WALLS AND FENCES section acknowledgments and photo credits

Thanks to the following people for their generous help with this section:

Don Osby, for his wonderful illustrations, help above and beyond the call of duty, and endless patience.

Richard Freudenberger, for his expert technical contributions.

Dean Riddle, for allowing us to show his beautiful stick and woven willow fences and for telling us how he built them and Anita Matos, whose bamboo fence appears on page 284.

The following landscape architects generously allowed us to feature photographs of their work:

J. Dabney Peeples, Arthur Campbell, and Graham A. Kimak of J. Dabney Peeples Design, Associates, Inc., Easley, SC

Jane O'Neal Spector, JOS Landscape Architect, Newton, PA

Photo Credits:

Walpole Woodworkers, Walpole, MA, (800) 343-6948, supplied the photographs of the beautiful fences found on pages 241 (top and bottom), 248, 277, 278, 279, 280, 283, 285, 296

Keystone Retaining Wall Systems, Minneapolis, MN; (800) 747-8971, supplied the photographs of the walls on pages 255 and 265

Richard Babb: page 239

Evan Bracken: pages 240, 246, 256, 268

Walter Chandoha: page 255 (top)

Alan & Linda Detrick: pages 287 and 302

Derek Fell: pages 245, 250–251, 286

Dency Kane: pages 236, 274–275, 276

Richard Hasselberg: pages 238 (top), 242, 244, 249, 252, 271, 281, 282

Charles Mann: pages 253, 254 (top and bottom)

Jane O'Neal Spector: page 247

Sandra Stambaugh: page 284

Thanks to the following homeowners for allowing us to photograph their wonderful examples of walls and fences:

Dr. Julie Newburg and Patrick Bralick, Liberty, SC

Gay and Stewart Coleman, Biltmore Forest, NC

Hedy Fischer and Randy Shull, Asheville, NC

Dr. Peter and Jasmin Gentling, Asheville, NC

Carol Hire, Asheville, NC

Bill and Pat Kuehl, Asheville, NC

Ed and Trena Parker, Biltmore Forest, NC

Paul and Hazel Sanger, "Carlsbad," Highlands, NC

Mary Sheldon, Asheville, NC

Mr. and Mrs. Glen and Jan Spears, Greenville, SC

Jodi Tuuri, Asheville, NC

Sandra Wallace and Roger Dean Camp, Asheville, NC

GARDEN SEATING section
acknowledgments and photo credits

Many thanks:

To the designers who created our how-to projects, to the friends who literally opened their homes and gardens to us, and to the artists and landscape architects who shared images of their work. I owe a special thank you to Dabney Peeples, Graham A. Kimak, and Arthur Campbell for their expertise and Southern hospitality.

We were fortunate to have technical, editorial, and artistic help from Jerald Snow, Joe Archibald, Kevin Barnes, and Perri Crutcher. Thank you as well to Evan Bracken for his photography, to artist Olivier Rollin for ces dessins magnifiques, and to Orrin Lundgren and Lark production assistant Hannes Charen for their informative visuals.

We were also fortunate to work with colleagues here at Lark who share a common interest in making beautiful and meaningful books. Thank you, Terry Taylor, for reaching into that amazing Rolodex of yours, and thank you, Dana Irwin, for bringing a passion for excellence and a remarkable artistic eye to its art direction. The skills of assistant editors Veronika Alice Gunter, Heather Smith, Roper Cleland, and Emma Jones were essential. And finally, a big thank you to Andy Rae, for his timely and expert advice.

Landscape Architects and Designers:

J. Dabney Peeples and Graham A. Kimak, J. Dabney Peeples Design Associates, Inc., Easley, SC

Arborsmith Studios, Williams, OR

Jerald A. Snow, ASLA, Asheville, NC

Ken Smith, Landscape Architect, New York, NY

Landplan Studio, Fair Lawn, NJ

Martina Meyer Interior Design and Hawthorne Studio, Santa Fe, NM

Steven J. Young, ASLA, SJY Design, Oakland, CA

Terry Broussard, ASLA, Broussard Associates Landscape Architects, Clovis, CA

Photo Credits:

Page 308 (middle left): J. Dabney Peeples Design Associates, Inc., Easley, SC; Graham A. Kimak, photographer

Page 308 (right): Thom Gaines, photographer

Page 309 (bottom): J. Dabney Peeples Design Associates, Inc., Easley, SC.

Pages 315 (top), 339, 372, 374 (top), 375 (left), 415 (top): Richard Hasselberg, photographer

Page 312 (bottom): Broussard Associates Landscape Architects, Clovis, CA; Terry Broussard, ASLA, architect; Larry Falke, photographer

Pages 315 (bottom right) and 416 (top left): Dana Irwin, photographer

Page 314 (top): Charles Mann Photography, Inc., Santa Fe, NM

Pages 316, 317, 318, 319, 337: Enid Munroe, photographer

Pages 324–325, 326, 356 (top) Janice Eaton Kilby, photographer

Pages 332 (bottom), 357 (top and middle): used with permission from Biltmore Estate, Asheville, NC. Evan Bracken, photographer

Pages 334 and 342: Derek Fell, photographer

Pages 344 and 346: Richard Charles Reames, photographer

Pages 369: Robert Cheatham, photographer

Pages 401 (left) and 406–407: Hays Cash, Tampa, FL; Reed Photography, Umatilla, FL, photographer

Page 409: Chuck Pearson, Key West, FL, photographer

Page 416 (bottom): Laura Spector, Laura Spector Rustic Designs, bench with market umbrella. Enid Munroe, photographer

Locations:

Roger Bakeman, Atlanta, GA

Brad Lawley, Decatur, GA

Carolyn Krueger, Decatur, GA

Charles and Gail Jones, Greenville, SC

David and Geri Laufer, Roswell, GA

Don and Ellen Wall, Greer, SC

Mr. and Mrs. David Lichtenfelt, Easley, SC

Elizabeth Lide and Paul Kayhart, Atlanta, GA

Frank and Emme Gannon, Greer, SC

Heather Spencer and Charles Murray, Asheville, NC

Hedy Fischer and Randy Schull, Asheville, NC

James Hiram Malone, Atlanta, GA

Jasmin and Dr. Peter Gentling, Asheville, NC

John Cram, Asheville, NC

John and Mary Dinkel, Greer, SC

Norma Cheren, Decatur, GA

Patrick Bralick and Dr. Julie Newberg, Liberty, SC

Scott and Amy Eller, Salisbury, NC

Teri Stewart and Iris Hale, Atlanta, GA

Robin Van Valkenburgh, wa wië, Asheville, NC

Christopher Mello, Asheville, NC

GARDEN SEATING section
designers and contributors

ROBERT CHEATHAM began his artistic career designing and building sculptural furniture from wood. He later adopted concrete and ferrocement techniques, which he uses in his studio and garden constructions, often adding mosaic tile and painted finishes.

DEREK FELL is a widely published garden photographer with more awards from the Garden Writers' Association of America than any other person. His own garden, Cedaridge Farm in Pennsylvania, has also won numerous awards for landscape design.

GEORGE HARRISON has been a professional woodworker for 37 years. He lives in the historic Ox Creek area of Weaverville, NC.

DOUG HAYS and **PENNY CASH** work from their joint Florida studio to produce works of art in steel, glass, and clay. Partners in life and art, they move freely among their mediums and will soon introduce new pieces incorporating blown, fused, and cast glass with raku and steel.

ALAN MICHAEL HESTER has been a custom woodworker since 1978 and works mostly in hardwoods. He lives with his wife and son in Asheville, NC, where he runs Lothlorien, a woodworking shop.

SHERRI WARNER HUNTER is a sculptor who has been working with concrete for a decade. Her large-scale concrete and mosaic public sculptures are featured at the Memphis/Shelby County Public Library, Nashville International Airport, and Vanderbilt Children's Hospital in Tennessee. She is the author of the Lark book, *Creating With Concrete: Yard Art, Sculpture, and Garden Projects*. She lives in Bell Buckle, TN, with her husband, Martin.

JOHNNY LEE JONES is a self-taught furniture refinisher/builder whose store, Classic Antiques, in Raleigh, NC, has been in business for more than 20 years. He specializes in architectural iron.

LISA MANDLE is the owner and principal designer of Only One, a custom clothing and accessories business in Madison County, NC. Before she moved to North Carolina, she was selected as one of the top 10 designers in Washington, DC.

CHRISTOPHER D. MELLO is a horticulturist by trade (but prefers to call himself a gardener), and he gained much of his experience on the grounds of the historic Biltmore Estate in his hometown of Asheville, NC. He is also an accomplished metal sculptor and floral designer.

JEAN TOMASO MOORE has been creating art in various forms for as long as she can remember. A part-time multi-media artist, she lives in Asheville, NC, with her patient and humble husband.

ENID MUNROE is the author of *An Artist in the Garden: A Guide to Creative and Natural Gardening*. (Henry Holt and Company, 1994). Her paintings, drawings, and collages are in numerous private and corporate collections. She lives in Fairfield, CT, with her husband and co-gardener, Harry.

ERIC O'LEARY is an accomplished ceramicist and member of the New Hampshire Potters' Guild, League of New Hampshire Craftsmen, and National Council on Education for Ceramic Arts. His work is in the collections of the Museum of Fine Arts, Boston, the White House, and the Currier Museum.

J. DABNEY PEEPLES is president and senior landscape/garden designer of J. Dabney Peeples Design Associates, Inc., of Easley, SC. The firm works throughout the Southeast. Peeples' residence, a 30-acre farm in Easley, serves as a design studio.

DANIEL O. PETERSEN has more than 25 years of experience in the tree care industry. His company, Petersen Tree and Landscape Management, is located in Swannanoa, NC.

ROB PULLEYN is an executive at Lark Books, and is usually a very hands-off manager. But when the spirit moves him, he can't help using his hands to create projects for our books. He lives in the mountains of western North Carolina.

RANDALL KAY works from his furniture studio in Asheville, NC. He pursues woodworking in many different forms, including boatbuilding, cabinetry, restoration, reproduction, and contemporary works.

RICHARD CHARLES REAMES owns and operates Arborsmith Studios in Williams, OR, where he designs, plants, bends, and grafts trees to form living houses, furniture, fences, gazebos, and other constructions. Author of the book *How to Grow a Chair: The Art of Tree Trunk Topiary* (Arborsmith Studios, 1995), he has been practicing "arborsculpture" for more than 10 years.

JANICE SHIELDS has worked as a dress shop manager and foreign car mechanic, and she credits her mother with her love of tinkering. She started her rustic furnishings business, Cut It Out, in 1995, and works with saplings and oriental bittersweet vines.

LAURA SPECTOR has been building rustic furniture for six years. Her whimsical and romantic creations are inspired by the natural curves, twists, and knurls of oriental bittersweet vine.

CAROL STANGLER is an environmental artist. She lives in and maintains a studio in Asheville, NC. Her work is featured in *Making the New Baskets* (Lark Books and Sterling Publishing Company, Inc., 1999) and she is the author of *the Craft & Art of Bamboo* (Lark Books and Sterling Publishing Company, Inc., 2001).

JIMMY STRAELA makes artwork from found materials and old lumber salvaged from house demolitions or burn piles. He also uses granite from a quarry in nearby Tinytown, GA.

TERRY TAYLOR specializes in creating art for the garden using the pique-assiette, or shard art, technique. Terry is known for his willingness to try any craft, and does a fabulous job at whatever he tries. He collects, creates, and carves from his home in Asheville, NC.

SUE and **ADAM TURTLE** publish the international journal *Temperate Bamboo Quarterly*. They also offer courses in working with bamboo at Earth Advocates Research Farm and operate "Our" Bamboo Nursery, a wholesale source of landscape-grade bamboo plants in Summertown, TN.

JANE WILSON spent many years as a studio designer, after studying art history and design at East Tennessee University and technical drawing and drafting at Eastern Kentucky University.

CYNTHIA WYNN began metalworking in 1990. Her work started winning awards during her second semester at the University of North Carolina at Asheville, and two years later Wynn had her own shop. She did the installation of the Rework Museum in Key West, FL, and she continues to divide her time among Key West, Asheville, and street festivals.

index